Resale Price Maintenance

Resale Price Maintenance

A Comparative American-European Perspective

edited by
B. S. Yamey

AldineTransaction
A Division of Transaction Publishers
New Brunswick (U.S.A.) and London (U.K.)

First paperback printing 2008

This book is printed on acid-free paper that meets the American National Standard for Permanence of Paper for Printed Library Materials.

Library of Congress Catalog Number: 2008001545
ISBN: 978-0-202-36227-4
Printed in the United States of America

Library of Congress Cataloging-in-Publication Data

Resale price maintenance : a comparative American-European perspective / B.S. Yamey, editor.
p. cm.
Reissue. Originally published: 3rd ed. Chicago : Aldine Pub., 1966.
Deals with selected countries: Canada, the United States of America, Sweden, Denmark, Ireland, and the United Kingdom.
Includes bibliographical references and index.
ISBN 978-0-202-36227-4 (alk. paper)
1. Price maintenance. 2. Price maintenance—United States. 3. Price maintenance—Europe. I. Yamey, Basil S.

HF5317.Y34 2008
338.5'23094—dc22 2008001545

CONTENTS

PREFACE

Six of the studies in this book deal with resale price maintenance in selected countries: Canada, the United States of America, Sweden, Denmark, Ireland and the United Kingdom. In each of these studies the main emphasis is placed on two subjects: the effects of resale price maintenance, and of its termination where this has taken place, as disclosed in official and private investigations; and the development of public policy measures, including some consideration of the problems encountered in their implementation. Some attention is also given to the historical development of the practice, and its extent and scope when at its height. A seventh study deals with resale price maintenance in the European Common Market. Dealing, as it does, with the practice in the constituent countries and also as it is affected by the emerging Common Market policy towards restraints on competition, the focus is more narrowly on developments in public policy.

Taken together, the several 'country' studies constitute a compendium of the arguments which have been deployed in the debates on resale price maintenance: all the major issues and most of the minor ones are considered or at least mentioned in one or more of the studies in the course of the review of developments in public policy. Editorial efforts have been aimed at avoiding repetition. It will be appreciated, however, that some topics and arguments are central and therefore recur. An introductory chapter, by the editor, sets the scene with an analytical discussion of the major economic issues.

The editor warmly acknowledges the co-operation of the contributors to this book: they were prompt and helpful, friendly and efficient. He is indebted to Professor Søren Gammelgaard, Dr James B.Jefferys and Professor W.J.L.Ryan for helpful advice. He is also indebted to Miss J.Bulman for translating several sections of the chapter on Sweden. Finally, he is grateful to Mr Nicolas Thompson for having given him the idea for this book. B.S.Y.

1

INTRODUCTION: THE MAIN ECONOMIC ISSUES

B. S. Yamey

Introduction

Resale price maintenance is a restrictive business practice: it restricts or eliminates price competition in the distributive trades affected. In the typical situation it raises retail prices and narrows consumers' choice; and by widening the gross margins of distributors without at the same time eliminating all forms of competitive behaviour, it attracts more labour and other resources into distribution. It is not surprising, therefore, that in the post-war period there has been growing public and official concern with r.p.m. in all Western countries which are experiencing strains on their national resources in conditions of full or over-full employment.

Further, since r.p.m. bears directly on retail prices, the practice provokes mounting criticism in periods of inflation, more particularly when, as is increasingly the vogue, governments attempt to introduce and implement general prices and incomes policies. It should be clear, however, that the relationship between r.p.m. and the process or the control of inflation is tenuous. The practice has little, if any, influence on *total* national money expenditure or on the availability of *total* national resources. It is relevant to the economy-wide issues of inflation mainly in so far as it affects the flexibility of particular prices. Moreover, the act of eliminating r.p.m. may create a situation of price reductions which may be favourable tactically for particular measures of policy to control or to contain inflation. But this in its nature can be no more than a once-for-all possibility. One cannot abolish r.p.m. every few years. The real importance of r.p.m., or of its prohibition or reduction, lies in its effects on the prices of particular goods and the deployment of resources between different economic activities. It is to be judged primarily in these terms, seen in the wider context of competition in industry and trade, and also in the yet wider context of the interests of consumers.

Distributors' Margins and Retail Prices

The proposition that r.p.m. raises retail prices and retailers' margins turns on the proposition that competing retailers do not have uniform costs per unit of sales.[1] Inter-firm differences in cost provide the basis for price competition; the independent pricing decisions of competing retailers and the responses of consumers lead to the elimination of the least efficient retailers, to the expansion (including the establishment) of more efficient firms, and to the availability of a range of competing offerings of different combinations of retail prices and services to meet the varied and varying preferences of consumers. Resale price maintenance obstructs the process of price competition. It therefore keeps distributive margins and resale prices higher than they would otherwise be and involves more resources in distribution.

The basic proposition is sometimes called in question. Thus it has been suggested or implied that the costs of retailing (or of distribution) are almost wholly fixed, and the elimination of r.p.m. would mean simply that the prices and gross margins of certain articles are reduced, while those of other articles are raised, with the average level of prices and gross margins left much the same as before. In other words, it seems that consumers as a body have to bear a given quantum of retailing costs whatever happens; the presence or absence of r.p.m. affects merely the distribution of the total costs among the various goods bought by them. If this were so, the case for the abolition or reduction of r.p.m. would be weakened, though even then it is not obvious that the distribution of the total costs with r.p.m. is in any sense better than that without r.p.m. But the thesis of the fixed quantum of distribution costs, or any analysis implying its validity, is untenable on several grounds.

The thesis of the fixed quantum seems to be derived from the proposition that the costs of running a particular shop are almost all in the nature of fixed overheads. This proposition is, however, seriously inadequate, if only because a large part of the gross profits of small-scale retailing consists of the earnings of the proprietors; and this element is not fixed. But even if, *arguendo*, the proposition be accepted that the running costs of any one shop is a fixed quantity, it would not follow that each shop has the same level of fixed costs.

[1] For convenience in exposition, the discussion proceeds in terms of 'retailers' rather than the more embracing and strictly more relevant 'distributors'. The argument applies, *mutatis mutandis*, also to 'wholesalers'.

Location, density of shopping traffic, range and quality of services, scale of operation and efficiency are among the factors affecting the level of the (assumed) fixed costs, both absolutely and also relatively to turnover. The thesis would apply only if the abolition of r.p.m. and the restoration of retail price competition did not affect the number, distribution, size, and ownership of shops and the level of services provided in them. A prediction of such an outcome cannot be entertained seriously in the representative case. Retailer supporters of r.p.m. would certainly not subscribe to it: and several of the standard arguments for r.p.m. reject implicitly the thesis of the fixed quantum of retailing costs. The thesis would have relevance, indeed, only if retailing were different from all other forms of business activity, because it postulates both that the requirements of customers are uniform and also that the unit costs of suppliers are uniform, or sufficiently so as to rule out the possibilities of competitive substitution.

It is the disregard, in a system of r.p.m., of differences in consumer requirements and preferences and of differences in costs of retailing which points to the conclusion that r.p.m. keeps the retail prices of the goods in question higher than they would otherwise be. By stopping price competition in retailing, the practice impedes the replacement of high-cost by low-cost forms of retailing, and of less efficient by more efficient firms. The brake on price competition is especially severe on the development of new forms of retailing.[2]

Although one can assert with some confidence that, typically, r.p.m. raises retail prices and retail gross margins above their competitive levels, it is more difficult to measure the extent of these effects. Thus it is difficult to predict with confidence by how much prices and margins would fall in a particular trade if r.p.m. were to be abolished in that trade. Examination of such matters as the shopping behaviour of consumers or the costs and profits of retailers engaged in the trade in question would be of little help in guiding the prediction, because they are conditioned by the practice of r.p.m. itself. Moreover, it is not easy to determine the effects of r.p.m. on prices and margins even

[2] The last three paragraphs are taken, with minor changes, from my 'Resale Price Maintenance: Issues and Policies', *Three Banks Review*, December 1960. The *Review* is a publication of the Royal Bank of Scotland, Glyn Mills & Co. and Williams Deacon's Bank Limited, to whom I am obliged for permission to use material from this article in the present chapter.

after it has been terminated in a particular trade. The more immediate effect on prices can, of course, be observed; but then it is not always easy to distinguish the more lasting price reductions from the more spectacular price cuts executed by high-spirited and publicity-conscious retailers released from the irritations of r.p.m. As, however, the date of the end of r.p.m. recedes into the distance, the particular effects of r.p.m. and of its termination are increasingly difficult to gauge. Thus the relative costs of factors of production used in manufacturing and in distribution do not stand still; consumer preferences change; and the general price level rises or falls for reasons quite unconnected with r.p.m. or its absence.

Even where, miraculously, there are no disturbances of this kind, time-series of retailers' margins, in particular, may contain pitfalls for the incautious. These arise from the fact that different retailing enterprises engage to a greater or lesser extent in what can be called wholesaling activities. Thus, broadly, large-scale retailing enterprises tend to do all or most of their own wholesaling, buying direct from manufacturers, whilst the smallest-scale retailing enterprises use extensively the services of independent wholesalers; and there are endless gradations between the two poles.[3] The gross margin of a retailing enterprise, which in reality is a vertically integrated wholesaling-retailing enterprise, refers to a span of economic activity which is wider than that of a more strictly retailing enterprise. Censuses of distribution do not ask vertically integrated distributors to split their over-all margin, the difference between final selling prices and initial buying prices, into separate 'retail' and 'wholesale' margins (and if they were required to do so, the split would be arbitrary). Hence a census average of gross margins in a trade is an average of individual margins which do not relate to the same span of activity. This would not matter if, over time, the relative proportions of different categories of retailer remained substantially unchanged and if retailers in a particular category did not change their degree of vertical integration with wholesaling. But these conditions are not likely to be satisfied, except within the limits of very short periods. Indeed, if the analysis of r.p.m. and its effects is correct, the abolition (or introduction) of r.p.m. would be likely to change the relative proportions of different categories of retailer and might also induce

[3] For this reason, among others (specially the relative expenditures on sales promotion), comparisons of retailers' margins on price-maintained brands and distributors' own brands are uninformative.

changes in the extent of vertical integration engaged in by some of them. In such a situation, a recorded change in *average* retail gross margins would be difficult if not impossible to interpret. Paradoxically, the average retail gross margin of a group of retailers may increase even where the average gross margin of each constituent category of retailers has fallen.

To escape from the complications introduced by the passage of time, it may seem more promising to make price comparisons between pairs of territories, only one of which has r.p.m. in a particular trade.[4] Such comparisons are valid for the purpose of measuring the effects of r.p.m. only where the two territories are substantially the same in all relevant respects such as density of population, consumer preferences, costs of factors of production, intensity of manufacturers' advertising, and taxes on goods and transactions, and different only in respect of the presence and absence of r.p.m. There is therefore not much point in comparisons between, say, the United States and the United Kingdom. The United States itself, however, provides scope for more relevant comparisons, since some states allow r.p.m. and others do not. As Professor Hollander shows, several studies on this basis have been made; and he discusses their findings and limitations (pp. 95 to 98, below).

Confidence in the proposition that r.p.m. has the typical effect of raising retail prices would be severely shaken if such studies, when carefully conducted in appropriate situations, found in favour of r.p.m. In fact, they have not done so. Confidence would be even more seriously shaken if consumers could be seen to be behaving in a way which contradicted the proposition. Such behaviour would be where consumers living in an area without r.p.m. in a particular trade bought the goods in question from a near-by area with r.p.m. (and otherwise reasonably comparable in relevant respects) either by making systematic shopping forays into that area or by mail-order buying from retailers operating from that area. There is no evidence of this kind. There is, on the contrary, evidence of inter-area trade in the opposite direction, as the proposition would lead one to expect. Professor Hollander refers to the importance of such trade in the United States; and Mr Boggis draws attention to analogous developments undermining r.p.m. in some countries within the European Economic Community.

[4] The complication considered in the preceding paragraph applies equally to comparisons of gross margins in pairs of territories.

The preceding discussion has been conducted explicitly in terms of the typical working of r.p.m. This qualification is necessary because special circumstances are conceivable in which r.p.m. may have little or no effect on prices, and yet more exceptional circumstances in which it may serve to keep retail prices (and margins) *lower* than they would be otherwise. The conceivable exceptions considered here fit into the general analysis; they depend on the presence of conditions in which price competition (or, indeed, any form of competition) among retailers for some reason or other is weak or non-existent regardless of whether or not there is r.p.m.

Competitive pressures may be low in a trade because of its peculiar structure: the 'shopping' mobility of consumers of the goods may be so low and their total demand so limited that the retailers in each locality are few in number, uncompetitive in behaviour, and protected from the competition of retailers in other localities. The abolition of r.p.m. in such situations may leave prices, margins and the structure of retailing virtually undisturbed. In this connection the role of resale price *recommendations* (not enforced by the manufacturers) may be important. They may provide a framework of retail pricing to support and to strengthen the non-competitive tendencies and behaviour of the retailers. But this is not the inevitable effect of resale price recommendations. In other circumstances they may encourage and accentuate retail price competition. It is interesting that in Ireland the retailer in some cases is not allowed to advertise his own selling price together with that of the manufacturer's recommended price: the purpose of the prohibition is to mitigate price competition. (See below, pp. 229 and 245. See also pp. 57 to 60, for the Canadian experience. The Danish and Swedish chapters also include discussions of price recommendations.)

The most exceptional and unusual situations are those in which the termination of r.p.m. may cause the retail prices of the goods in question to be higher than otherwise by causing retail margins (for a given span of distributive activity) to be higher than otherwise. Consider a situation in which each retailer has an effective monopoly of the sale of goods in his market area, and does not have to fear actual or potential competition. The resale prices he would set in his own interests might conceivably be higher than those which the manufacturer would wish to set in his own interests. The retailer's optimal resale prices would reduce sales below the level which would be optimal for the manufacturer. Should the manufacturer be able to prescribe fixed resale prices for his goods, he could force the retailer away from his optimal position towards his own optimal position, reduce the retailer's profits and increase his own. Here, r.p.m. would reduce retail prices. The manufacturer, it may be noted, could achieve the same object not by fixing his resale prices but by prescribing and enforcing *maximum* resale prices; and yet another method would be the stipulation of a minimum sales quota for each local monopolist stocking his goods, a device which, applied effectively, would indirectly allow the manufacturer to set an upper limit to the retailer's price.

The situation has been considered above in terms of local retail monopolies. The analysis is largely applicable also to local groups of retailers agreeing effectively to concert policy on pricing, as in the Swedish tobacco trade discussed by Professor af Trolle (p. 142, below). It is unlikely, however, that such situations (and those discussed in the paragraph preceding the last) are common in a modern economy, though national differences in the density of population preclude broad generalisations. Many shoppers are mobile and have easy access to important market centres. Mail-order business also breaks down the power of local monopolies or monopoly groups. The important and persistent cases are likely to be those where entry into retailing or changes in the number of retailers handling a particular important brand of products are controlled restrictively, either as a by-product of official control over the use of sites for business purposes or in pursuance of a manufacturer's policy of marketing through selected exclusive dealers, each with a sales territory assigned to him. A possible example in which both influences are combined is noted briefly in the chapter on the United Kingdom (p. 292, note 89, below).

Retail Price Competition and Manufacturers' Price Competition

The economics of r.p.m. are generally discussed in terms of its effects on competition in the distributive trades. The practice may, however, also affect price competition among manufacturers. Although it is difficult to assess the significance of r.p.m. in this respect, it nevertheless seems improbable that r.p.m. is less important for its effects on competition in distribution than for its effects on competition in production.[5]

[5] For a different assessment of the position (in the United Kingdom) see letter

The control of resale prices may affect price competition in manufacturing industry in various ways. The most direct way is where manufacturers who have a price agreement sell part of their output direct to consumers or users and part to resellers. For the agreement to be effective, the manufacturers have to fix both their price to the trade and their (higher) price to be charged on direct sales to users. Their reseller customers are, however, also their competitors in relation to sales to some or all final buyers. Insistence on r.p.m. ensures that the resellers, whatever their wishes may be, in effect become parties to the price agreement. If r.p.m. were not practised manufacturers would tend to become involved in price competition in sales to final consumers or users. This competition might, in turn, weaken or undermine the entire price agreement, and so provoke price competition among the manufacturers both in sales to resellers as well as in sales to final consumers or users. Whether such disruptive effects need be serious in the long run depends on the considerations discussed at the end of this section.

Resale price maintenance can serve the purposes of a group of manufacturers acting together in restraint of competition by being part of a bargain with associations of established dealers to induce the latter not to handle the competing products of excluded manufacturers. Collective policies of r.p.m. have often been part and parcel of agreements among manufacturers, as is illustrated in several of the succeeding chapters.[6]

Resale price maintenance may affect competition in manufacturing in a different way. By eliminating or restricting price competition in retailing, it may prevent or retard the growth of large firms in retailing, and thereby inhibit the building-up or strengthening of bargaining power which could be used to disrupt price agreements or non-collusive oligopolistic price structures in supplying industries. A weaker explanation sometimes encountered (for example, pp. 279 and 281, below) is that large distributors who possess bargaining power are under less pressure to use it when their own margins and selling prices are protected by r.p.m.; the removal of r.p.m. and the release of price competition in retailing force them to use their bargaining strength to the full. This explanation is weaker because

by Mr N.Kaldor, *The Times*, 17 March 1964: '. . . The really important issue is not price competition in retailing, but price competition among manufacturers'.

[6] See also L.G.Telser, 'Why Should Manufacturers Want Fair Trade?', *Journal of Law and Economics*, 3 (1960), pp. 86–105.

it assumes that large distributors would not use their bargaining power unless they themselves were subject to competitive stress.

Retail price competition may provoke price competition in manufacturing in yet another way. Especially in industries in which there are only a small number of manufacturers, non-competitive price policies (whether the result of formal or informal price agreements or the result of individual restraint induced by the logic of an oligopolistic situation) may be subverted by price competition in the retail markets. This comes about when price competition among retailers has the effect of causing changes in the relative sales (market shares) of the brands of the members of the oligopoly group. Such changes occur whenever retail price-cutting is not spread evenly over all brands, but favours the sale of some brand(s) at the expense of the others. Changes in relative sales, if they are material and also not ephemeral, are likely to weaken the restraint of the particular manufacturer(s) who is at a disadvantage; and to that extent concealed (or even open) reductions in trade prices are likely to be offered to selected (or all) retailers in attempts to recapture business. Should retail price-cutting shift from brand to brand, the resulting instability in market shares may well disrupt established non-competitive price policies and make it difficult to resurrect them. Furthermore, experience of increased instability in the market shares of the leading brands brought about by retail price competition may embolden each individual manufacturer to seek to increase his share (and not merely to maintain a given share) by concealed and possibly selective reductions in his trade price. Each of them may reckon that his competitors might desist from retaliation for some time because they might be more likely to ascribe an observed change in market shares to disturbances emanating independently in the retail market than to infer that he was attracting more business by cutting his price to retailers; and price competition would ensue from such (mutually frustrating) tactics. In general, the wider the 'normal' expected fluctuations in market shares, the less likely are price agreements or non-competitive price policies to be effective.[7]

[7] See G.J.Stigler, 'A Theory of Oligopoly', *Journal of Political Economy*, 72 (1964), pp. 44–61, for a formulation and general discussion of this proposition.
Kaldor's explanation of the way in which r.p.m. helps maintain manufacturers' non-competitive price policies is as follows: 'In transactions within the trade there are so many ways of making a price concession – through concealed discounts, the offer of easier credit terms, etc. – that no manufacturer will feel "safe",

Resale price maintenance, by eliminating one external source of instability, to that extent tends to support price agreements or pricing arrangements in manufacturing industry. It is extremely difficult to judge the importance of this effect in general terms.[8] To give much importance to it is to imply a high degree of 'instability' in price competition in retailing. Instability of this kind does not seem to be a prominent feature of retail price competition.[9]

The Supply of Retail Services

That r.p.m. restrains price competition in retailing, and that it sometimes has the effect of restraining price competition in manufacturing industry, constitute two serious charges against the practice. In defence of the practice, on the other hand, a number and variety of claims in favour of r.p.m. have been developed over the decades, ranging from the claim that it (in specific cases or in general) is necessary to protect certain trading or manufacturing interests from price competition to the claim that price competition as such harms the interests of consumers as well as of the economy at large. Many

and each will be tempted to shade his price to the wholesaler or retailer in order to forestall his competitors. Hence the importance of resale price maintenance to the manufacturer – it is the only sure guarantee against price wars.' (Letter in *The Times*, 17 March 1964.) This explanation, however, is inadequate, since it does not explain what it is that makes the individual manufacturer feel more 'safe' with r.p.m. than without it.

[8] It may be noted that manufacturers can avoid the generation of this effect without r.p.m.; it is sufficient if each stipulates that retailers may not re-sell this brand at a *higher* price than that of any competing brand in the same price-bracket, though they are free individually to set their resale prices at any level. American cigarette manufacturers are reported to have used such a device in the inter-war period. (See R.B.Tennant, *The American Cigarette Industry* [New Haven, 1950], pp. 312–4; W.H.Nicholls, *Price Policies in the Cigarette Industry* [Nashville, 1951], e.g. p. 118.) Where individual manufacturers choose to market their products through exclusive dealers (who do not stock competing lines), this device would not serve this purpose. More generally, it would seem that exclusive-dealing channels of distribution are likely to enhance the 'disruptive' effects of retail price competition on manufacturers' price policies.

[9] The sale of cut-price 'specials' for very short periods is a feature of the grocery trade in some countries. Since each bout is short-lived, however, and since bouts are frequent, market shares are not likely to be disturbed seriously or long enough to upset manufacturers' price policies. It is interesting that r.p.m. has rarely been strong in the grocery trade at times when the practice was available to manufacturers.

of these claims are referred to in one context or another in the remaining chapters of this book, and Professor af Trolle presents an analysis of a number of them in his chapter. No exhaustive catalogue or examination will be attempted here. The multiplicity and multiformity of the claims are not correlated with the cogency and weight of the case for r.p.m. It is more to the point to consider a group of claims which have analytical interest and have some bearing on a number of types of market situation which have been prominent in the devising and implementation of official policies towards r.p.m. These claims all relate to the supply of services by retailers to consumers. They are not as a rule applied by their advocates indiscriminately to all situations in which r.p.m. is or has been practised, but only to those situations in which particular retail services are, more or less plausibly, considered to be important for consumers or for manufacturers of the goods in question.

The underlying idea is that, because r.p.m. ordinarily widens their gross margins and safeguards them against erosion, retailers are in a position to give more services to their customers together with the sale of the goods; and that, because competition (apart from price competition) is not prevented by r.p.m., retailers are obliged to give more services in order to win or retain customers. Thus consumers have the benefit of competition in the form of more retail services; they pay for them in the prices of the goods they buy.

While this effect of r.p.m. in enlarging the provision of retail services seems indisputable, it is difficult to establish that it is in the consumers' interest, and less difficult to suggest that it is unlikely to be in their interests when the general implications of r.p.m. are kept in mind. First, in order to show that the effect is in the interests of consumers, it must be shown that in the absence of r.p.m. consumers would not be supplied with the same volume of services on the same or better terms if it is assumed (as the claim must assume) that the consumers in some collective sense want that volume of services and are prepared to meet its costs. Second, it is realistic to suppose that not all consumers want the same amount and kinds of retail services; some of them would be willing to do without certain services if they were free to choose from among several competing combinations of retail price and type and quantity of retail service. With r.p.m., they cannot exercise such a choice and express their preferences. In this respect, r.p.m. involves the subsidisation of some consumers by those others who in fact do not use their 'share' of the services for which they pay. Third, while it is reasonable to say that r.p.m. increases the total expenditure by retailers (and hence by consumers) on retail services, it does not follow that the practice is effective in increasing expenditure on any particular kind of retail service. In so far as a particular claim for r.p.m. is that it augments the supply of a certain kind of service desired by consumers, there is a gap in the reasoning. The retailer is not required by r.p.m. as such to use his additional margin to increase his expenditure in any particular way. Should a manufacturer wish to see the supply of a certain kind of retail service increased, he may well find it more effective to achieve this end by rewarding only those retailers who carry out his wishes. He can do this by confining the sale of his goods to retailers who do what he wants or by giving better terms to those retailers who meet his requirements. (He can also himself supply the 'retail' services to consumers, regardless of the retail outlet patronised.) These practices are independent of a policy of r.p.m.

The analysis sketched above can be applied to various categories of retail service. Services such as credit, delivery, installation and maintenance provide no support to the case for r.p.m. There is no difficulty in the way of retailers to make separate charges, by charging higher prices, for those of their customers who want the services. Services such as the availability of selections, demonstrations and stocks of goods and the provision of advice to customers are, however, in a different category. They cannot be charged for separately; and those who use the services need not buy the goods from the shops which incur the costs of providing them, but may patronise, instead, shops which avoid these costs and reduce their prices accordingly. Thus r.p.m., it seems, would stimulate the supply of such before-sales services, to the benefit of those consumers who want them and would be prepared to meet their costs (and to the disadvantage of those other consumers who do not want them). The difficulty remains, however, that r.p.m. by itself cannot ensure that pre-sales services will be increased: it is possible, and sometimes highly probable, that competing retailers will find it in their interests to use the additional margin of r.p.m. on other services such as more convenient and more expensive locations, more attractive decor and amenities and more credit.

Two more specialised claims for r.p.m., in which the subsidisation effect of r.p.m. is recognised to be at the heart of the matter, require some discussion. The first claim is the tendency for r.p.m. to increase the number and the geographical dispersion of shops selling the goods or brands in question. In this way retail service to consumers is improved: they have more convenient access to more numerous sources of supplies. It may be thought that, in the absence of r.p.m., the number and dispersion of outlets would be adjusted more accurately to the varied and varying preferences of consumers, and that the optimal amount of shopping convenience would ensue, with each consumer in the position of being able to choose from among a variety of combinations of retail price and shopping convenience. At this point, however, the subsidisation effect has to be introduced specifically into the analysis. It is conceivable that, without r.p.m., some localities may be denuded of shops selling the particular goods. If many of the consumers living in the locality find it profitable to buy their needs elsewhere, too few less mobile consumers may be left to support the stocking of the goods in that locality.[10] Resale price maintenance would be in the interests of such groups of consumers if, given the uniformity of retail prices imposed by r.p.m., more of the consumers would prefer to buy locally and hence make profitable the stocking of the goods. The advantages gained by these groups would, however, be paid for by the rest of the consumers.[11]

Although both claims involve the subsidisation of some consumers at the expense of others, the second claim differs from the preceding one in that it refers to subsidisation of the sale of some goods at the

[10] Or the price may be higher (than under r.p.m.) because of higher costs per unit on a small turnover or because of the local monopoly power of the retailer.

[11] The relationship between r.p.m., the number of shops, and prices is examined formally, in the context of a simple analytical model, in a recent article: J.R. Gould and L.E.Preston, 'Resale Price Maintenance and Retail Outlets', *Economica*, 32 (1965), pp. 302–12. In terms of this model it is shown that, given certain assumptions about the monopolist manufacturer's marginal costs and/or the effect of r.p.m. on the elasticity of demand for his product, r.p.m. may reduce the manufacturer's trade price and even his retail price below their levels in the absence of r.p.m. *Ibid.*, pp. 310–11. For an earlier, analytically less formal, discussion, see T.H.Silcock, 'Some Problems of Price Maintenance', *Economic Journal*, 48 (1938), pp. 41–51, esp. p. 50.

It may be noted that, in the absence of r.p.m., a manufacturer could increase the number and dispersion of outlets stocking his brands by subsidising particular outlets which would otherwise not find it worthwhile to be in business or to stock his brands. It may be said then that such subsidisation would be discriminatory. It would not, however, in principle, be more discriminatory than r.p.m. in relation to various categories of consumers.

expense of others, not some places of sale at the expense of others. Thus it is sometimes said that while r.p.m. in certain trades raises the retailers' gross margins on some articles (the fast-moving popular articles), it enables the gross margins on other articles (the articles in less popular demand) to be lower then they would be otherwise. The retailer obtains a satisfactory average gross margin, even though the sale of the less popular articles is subsidised. Two comments are in point. The first comment is that it is not clear why the manufacturers of the goods in question should find it desirable or expedient to bring about this cross-subsidisation. It is not clear, that is, why those manufacturers who are predominantly interested in the sale of the popular items should wish to burden them with higher retail margins and prices than they thought necessary for *their* effective distribution, simply in order to facilitate the reduction of the gross margins on less popular items, predominantly supplied by other manufacturers. It would appear, therefore, that the cross-subsidisation can at best be expected to be found in those situations in which all or most of the manufacturers are as interested in the production of the slow-moving as they are in that of the fast-moving lines: specialists concentrating on the latter would have no reason to follow the pricing pattern voluntarily. Even where this condition were satisfied, it is not obvious that the implied cross-subsidisation would be profitable for the manufacturers. The purposive adoption of pricing practices to achieve cross-subsidisation would seem to require, further, that the manufacturers have some non-pecuniary interest in the production and sale of the slow-moving lines.

The second comment echoes a point made earlier, namely, that r.p.m. as such does not ensure that the additional margin allowed, *ex hypothesi*, to retailers on the sale of the fast-selling lines will be used by them to stock and sell the slow-selling lines, the sale of which, again *ex hypothesi*, has been made unprofitable for them. The implied over-generous rewarding of the resale of the fast-sellers would seem to encourage retailers to concentrate on their sale; and would achieve the unintended subsidisation of retailers rather than the intended subsidisation of slow-selling lines. It is of interest, in this connection, to refer to the earlier temporary exemption of the book trade in Sweden from the prohibition of r.p.m. (discussed below, pp. 129 to 132). The argument based on the cross-subsidisation of slow-selling books by fast-selling books was accepted by the authorities; but, in addition to r.p.m. in the book trade, there were other trade regulations which required booksellers to take copies of all new books at their publishers' discretion and on consignment terms. Such regulations helped to ensure that whatever cross-subsidisation was inherent in resale pricing was made more effective in achieving a desired purpose.

In the preceding discussion in this section various claims made for r.p.m. have been examined critically and their limitations explained. The criticism cannot, however, establish that there can be no special cases in practice, and that, where the special effects of r.p.m. are achieved, they cannot in some sense be in the interests of consumers collectively. Indeed, the possibility of special cases perhaps helps to explain why only one country, Canada, has yet seen fit to prohibit all r.p.m. without any exceptions or provisions for possible exceptions, although Sweden will soon have reached the same result by a different route. The more common post-war approach, exemplified in the policy measures considered in several of the succeeding chapters, is to provide, in some way or other, for exceptions from the general principle that r.p.m. is against the public interest. It must be a matter of judgment whether it is worth while to devise elaborate arrangements for the discovery and exemption of exceptional cases.

Loss Leaders

In an undated manuscript, published after his death, Alfred Marshall wrote that 'there must always be a good many movements of retail price which stand in no relation to changes in the wholesale trade [meaning, in the context, changes in the wholesale price], or are even in opposite directions'. Included in the examples given is that of the individual retailer who 'may move the price of a certain commodity apparently at random, when he or a neighbouring rival begins or ceases to make it a catch article'. Marshall concluded: 'But all cases of this kind put together cover a very small part of the transactions of life: and it would not have been worth while to call attention to them at all, were it not that they have furnished sensational material to writers who have argued that retail prices generally are arbitrary and scarcely at all subject to economic law.'[12] Similarly, but in a different context, it would not have been worth while to consider here, how-

[12] 'Retail Prices', in A.C.Pigou (ed.), *Memorials of Alfred Marshall* (1925), pp. 356–7.

ever briefly, the practice of loss-leader selling were it not for the prominent place it frequently has assumed in public discussion and political debate on the subject of r.p.m. The attention paid to loss-leader selling in those discussions of r.p.m. has been wholly disproportionate to the intrinsic importance and quantitative extent of loss-leader selling (unless it is meaninglessly equated with all retail price competition).

The charges laid at the door of loss-leader selling – and constituting defences of r.p.m. – are directed against three types of effect it is said to have. First, it is said to jeopardise the goodwill of established brands, to disturb their steady supply and thereby raise costs, affect their ready availability or prejudice the maintenance of their quality. Second, it is said to be a device by which large-scale retail firms can drive their competitors out of business and so establish effective monopoly positions. Third, it is said that consumers, as shoppers, are confused and misled by loss-leader selling. Having listed the charges, it will not be necessary to go into an examination of them, either analytically or in terms of the available evidence. Professor Skeoch's chapter includes an extended discussion of the loss-leader question, and several of the other chapters also refer to it. Moreover, the tendency in public policy, as demonstrated in the chapters which follow, is to divorce the issue of r.p.m. from that of loss-leader selling. Thus where loss-leader selling is considered to be a problem requiring control in the public interest, it is being treated separately without involving the retention of r.p.m. This is both reasonable and sensible, because r.p.m. is at best a crude instrument with which to attempt to curb or to control loss-leader selling. It is more questionable whether it is necessary, in the interests of consumers or of the economy as a whole, to have any controls over loss-leader selling, since these controls may have unintended consequences to the detriment of the public.

The Stability of Resale Price Maintenance

It is sometimes said that r.p.m. is inherently unstable in the sense that it creates the conditions for its own eventual collapse or weakening. The long-run forces of competition will destroy or circumvent r.p.m. even where this is practised by manufacturers who are intent on retaining it and enforcing it. The thesis is that those distributors who do not need or want the higher margins given by r.p.m. will in due course disrupt the system by selling the goods at the lower margins and retail prices made possible by their own efficiency or low-cost methods of operation.

The historical evidence on the stability of r.p.m. is not easy to interpret. On the one hand there is the record of effective r.p.m. in several branches of trade in the United Kingdom and some other countries: r.p.m. has prevailed for half a century or more, with at most occasional temporary setbacks, despite changes in general economic conditions, in methods and organisation of production, in the organisation of distribution, in the share of price-maintained goods in the total trade, and in the methods of enforcement open to price-maintaining manufacturers. There is ample evidence, that is, of persistent and enduring r.p.m. There are, on the other hand, several instances of the collapse of r.p.m. The United States provides some major examples. But it is not simple in such cases to decide the relative contributions to the breakdown made by the long-run pressures of competition and by the peculiar difficulties of enforcement caused by the multiplicity of jurisdictions and differences in state policies which played into the hands of price-cutting retailers. Professor Hollander reviews this problem in his chapter. Differences in national policies towards r.p.m. in the member-countries of the European Economic Community may result in similar problems of enforcement, as Mr Boggis explains (p. 214). In yet other examples it is not easy to decide whether the withdrawal of r.p.m. by certain manufacturers was due to a recognition of its imminent collapse under the stress of changing competitive conditions in the distributive trades, or whether it reflected little more than voluntary submission to changes in public opinion. The German experience of extensive breakdown of r.p.m. does, however, seem to be unambiguous, although the law and its administration made some contribution.

Assuming no such disturbance as a change in the law, r.p.m. in a particular trade may be expected to crumble or to decline in importance in certain circumstances, whatever the manufacturers may prefer. Thus where one or a few important retailers, who already have built up a large volume of trade in the price-maintained goods, decide to cut their prices, the manufacturers may find it expedient to give way. Historically, however, situations of this type do not seem to have been common. The threat to r.p.m. has not usually come from well-established large-scale retailing firms with a large stake in the distribution of the particular goods. More frequently, it seems, the threat has come from newly established firms wishing to try new methods of distribution or different price policies. (This is also true, though perhaps to a smaller extent, of the exploitation of the new opportunities opened up by an official prohibition of r.p.m., as is illustrated, for example, by Mr Kjølby in his chapter on Danish experience.) But threats from such a source are generally not serious. Newcomers to the retail trades tend to be operating on a small scale initially. Moreover, because of r.p.m., they cannot quickly build up a large volume of business in the goods while conforming to the resale price conditions, and then change their spots by becoming price-cutters. The most likely threat in this context possibly comes from large-scale retailers who are well-established in some branch of trade operating on a low-cost low-price basis and who then turn their attention, making use of their goodwill, to the price-maintained lines of another branch of trade. But even they would be up against the difficulty of building up a large volume of sales in the new lines when they, in the process, cannot offer competitively attractive price reductions on them; and until they have achieved such sales, their power to challenge the manufacturers is limited.

Another set of circumstances in which r.p.m. may be expected to crumble is where low-cost retailers can gain access to competing goods which they can market as their own 'private' brands and which they can price as they like. A necessary condition is that entry into the industry manufacturing the goods is not difficult, whether it is entry by an independent manufacturer or by the distributor. Where entry is relatively easy, in fact r.p.m. has rarely been important, as in many food and textile products. Resale price maintenance has been strong where private branding is handicapped, if not rendered impossible, by the presence of significant economies of large-scale production, by the need for large-scale sales promotion for the success of a brand, or by institutional constraints such as the laws relating to patents and copyright. Moreover, in so far as r.p.m. inhibits the establishment and growth of large competitively aggressive retailing firms, it makes it more difficult for private brands to be developed in effective opposition to the national brands. The ease of entry into private branding is in part a matter of the scale of requirements.

It should be added that the development of private brands by one or several large distributors need not always undermine r.p.m. In some situations it may be the most profitable course for the private-branding distributor(s) not to price his private brands so competitively as to force the manufacturers of the national brands to jettison their r.p.m. or to reduce their prices. The private brander may find it expedient to act as if he were part of the oligopoly group. Alternatively, a large-scale distributor may find it profitable to refrain from having private brands – even where this would present no difficulties on the supply side – if the manufacturers of the national brands recognise that he presents a threat by granting him specially favourable terms on the purchase of their price-maintained brands.

The Diversity of Policies

Whatever the strength of the long-run forces of competition and economic change might be, it is apparent that governments which have been worried about r.p.m. in the post-war period have not been prepared to rely on those forces either to cause the breakdown of the practice or the moderation of its exercise. For one reason or another, to achieve one purpose or another, various governments have intervened with compulsory prohibition, curtailment or amendment of r.p.m. A variety of policies has ensued. The differences reflect a number of considerations, pressures and influences. There have been differences in the assessment of the economic effects of alternative policy measures; differences in the weights attached to various interest groups; differences in legal institutions and traditions; and differences in the approach to monopoly and restrictive arrangements generally. The seven chapters which follow have as one main theme the development of policy towards r.p.m. in a number of countries, and they illustrate a diversity of approach and method.

Despite the diversity of policies adopted and the differences in the economies in which they are applied, three conclusions emerge with some clarity. First, the termination of r.p.m. does not automatically and in every instance lead to price competition in distribution. Competitive pressures are sometimes low: there is little of them to be released. Further, it requires careful ancillary provisions in the law to ensure that something akin to r.p.m. does not operate after the practice itself has been formally discontinued. Moreover, where apprehensions about the depredations allegedly caused by loss-leader selling have given rise to measures to combat such activities, it is possible that 'genuine' price competition may be blunted in the process. Second, the termination or breakdown of r.p.m. has generally made it possible or easier for major changes to take place in the structure of retailing and wholesaling; it has facilitated or accelerated the kind of change which has been to the advantage of consumers. Third, subject to one or two documented exceptions (for example, p. 142, below), consumers do not seem to have been hurt by the termination of r.p.m. along the lines predicted by supporters of the practice, and frequently they have derived substantial advantages from such a course.

2

CANADA

L. A. Skeoch

The Background

In 1888, a select committee of the Canadian House of Commons began a broad investigation into a number of trades in which combinations or monopolies were suspected of limiting competition to an excessive degree. The inquiry was concerned with sugar and groceries, biscuits and confectionery, oatmeal, eggs, barley, coal, stoves, barbed wire, binder twine, agricultural implements, watch cases, coffins and fire insurance.[1] Although evidence of monopolistic restraints was found in all but two trades – barley and agricultural implements – only one trade – sugar and groceries – will be singled out for consideration here. The arrangements in this trade are of interest because they represent the first *documented* case of the use of resale price maintenance in Canada, and also because the arrangements were defended by Professor W.J.Ashley,[2] on grounds still being put forward by some trades.

In substance, the Dominion Grocers' Guild was formed in 1884 by almost all the wholesale grocers in the provinces of Ontario and Quebec to prevent price-cutting and to set resale prices in the grocery trade. The Guild made arrangements with manufacturers of a number of staple products, such as sugar, tobacco, starch, baking powder and so on, by which the manufacturers would give preferential buying terms to the members of the Guild, whilst, on their side, the members of the Guild undertook to make their purchases solely from the co-operating manufacturers and to resell to retailers at a specified mark-up.[3] In compiling lists of wholesalers for the direction of the

[1] The report of the Committee is found in the *Journal of the House of Commons*, 1888, XXII, appendix 3. A summary of its findings is given in V.W.Bladen, *An Introduction to Political Economy* (Toronto, 1941), pp. 198–200.

[2] W.J.Ashley, 'The Canadian Sugar Combine', *University Quarterly Review* (Toronto), February 1890, pp. 24–39. Reprinted in *Surveys Historic & Economic* (1900), pp. 361–77.

[3] There was some evidence that retailers organised a combine similar to that

manufacturers, the Guild eliminated the names of a number of very large retailers who had generally been accorded wholesale buying terms, as well as of dealers who were partly wholesale and partly retail in their operations, so that 'all retailers should be on the same footing'. The Guild disseminated to its members price information supplied by the manufacturers, thereby discouraging backsliding on the part of the latter in the form of secret price cuts.

Sugar was the strategic product in the scheme; in part, because it was the chief source of 'disturbance' in the wholesale and retail trades owing to its use as what would now be called a 'loss leader', and, in part, because on the supply side the industry was dominated by one refiner behind a substantial tariff wall, thereby facilitating 'stabilised' pricing. If 'orderly marketing' could be achieved by the Guild in sugar, its prowess would be clearly established.

In fact, it did enjoy a considerable measure of success. The use of sugar as a 'loss leader' was brought to an end, and, according to Professor Ashley's estimate, its price was increased by about one full cent per pound. The assessment of the Select Committee was decidedly unfavourable to the Guild: it was 'obnoxious to the public interest, in limiting competition, in enhancing prices, and by the familiar use of its growing and facile powers tending to produce and propagate all the evils of monopoly'.[4]

Professor Ashley was somewhat more lenient in his evaluation. It was his view that 'selling at a price which barely covers original cost' was a 'growing feature' of the grocery trade. When grocers, buying at the same prices, engaged in such a practice, 'one of four things must happen'. 'Either they must be content with a smaller profit than other grocers, which is not likely; or they must succeed in making so large a business as to be able to turn over their capital more quickly than other grocers, which is seldom likely to be the case; or the other articles must be either inferior in quality or dearer than those sold elsewhere.'[5] He considered that one or the other of the final two possibilities was likely to occur,[6] unless the retailer could obtain lower prices from his wholesaler. The attempt of all dealers to buy

of the wholesalers but it apparently broke up after a very brief career.

[4] Quoted in Bladen, *op. cit.*, p. 199.

[5] Ashley, *op. cit.*, p. 27.

[6] Current proponents of 'quality stabilisation' legislation adopt a similar position, as do many supporters of r.p.m. See e.g., *The Bargain That's Merely a Mirage* (Toronto, Retail Merchants' Association of Canada, Inc., 1958), p. 14.

at lower prices resulted in the condition which he described as 'the devil take the hindmost'.[7] This type of 'unrestricted competition' permitted 'businesses carried on with large capitals to drive lesser undertakings out of the field'. Hence, the Guild protected society against the triumph of those with 'large capitals' by preserving the competition of the many and the small.

However, Professor Ashley was clearly uncomfortable with his preliminary conclusion. He had already demonstrated that there was a tendency for entrants to move into the grocery trade at a very high rate in spite of its limited prospects (hence the danger of monopoly without price maintenance was not great), and to describe the sale of products at uniform and fixed prices as 'competitive' obviously leaves much to be desired. Thus, although Professor Ashley did not refer explicitly to either of these considerations, he hedged his conclusion by remarking: 'But I must confess, finally, that there does seem some force in the argument that though the wholesalers have not obtained too high profits as yet, the combination may possibly enable them to exact too high a price by and by'.[8] The danger of their doing so was somewhat diminished by the fact that a few wholesalers had not joined the Guild. In effect, the price maintenance scheme was made tolerable by the fact that a number of sellers did not adopt the practice.

The legislation that was enacted following the investigation of the Select Committee[9] did not deal specifically with the practice of r.p.m., although it did proscribe[10] conspiracies, agreements or arrangements which, among other things, unreasonably enhanced the price of, or unduly prevented or lessened competition in the sale of, any article or commodity which was the subject of trade or commerce.

Until 1952, the combines cases in which r.p.m. figured as an important element characteristically involved a restrictive 'horizontal' agreement or arrangement among manufacturers, wholesalers, or retailers, which was accepted tacitly or overtly by those at earlier or

[7] *Op. cit.*, p. 28.

[8] *Op. cit.*, p. 39.

[9] *An Act for the Prevention and Suppression of Combinations formed in Restraint of Trade, S.C. 1889, C.41.*

[10] The proscriptions proved, in practice, to be totally ineffective since the legislation was written so that the accused had to be convicted of doing certain acts 'unduly' which were 'unlawful' at common law; not until 'unlawful' was stricken from the legislation, in 1900, was effective prosecution possible.

later stages in the 'vertical' structure of manufacture and sale.[11] In general, both under the amended 1889 legislation (which was subsequently incorporated into the Criminal Code) and under the Combines Investigation Act of 1910 and its successor acts, the Commissioner and the courts held that *collusive* arrangements to adopt or impose a system of r.p.m. were illegal. In other words, joint and comprehensive schemes to enforce r.p.m. were clearly prohibited.[12]

[11] The following are examples of some of the early cases. *Rex v. McMichael* ((1907) 10 O.W.R.268) and *Rex v. Central Supply Association Ltd* ((1907) 12 C.C.C.371) involved prosecutions of organisations in the plumbing and steam-fitting trade which undertook to maintain prices, to protect the established channel of supply from manufacturer to retailer, and otherwise to suppress competition. Convictions were obtained in both cases. *Rex v. Clarke* ((1907) 14 C.C.C.46) was a prosecution involving the Alberta Retail Lumber Dealers Association which limited the sale of manufactured lumber to dealers who were members of the Association and established and maintained list prices. The accused was convicted. *Rex v. Beckett et al* ((1910) 20 O.L.R.401) involved the Dominion Wholesale Grocers' Guild, the Ontario Wholesale Grocers' Guild and certain individual wholesale grocers, who attempted to persuade manufacturers to set prices to the retailer and to give the wholesaler a proportion of the sale price for handling the goods. The only penalty for non-compliance was loss of membership in the Guild; non-members could buy from the manufacturers on the same terms as Guild members. The accused were acquitted. There is a suggestion in the judgment that if the manufacturers had been charged a different view of the case might have been taken. *Wampole v. Karn* ((1906) 11 O.L.R.619), which involved an action by a manufacturer against a distributor, arose from a detailed arrangement in which a contract form had been prepared by the Canadian Wholesale Druggists' Association and the drug section of the Retail Merchants' Association for use by manufacturers in all sales to retailers. The contract was used by committees representing a very large part of the wholesale and retail drug trade in Canada and covered almost every drug product. It provided for the fixing of retail prices, and manufacturers who failed to adopt the contract were unable to sell through association members. The court found the agreement contrary to the combines legislation in that the arrangements effectively eliminated competition and also enhanced prices unreasonably. For further discussion of these, and related cases, see S.F.Sommerfeld, 'Free Competition and the Public Interest', *The University of Toronto Law Journal*, VII (1948), pp. 423 ff.

[12] Despite the unambiguous position of policy and jurisprudence, attempts continued to be made to develop comprehensive r.p.m. schemes. Among the most noteworthy of the later instances brought to light under the Combines Investigation Act were: The Proprietary Articles Trade Association (which included retail and wholesale druggists and drug manufacturers), and the Fair Trade League (of similar scope to the P.A.T.A., but applying to the grocery trade), both of which were abandoned in 1927 when the P.A.T.A. was attacked by the Commissioner; a combine in radio tubes and sets which employed r.p.m. as an important element

The position of the individual supplier who adopted r.p.m. for his products was, however, less clear. The views of Mr F.A.McGregor, Registrar, and subsequently Commissioner, under the Combines Investigation Act from 1925–49, represent the consensus of informed observers as to the legality of this form of resale price maintenance prior to 28 December 1951: ' . . . There still remained the problem of dealing with the fixing of resale prices by a single manufacturer who insisted that no dealer should sell his goods below the minimum price which he, the manufacturer, established. It was still a serious limitation of price competition, but it was unilateral action, each manufacturer who adopted the practice applying it only to his own products. It was questionable then (i.e., in 1927), and still is questionable, if under the Combines Investigation Act the courts, dealing with only one arrangement of the kind between one manufacturer and his distributors, would declare that competition had been unduly lessened. Other manufacturers might be doing the same thing in the same trade, but their activities could not be brought before the court in the same action'.[13]

The strength of the doubts as to the possibility of successful prosecution under the Criminal Code or the Combines Investigation Act is indicated by the fact that no prosecution against the individual-supplier type of r.p.m. was instituted during the entire period 1889–1951.[14]

of its restrictive arrangements (1932); arrangements among tobacco manufacturers, wholesalers and retailers to enforce r.p.m., to limit entry by new wholesalers, and the like (1938); a combine between manufacturers and dealers in dental supplies to maintain prices (1947); arrangements among manufacturers, wholesalers and retailers to maintain prices for optical goods (control, in this case, was based, in part, on patents) (1948); arrangements among baking firms to maintain resale prices for bread in Western Canada (1948); the maintenance of resale prices for wooden matches by a monopolist (1949). In addition, there were other cases in which r.p.m. was employed as a more or less effective accessory of general restrictive arrangements.

[13] Joint Committee of the Senate and the House of Commons on Combines Legislation, *Minutes of Proceedings and Evidence*, No. 8, 28 November 1951, p. 389. A similar view was expressed by Mr T.D.MacDonald, the then Commissioner. *Ibid.*, No. 1, 13 November 1951, p. 16.

[14] To this there is one exception involving a situation in which the individual supplier was also a monopolist (wooden matches). However, this case embraced such a wide range of predatory and monopolistic practices that it is impossible to determine how much importance the court assigned to the practice of price maintenance in registering a conviction.

The Extent of the Practice of Resale Price Maintenance after 1945

The Second World War marked a significant shift in the approach to pricing in a number of divisions of trade, a shift which is frequently regarded as an aftergrowth of the regulatory activities of the Wartime Prices and Trade Board. For example, a witness from the Canadian Manufacturers Association appearing before the Joint Parliamentary Committee on Combines Legislation gave the following reply to a question dealing with business failures in the grocery trade: 'There have been less failures in the grocery business since the war years when the Wartime Prices and Trade Board imposed a considerable degree of price maintenance. There have been less grocery stores fail because of the very training which they received through the Wartime Prices and Trade Board'.[15]

The experience of some trade association secretary-managers as administrators under the Wartime Prices and Trade Board also tended to encourage the development of an attitude of 'regulated uniformity' with respect to pricing for entire trade categories.[16]

The Commissioner under the Combines Investigation Act was particularly concerned about the increase in the extent of r.p.m. in products sold through grocery stores. A survey by the Commissioner of some of the leading retail food chains in 1941 indicated that 425 items were subject in one form or another to resale price control.

[15] The witness, in his private capacity, was a manufacturer of fancy biscuits. Joint Committee of the Senate and the House of Commons on Combines Legislation, *Minutes of Proceedings and Evidence*, No. 12, 4 December 1951, p. 585.

[16] The following reply by a representative of the Canadian Electrical Manufacturers Association to a question about the justification for a recent increase in the retailer's mark-up on electrical appliances is characteristic of the approach adopted: 'These mark-ups here . . . cost the dealer . . . considerably more money in financial charges than he had to pay before, so he does need some mark-up to cover that. [During the war] they went to the Wartime Prices and Trade Board and submitted their prices and retailers were given a mark-up by the W.P.T.B. and this is, in theory, no different than what was granted to them by the government during the war.' *Ibid.*, No. 11, 3 December 1951, p. 509. The exposition is somewhat confused but the general meaning is probably clear.

Cf., also, the following questions to, and the replies of, the witness for the Allied Beauty Equipment Manufacturers' and Jobbers' Association:

'Q. What percentage, when you started in 1941, of your production or distribution was under resale price maintenance? – A. I could only guess.

Q. What would be your judgment? – A. Perhaps half.

Q. And that has advanced now to 90 per cent.? – A. That is right.'

Ibid., No. 3, 21 November 1951, pp. 87–8.

A similar survey in 1947 found that the number of items had increased to approximately 600, an increase of about 41 per cent. The principal increases took place in canned soups, tobaccos, floor and furniture waxes and polishes, and in the 'miscellaneous' group. Insistence on resale price adherence was marked in the case of all tobacco products, bread and other bakery products, milk, the better-known brands of floor and furniture waxes, polishes and cleansers, face and toilet tissues, and some brands of cereals. The average mark-up for similar categories of products showed only a slight increase from 1941 to 1947. However, the number of items in the higher mark-up groupings increased substantially: the 34 per cent. and over markup class, for example, showed an increase of more than 100 per cent. over 1941.

The pressure for the extension of r.p.m. was reported by a number of executives in the fields of grocery distribution and production to come from trade associations representing the smaller retailers and wholesalers facing increased competition from the rapid expansion of chain supermarkets. Manufacturers of new items particularly, apparently found it easier to obtain general distribution for their products if they fixed minimum resale prices when introducing them.

No precise estimate of the proportion of grocery-store sales subject to r.p.m. is available. A representative of the Retail Merchants Association (National Foods Division) did, however, testify that about 15 per cent. of food sales were price-maintained.[17] This would suggest that the percentage for total grocery-store sales would be in excess of 20.[18] In any event, whatever the exact percentage, the significant and incontrovertible fact is that the practice was rapidly expanding in the grocery-store field.

In other merchandising areas, representatives of the various trades appearing as witnesses before the Joint Parliamentary Committee on Combines Legislation provided estimates of price-maintained sales varying from 95 per cent. to about 15 per cent. of total sales. In the jewellery trade,[19] r.p.m. was said to apply to 95 per cent. of sales of silverware, 90 per cent. of sales of watches, and 75 per cent. of sales of diamond jewellery. With respect to supplies and equipment for

[17] *Ibid.*, No. 5, 23 November 1951, p. 262.

[18] A figure which, on the basis of calculations he made in 1951, the author considers improbably high. Something in the 12–15 per cent. range seems more likely.

[19] *Ibid.*, No. 13, 5 December 1951, p. 680.

beauty parlours and barber shops, at least 90 per cent. of sales fell in the price-maintained category.[20] Of total drug-store sales, over 60 per cent. were reported as constituting price-maintained articles.[21] Since this included prescriptions and soda-fountain sales, the percentage would be a good deal higher for proprietary medicines and toilet goods. In the field of electrical appliances, most manufacturers were reported as suggesting or recommending their retail selling prices.[22]

In the hardware field, estimates varied. A manufacturer of hardware products reported that about 37 per cent. of his firm's sales were price-maintained.[23] The cheaper qualities were those which were not price-maintained. Counsel for the Ontario Retail Hardware Association reported that 10 to 15 per cent. of the volume of hardware store sales were price-maintained, based on items listed by the manufacturer as price-maintained in the hardware price book.[24] However, it is important here to keep in mind that the Association, itself, published this price book, which recommended resale prices for about 26,500 items. These prices were 'substantially the same' as the resale prices established by manufacturers, in those cases where the manufacturer had adopted the policy of r.p.m. In the case of other products, 'men with practical hardware experience' were 'given sole responsibility of preparing for the members suggested resale prices'.[25] Although, apparently, no direct sanctions were applied to members not following the prices in the 'Price Book', the Association was very militant in its advocacy of 'fair competition' and considerable pressure by argument and persuasion was brought to bear on

[20] *Ibid.*, No. 3, 21 November 1951, p. 87.

[21] *Ibid.*, No. 4, 22 November 1951, p. 137.

[22] *Ibid.*, No. 6, 26 November 1951, p. 327. A representative of the Canadian Retail Federation was asked the meaning of suggested prices:

'Q. Is it just a suggested retail price? – A. I think that is a very mild way of putting it . . .

Q. Does suggestion mean that this is the price at which you will sell? – A. Yes.' *Ibid.*, No. 5, 23 November 1951, p. 285.

[23] *Ibid.*, No. 12, 4 December 1951, p. 567.

[24] *Ibid.*, No. 14, 6 December 1951, p. 719.

[25] *Ibid.*, p. 744. A spokesman for the Association emphasised that no collusion was involved in arriving at such prices: 'There was no suggestion on the part of the association, and no collaboration on the part of members or executive as to what these prices should be'. From this the rather improbable conclusion follows that the 'men with practical hardware experience' who prepared the suggested resale prices were not members of the Association.

retailers to observe the 'suggested' prices. In addition, where such large numbers of items were involved, many retailers would, no doubt, find it convenient to adopt the prices calculated by the Association rather than develop their own costing methods. Hence, price maintenance, in the sense of rigid and uniform prices throughout the trade, was undoubtedly much more widespread than the Association's estimate of 10 to 15 per cent. of sales.

Other categories of products in which r.p.m. was enforced were: cigarettes and other tobacco products, nationally advertised confectionery products, office supplies and fine paper products, books, nationally advertised lines of men's and boys' wear, nationally advertised lines of ladies' wear, nationally advertised lines of shoes for men, women and children, sporting equipment and supplies, cameras, films and photographic equipment, nationally advertised lines of toys, and nationally advertised lines of furniture, mattresses and springs.[26]

The impact of r.p.m. will not, of course, necessarily be the same for all categories of buyers. For example, the Canadian Federation of Agriculture made the following estimate for farm operators in its brief to the Joint Parliamentary Committee: 'More than half of all the purchases made by farmers for productive purposes come directly under some form of private resale price fixing'.[27] The list of items included farm machinery and parts; most items of general hardware such as small tools; many construction and building materials; fertilisers; truck and auto tyres; gasoline and oil; milking machines and parts; milk coolers; electric motors; all barn fixtures such as steel stanchions, water bowls, etc.; some brands of paint; woven wire, wire gates and barbed wire; and veterinary supplies and drugs for livestock.

Although it is not feasible from these data to arrive at an over-all estimate of the proportion which price-maintained sales constituted of total retail sales, it is apparent that the practice of r.p.m. was widespread and, furthermore, that the war and post-war years saw a rapid extension of the practice. In attempting to assess the significance

[26] For a list of some 500 types of nationally advertised merchandise subject to r.p.m., see the brief of the T. Eaton Company to the Joint Committee of the Senate and the House of Commons, *Minutes of Proceedings and Evidence*, No. 12, 4 December 1951, pp. 648–56. The T. Eaton Company operates a nation-wide chain of department stores and mail-order stores.

[27] *Ibid.*, No. 12, 4 December 1951, pp. 628–9.

of r.p.m., it is important not only to be aware of the scope of the practice but also, to use Professor G.C.Allen's words, to take account of 'the type of society or the economic environment with which the enquirer is concerned'.[28] In a small, homogeneous country where suppliers tend to be limited in number, there may very well develop a degree of conservatism and mutual restraint in competitive relationships which will exercise a serious check on important types of dynamic economic conduct.[29] Innovations which disturb established relationships and routines will tend to be discouraged. The longer-run consequences of restrictive practices will have a greater chance of becoming established in persistent and enduring fashion than in a larger and more dynamic economy where they will be uprooted in the early stages of their growth. Thus, the Canadian economy which has had a reputation – at least partly deserved – of being protectionist, imitative and unprogressive, is likely to suffer more from a given type and degree of non-competitive practice than will an aggressive, dynamic economy, such as the United States. It is highly significant that in the United States even the enactment of legislation incorporating the non-signer clause has proved to be incapable of establishing the practice of r.p.m. on an effective and enduring basis, whereas in Canada it spread and prospered even without strong private collective arrangements to enforce it.

The Legislation of 1951 and 1960

The Committee to Study Combines Legislation,[30] appointed by the Government in 1950 'to recommend what amendments, if any, should be made to our Canadian legislation in order to make it a more effective instrument for the encouraging and safeguarding of

[28] G.C.Allen, 'A Note on Monopoly and Economic Progress', *Economica*, 20 (1953), pp. 359–61. Although Professor Allen was primarily concerned with the element of monopoly and technical progress, his argument has a wider application to various kinds of monopolistic and restrictive practices. For a similar argument, see the evidence of E.T.Grether, *Loss-Leader Selling, Transcript of Evidence* (Restrictive Trade Practices Commission, Ottawa, 1954), vol. 20, p. 3305.

[29] Such attitudes are not necessarily limited to small societies. There are plain examples of their existence and maintenance in large societies. It seems safe to suggest, however, that they are more difficult to maintain in large societies, and more difficult to eradicate in small ones.

[30] Commonly referred to as the MacQuarrie Committee.

our free economy', submitted an interim report on r.p.m. on 1 October 1951.[31] The report, which can best be described as a library study of r.p.m., recommended 'that it should be made an offence for a manufacturer or other supplier: 1. To recommend or prescribe minimum resale prices for his products; 2. To refuse to sell, to withdraw a franchise or to take any other form of action as a means of enforcing minimum resale prices'.

It also expressed the cryptic views that the 'loss-leader device' (undefined) was a monopolistic practice which was not compatible with the public interest, that it was not, however, an immediate danger, that there were 'other effective and more desirable methods' of controlling it than r.p.m., and that 'present circumstances' (inflation and relative scarcity) afforded time to make a careful study of the practice and of methods to control it. Thus elevated to a position of major importance, the ominous, if shadowy, threat of loss-leader selling became the rallying cry of the supporters of r.p.m.

The Government promptly introduced legislation to ban r.p.m. unconditionally. Its case was based, essentially, on the familiar arguments (1) that r.p.m. tended to weaken the pressures for greater efficiency not only among retailers but also among wholesalers and manufacturers; and (2) that the small retailer did not require special protection, and furthermore, assuming that he did, that r.p.m. provided no effective protection because the apparently generous margins attracted excessive numbers into the price-maintained trades, and because costs tended to increase as competition in service and advertising developed as substitutes for competition in price.[32]

The opponents of the legislation (found largely, but not wholly, in the Conservative Opposition) based their case primarily on the argument that the legislation would open the flood-gates of loss-leader selling with disastrous consequences for small distributors.[33]

[31] Included as part of the *Report* of the Committee to Study Combines Legislation. (Ottawa, 1952), pp. 51–72.

[32] See the speech of the Minister of Justice on second reading, *Debates*, House of Commons, II, 1951 (Second Session), 17 December 1951, pp. 2090–2108.

[33] Some of the expressions of this position were distinguished chiefly by their vehemence. *Cf.*, the following statement by Mr E.D.Fulton, spokesman for the Official Opposition (and later Minister of Justice when the 1960 amendments to the Combines Investigation Act, including the defence against a charge of r.p.m., were enacted): '. . . I submit it is a reversal of history, a turning back of the clock, a retrograde step to the laws of the jungle to take away the protection of resale price maintenance and throw open the doors . . . to cut-throat competition, to

They argued, as supplementary issues, that the reputation of branded products would suffer serious damage as a result of cut-price selling, and, also by implication, that the banning of r.p.m. would make it more difficult for manufacturers to play the oligopoly game of 'spontaneous co-ordination'.

After one of the most bitter parliamentary struggles in recent years, the amendment to the Combines Investigation Act banning r.p.m. was adopted on 28 December 1951. Section 34 embodying this amendment was formulated as follows:

> 34. (1) In this section 'dealer' means a person engaged in business of manufacturing or supplying or selling any article or commodity.
>
> (2) No dealer shall directly or indirectly by agreement, threat, promise or any other means whatsoever, require or induce or attempt to require or induce any other person to resell an article or commodity
>
> (*a*) at a price specified by the dealer or established by agreement,
>
> (*b*) at a price not less than a minimum price specified by the dealer or established by agreement,
>
> (*c*) at a markup or discount specified by the dealer or established by agreement,
>
> (*d*) at a markup not less than a minimum markup specified by the dealer or established by agreement, or
>
> (*e*) at a discount not greater than a maximum discount specified by the dealer or established by agreement, whether such markup or discount or minimum markup or

unfair trade practices . . .'. *Debates*, House of Commons, *ibid.*, 21 December 1951, p. 2341.

Cf., also, the following answers by Mr J.W.Preston, Secretary-Manager, Canadian Pharmaceutical Association, to Mr Fulton:

A. Well, we assume that the minute the government were to legislate against price maintenance every article that is now price-maintained would become overnight a loss leader.

Q. Did you say "would" or "might"? – A. In my opinion "would" – every item that is now price-maintained would become a loss leader tomorrow morning.' Joint Committee of the Senate and the House of Commons on Combines Legislation, *Minutes of Proceedings and Evidence*, No. 4, 22 November 1951, p. 151. Since the same witness had estimated that 60 per cent. of drug-store sales were in price-maintained articles, the incongruous nature of his position becomes obvious.

maximum discount is expressed as a percentage or otherwise.

(3) No dealer shall refuse to sell or supply an article or commodity to any other person for the reason that such other person

(*a*) has refused to resell or to offer for resale the article or commodity

(i) at a price specified by the dealer or established by agreement,

(ii) at a price not less than a minimum price specified by the dealer or established by agreement,

(iii) at a markup or discount specified by the dealer or established by agreement,

(iv) at a markup not less than a minimum markup specified by the dealer or established by agreement, or

(v) at a discount not greater than a maximum discount specified by the dealer or established by agreement; or

(*b*) has resold or offered to resell the article or commodity

(i) at a price less than a price or minimum price specified by the dealer or established by agreement,

(ii) at a markup less than a markup or minimum markup specified by the dealer or established by agreement, or

(iii) at a discount greater than a discount or maximum discount specified by the dealer or established by agreement.

(4) Every person who violates subsection (2) or (3) is guilty of an indictable offence and is liable on conviction to a fine in the discretion of the court or to imprisonment for a term not exceeding two years or to both.

The legislation, in itself, neither permits nor prohibits the use of suggested resale prices. In the committee stage, however, the Minister was asked whether a manufacturer would be permitted to suggest resale prices for his products, and he replied as follows: 'I think there is no doubt at all that he can do so provided that the manner in which he does it does not constitute an attempt to require or induce the retailer to sell at that price . . .'.[34] There was, significantly,

[34] *Debates*, House of Commons, II, 1951 (Second Session), 28 December 1951, p. 2458.

no discussion of the possibility that the use of suggested resale prices might, in the circumstances of a number of Canadian distributive trades, facilitate the effective adoption of a high degree of r.p.m.

With the defeat of the Liberal government in 1957 and the coming to power of the Conservatives who had so strenuously opposed the ban on r.p.m. in 1951, the advocates of price maintenance mounted a more intense attack on Section 34. Once again, their central thesis was that loss-leader selling was threatening the existence of the small dealer.[35] The manufacturers of small electrical appliances, in particular, supported this position, and supplemented it by the argument that since 1951 the distribution of their products had fallen into the hands of a small number of large 'discount-type' distributors, thus altering the bargaining relationship that had formerly prevailed.[36] In response to these pressures, the Government had open to it a number of possible courses of action.

(1) It could accept the evidence and conclusions of the Restrictive Trade Practices Commission to the effect that loss-leader selling did not, in fact, present a problem, and decline to amend Section 34.[37]
(2) It could adopt some form of minimum markup legislation.
(3) It could prohibit certain defined categories of loss-leader selling, the prohibition to be enforced by the public authorities.

[35] This, despite the two-year inquiry into loss-leader selling by the Combines Branch which found that the practice was almost non-existent. See *The Green Book on Loss-Leader Selling* (Ottawa, 1954), pp. xvii, 308, written by the present author; and *Report on an Inquiry into Loss-Leader Selling* by the Restrictive Trade Practices Commission (Ottawa, 1955), pp. xxi, 278. A similar view was expressed by the President of the Board of Trade of Metropolitan Toronto (Mr W.E. Williams): 'I know virtually of no major area in which there is so-called below cost selling. There is a lot of competitive selling where the normal profit level is 33⅓ per cent. and someone sells at 10 per cent.' Standing Committee on Banking and Commerce, *Minutes of Proceedings and Evidence*, No. 6, 28 June 1960, p. 404. In his private capacity, Mr Williams was then president of the Procter and Gamble Company of Canada.

[36] See the statement by a spokesman for the Retail Merchants' Association of Canada, Inc., before the Standing Committee on Banking and Commerce, *Minutes of Proceedings and Evidence*, No. 2, 16 and 17 June 1960, p. 74.

[37] Logically, it could be argued that the government could also repeal Section 34; however, such a direct move against the section would have encountered strong resistance from consumer and farm groups, as well as being unpopular among some distributors and manufacturers.

(4) It could permit suppliers to refuse to supply dealers who were using the supplier's products as (undefined) loss leaders.[38]

In the event, the government adopted a version of the fourth procedure, by enacting the following amendment to Section 34:

(5) Where, in a prosecution under this section, it is proved that the person charged refused or counselled the refusal to sell or supply an article to any other person, no inference unfavourable to the person charged shall be drawn from such evidence if he satisfies the court that he and anyone upon whose report he depended had reasonable cause to believe and did believe

(*a*) that the other person was making a practice of using articles supplied by the person charged as loss leaders, that is to say, not for the purpose of making a profit thereon but for purposes of advertising;

(*b*) that the other person was making a practice of using articles supplied by the person charged not for the purpose of selling such articles at a profit but for the purpose of attracting customers to his store in the hope of selling them other articles;

(*c*) that the other person was making a practice of engaging in misleading advertising in respect of articles supplied by the person charged; or

(*d*) that the other person made a practice of not providing the level of servicing that purchasers of such articles might reasonably expect from such other person.

This amendment, particularly clauses (*a*) and (*b*), was criticised in detail by all the economists making representation to the Standing Committee on Banking and Commerce,[39] as well as by associations

[38] The rationale of this fourth policy was expressed by the spokesman for the Retail Merchants' Association of Canada, Inc., as follows: 'I mean that right now the manufacturer is put in the position that he can accept no responsibility for what happens to his products in the market place and we feel some provision must be made whereby the manufacturer can be held responsible for his marketing practices . . . Retailers, wholesalers and distributors are going to determine at that point whether the manufacturer's marketing policy is the policy that is satisfactory to him [*sic*] and whether his products are the ones they wish to sell . . . it was our opinion there should be no law in Canada which would force the manufacturer to sell a second order of goods to that retailer if the retailer's methods of merchandising were disrupting the manufacturer's system of distribution'. *Ibid.*, pp. 80–1.

[39] See the evidence of the following witnesses: Professors T.N.Brewis, H.E.

of consumers, co-operatives, and by at least one business executive. One general criticism related to the ambiguity of the provision that the accused supplier was required to establish only that he 'and anyone upon whose report he depended had reasonable cause to believe and did believe' that a dealer was engaged in certain vaguely defined practices. The amendment was also criticised for permitting the supplier to refuse supplies without first establishing to the satisfaction of a court (or perhaps the Restrictive Trade Practices Commission) that his products were being used by the dealer in the ways specified in the amendment.[40] Perhaps the most glaring weakness of the subsection – particularly clauses (*a*) and (*b*) – is the assumption that dealers can and should compute costs and profits for each individual item in their array of goods. Distribution cost accounting – as the 'cost justification' cases in the United States have made clear – is not equal to the task. This point is well made in the following reply of a distributor in connection with the loss-leader inquiry: 'In some places we have to sell some lines such as butter and shortening with about a 3 to 4 per cent. mark-up. Most of our lines are priced at 16–4/16 to 25 per cent. and to tell you the truth I am not able, for the life of me, to tell you what percentage it costs us to handle a pound of butter as against a can of peaches or a dozen of oranges. I know these items represent three different costs in handling, but

English and H.Scott Gordon, *ibid.*, No. 8, 5 July 1960, pp. 484–520; Professor Gideon Rosenbluth, pp. 465–84; Professor L.A.Skeoch, No. 7, 30 June 1960, pp. 427–64. See also the submission by Professors G.E.Britnell, V.C.Fowke, N.M.Ward, K.A.H.Buckley and A.E.Safarian, *ibid.*, Appendix to Proceedings, pp. 15–18.

[40] To this criticism the official reply is that the dealer can lodge a complaint with the Director of Investigation and Research, and an investigation under Section 34 will be launched if the facts appear to justify it. This is scarcely adequate, however. In the first place, subsection 5 is drawn in such vague terms that the dealer is in real difficulty in determining what he is prohibited from doing. Second, the process of determining what is permitted and what prohibited is so long drawn out that the dealer may be out of business before a decision is reached. For example, on 1 September 1960 Sunbeam Corporation (Canada) Limited, wishing to take advantage of the amendment to Section 34, advised its distributors and retailers that it would consider as loss-leading sales of its products at less than certain specified prices (so-called 'Minimum Profitable Resale Prices'). An investigation was launched by the Combines Branch; the report of the Restrictive Trade Practices Commission was issued in October 1962; a true bill was returned by an Ontario Supreme Court grand jury on 14 September 1964 and a trial court decision has not yet been rendered. In the meantime, the company can refuse to supply non-co-operating dealers.

I do not know . . . how we could arrive at a cost for each item.'[41]

The prospect that the courts, in interpreting the amendment, will lay down some rough rule-of-thumb to apply to markups for all products in a given trade, or, even worse, to all products in all trades, is one that any person interested in efficiency in distribution can only view with deep concern.

Finally, the protests of the Minister that the amendment does nothing to weaken the ban on r.p.m. are surely not to be taken seriously. At the very least, the amendment offers scope for the manufacturer who favours r.p.m. to put pressure on the price-cutting distributor, and, perhaps more seriously, it permits associations of retailers and wholesalers to put pressure on all manufacturers to take action against price-cutters.[42] How much scope it offers can, of course, only be determined by an intimate knowledge of developments in a wide range of trades[43] and, also, of course, by the judgments of the courts in contested cases as they become available.

Loss-Leader Selling

Almost without exception, briefs in support of r.p.m. presented to the two parliamentary committees began their presentation by quoting the undocumented and unqualified generalisation in the MacQuarrie Committee *Report* to the effect that the loss-leader device was a monopolistic practice which did not promote the general welfare and thus was not compatible with the public interest. Inasmuch as the Committee did not define a loss leader, its view of the practice could be accepted by persons with widely differing conceptions of what constituted desirable or defensible price behaviour in a competitive society. The supporters of r.p.m. tended to define a loss leader as a sale at anything less than the 'regular' price, or at less than the net acquisition cost plus the average markup for the trade in question. Opponents of r.p.m. tended to define it as a sale at less than acquisition cost. The difficulty with the former definition is that it leaves no scope whatever for normal aggressive price

[41] *The Green Book on Loss-Leader Selling*, p. 80.

[42] See the statement of the Managing Director of the Retail Merchants' Association of Canada, Inc., quoted in footnote 38, above.

[43] A preliminary judgment based on complaints which the author has received would suggest that 'suggested resale prices' are more generally observed than was the case before the amendment was passed. See also pp. 47–51, below, esp. footnote 63.

competition; it also ignores the fact that within any trade there are marked variations in costs of handling and selling individual products or, in some cases, even particular brands of an individual product. To accept such a definition would be to impose an extremely inflexible and unadaptable pricing system on the entire mechanism of distribution. Hence, in what follows, when reference is made to a loss leader, unless the context indicates a special meaning, the expression will be used in the sense of a sale below net acquisition cost.

The central thesis of the parties expressing a concern about the consequences of loss-leader selling (particularly after r.p.m. was banned) was that because of the high degree of 'interdependence of demand' for the sale of goods at retail, it was possible for firms with large financial resources to resort to selling a few items below cost and to offset the resulting loss by increased sales of other goods at normal markups.[44] The effect on the smaller retailer was claimed to be especially serious.

The extent and consequences of loss-leader selling became matters of fact to be established by investigation. In an attempt to explore this area of controversy, the Combines Branch undertook a searching and comprehensive inquiry into loss-leader selling.[45]

The instances of actual loss leaders were extremely limited. Eight grocery items were identified as being sold below net purchase cost – four by chains and four by independents – as week-end specials in all cases, except for one product which was sold by independent stores for an extended period of time.[46] Three instances of household electric appliances being sold as loss leaders were also established. One further example which is of special interest developed after the publication of *The Green Book*; this involved the sale of bread in Montreal. Cigarettes were widely sold at reduced prices but very rarely below net purchase cost.

From this broad and intensive inquiry the Commission concluded that '. . . the practice of selling articles at prices below net purchase cost is not prevalent in any of the lines of trade for which

[44] Some versions claimed that the 'other goods' were marked up excessively, that the loss-leader item was usually available only in limited amounts, and so on. However, no evidence of such 'bait' advertising or excessive markups was presented. There is also reason to believe that such tactics, if persisted in, would be self-defeating.

[45] The results of this inquiry are reported in *The Green Book on Loss-Leader Selling*, the twenty-five volumes of evidence in the public hearings conducted by the Restrictive Trade Practices Commission, and the Commission's *Report on an Inquiry into Loss-Leader Selling*.

[46] See *The Green Book on Loss-Leader Selling*, pp. 72–3.

information was obtained in the inquiry. In fact, it appears that sales on such a basis are made infrequently and the evidence does not suggest in any way that selling of this sort is a practice in any line of trade, even among a minority of the dealers'.[47]

One factor accounting for the limited use of the loss-leader device may be found in the instance of loss-leader selling of bread in Montreal. The facts were, briefly, as follows. On Monday, 25 January 1954, the Montreal daily newspapers carried advertisements by a chain store offering its private brand bread for 'this week only' at a reduction of 5 cents per loaf (from 15 cents to 10 cents, with its regular buying price being 12.25 cents). Three other major chain stores also reduced the price for their private brand bread to 10 cents in retaliation: one on 25 January, one on 26 January, and one on 28 January. The following table brings together data on the sales of private brands and bakers' brands of bread, and on total sales for the four chains involved; separately, for chain store 'A', the store that initiated the price reduction and advertised it most extensively, and in the aggregate for the other three:

	Weekly average for the two weeks preceding price reduction	During the week of reduced bread prices	Weekly average for two weeks following price reduction
Sales of Private Brand bread	(loaves)	(loaves)	(loaves)
(1) Chain store 'A'	67,830	149,490	71,450
(2) Three other chains	52,870	75,725	60,550
Sales of Bakers' Brand bread			
(1) Chain store 'A'	26,800	14,700	26,700
(2) Three other chains	12,500	11,300	11,600
Total Sales (all products)	(dollars)	(dollars)	(dollars)
(1) Chain store 'A'	1,640,500	1,706,900	1,644,900
(2) Three other chains	1,190,000	1,236,100	1,212,000

[47] *Report on an Inquiry into Loss-Leader Selling*, p. 244.

It will be noted, by way of background, that chain store 'A' was much the largest of the four chains, accounting in the two weeks preceding the price reduction for approximately 58 per cent. of the total sales for the four firms. In other words, something in the nature of the 'classic' loss-leader setting prevailed.

Dealing, first, with the figures for the average of the two weeks preceding the price reduction and the figures for the week of the price reduction (25–30 January), the following changes occurred.

(1) an increase in sales of private brand bread of approximately 104,500 loaves, of which chain store 'A' accounted for roughly 80 per cent.;
(2) a decrease in sales of bakers' brand bread of approximately 13,300 loaves of which chain store 'A' accounted for approximately 90 per cent.; and
(3) an increase in total value of sales of approximately 112,500 dollars, of which chain store 'A' accounted for approximately 60 per cent.

Hence, despite the fact that chain store 'A' gained a very large proportion of the increase in sales of bread, it did little better than to obtain the same proportion of the *increase* in total sales (that is of all products) for all four chains that it possessed of total sales before the price reduction. In evaluating the significance of the increase in total sales, it is important to recall that the week of 25–30 January was a 'pay-day' week when some increase in sales could be anticipated. In fact, the increase in sales during the period 25–30 January 1954, compared with average sales in the two preceding weeks, appears to be of much the same magnitude as the increase in sales during the corresponding period a year earlier, 26–31 January 1953, as compared with average sales in the two weeks preceding that period. Hence, it is not clear what part, if any, of the increase in sales of all chain-store products in the period 25–30 January 1954 can be attributed to the loss-leader selling of bread during that period.

Dealing, second, with average sales for the two weeks preceding the loss-leader bread week, and those for the two weeks following it, the following changes occurred.

(1) Average sales of private brand bread for the two weeks following 25–30 January were approximately 11,000 loaves higher than

the average for the two weeks preceding the price reduction. Of this increase, chain store 'A' accounted for approximately 33⅓ per cent., whereas its share of total sales of private brand bread in the two weeks preceding 25–30 January had amounted to about 56 per cent.

(2) Average weekly sales of bakers' brand bread in the later period recovered to within 1,000 loaves of the average for the earlier period. Somewhat paradoxically, chain store 'A' suffered only about 10 per cent. of this decline.

(3) Average total weekly sales of all chain-store products in the later period showed an increase of roughly 26,000 dollars, or less than 1 per cent., over average weekly sales for the earlier period. Chain store 'A' was able to acquire only about 17 per cent. of this increase, compared with its share of total sales for all four chains of about 58 per cent. in the period before the price reduction. In other words, 'A''s very large proportion of the increase in sales of the loss-leader item failed to gain for it anything like its 'normal' share of the increased sales in the period after the price reduction.[48]

As the author has argued elsewhere,[49] the rise in many retail fields of a group of large retailing firms, no one of which will readily be undersold by its competitors, has substantially, if not wholly, undermined the effectiveness of loss-leader selling. Loss-leader selling is no longer a monopolistic practice incompatible with the public interest. It is, clearly enough, an ineffective merchandising practice, and this, in all probability, accounted for the failure of the inquiry by the Combines Branch to uncover more than a few scattered instances of its existence. Continued claims of widespread damage due to loss-leader selling reflect rather the cumulating pressures associated with the accelerating rate of change in many fields of distribution and, perhaps, with certain discriminatory pricing practices.[50] These

[48] The above data are taken from a mimeographed supplement to *The Green Book on Loss-Leader Selling* (Ottawa, 1954), p. 19. A similar experience has been documented for cut-price (but not loss-leader) selling of cigarettes by a chain-store in Vancouver. See *The Green Book*, pp. 229–31.

[49] L.A.Skeoch, 'Resale Price Maintenance in Great Britain', *The Canadian Journal of Economics and Political Science*, 19, 1953, p. 84.

[50] That this is to some extent appreciated by some observers is indicated by the following quotation from the submission of the National Foods Division of the Retail Merchants' Association of Canada, Inc., to the Minister of Justice, 30

pressures are real and painful, especially for the smaller dealer; to look to r.p.m. for their elimination is to confuse symptoms with causes.

Price-Cutting and Damage to the Reputation of a Product

Price-cutting of former price-maintained products which fell short of the loss-leader level (in the strict sense) was the object of strenuous criticism by certain manufacturers[51] before the Joint Parliamentary Committee in 1951, the Combines Branch inquiry, 1952–4, and, with some modification of viewpoint, before the Standing Committee on Banking and Commerce in 1960. The essence of the charge was that widespread price-cutting of their branded lines was causing retailers to cease stocking them, consumers to become suspicious of their quality, and, therefore, their sales to suffer.[52] The Restrictive Trade Practices Commission examined this issue in close detail and, on the basis of sales and production data submitted by the companies at the request of the Director of Investigation and Research, concluded that the complaints were without substance. Of the sales record of one company, the Commission remarked: 'It will be seen that sales of the three small appliances [in which price-cutting was alleged to be most damaging] by Canadian General Electric increased in each of the two years following 1951, and in the case of floor polishers there was an increase in 1951, compared with 1950. There is little indication that Ontario and British Columbia, despite the fact that Toronto and Vancouver were regarded as the centres of price-cutting activity, have significantly different sales records from Saskatchewan and the Maritime Provinces, where it was suggested that little price-cutting had taken place'.[53]

At the same time, criticism of the *advertising* of cut prices was developing on a more general basis. A spokesman for the Canadian Jewellers' Association expressed his views in the following terms: 'The only harm in price-cutting is in the advertising of it. A man

October 1959: 'What may be regarded superficially as important problems in merchandising, including some instances of loss-leader selling, are surface indications of the basic problems created by discriminatory merchandising practices'.

[51] Chiefly manufacturers of electrical household appliances, but also manufacturers of jewellery.

[52] See, e.g., *The Green Book on Loss-Leader Selling*, pp. 167–9.

[53] *Report on an Inquiry into Loss-Leader Selling*, p. 165.

may give a liberal trade-in allowance. There is no manufacturer's scout present to find out how I operate my business. I think that the harm is done when I advertise, let us say, a 15 per cent. discount'.[54] Similarly, a representative of the Canadian Electrical Manufacturers Association remarked: 'If you went into any retailer and wanted to buy an appliance he would give you 10 or 15 per cent. off if you did not tell anybody'.[55]

An attempt to adopt a policy giving effect to the belief that advertising price-cuts was damaging but unadvertised selling at cut prices was not resulted in an investigation by the Combines Branch and a subsequent prosecution under Section 34. The case involved the Moffat Company which manufactures and sells through dealers well-known lines of electrical and gas household appliances.[56] After the enactment of Section 34, Moffat's had adopted the practice, under its 'co-operative advertising plan', of contributing to the cost of certain newspaper advertising by its dealers, provided the prices mentioned met with Moffat's approval.[57] The Moffat Company took the position that advertisements featuring prices which it was not prepared to approve were disturbing to its dealer organisation and did not promote the general business of the company. It also argued that an attempt to have an article advertised at or above a particular price should be distinguished from an attempt to have the article actually sold at that price. The company claimed not to be concerned about the latter.[58]

[54] Joint Committee of the Senate and the House of Commons on Combines Legislation, *Minutes of Proceedings and Evidence*, No. 13, 5 December 1951, p. 683. In response to a question as to why, in such circumstances, a policy of price maintenance should be pursued, the witness said: 'Well, it is a nice orderly way to do business'. *Ibid.*, p. 687.

[55] *Ibid.*, No. 6, 26 November 1951, p. 325. In his private capacity, the speaker was general manager of Renfrew Electric and Refrigerator Company.

[56] *Report concerning a Manufacturer's Advertising Plan alleged to constitute Resale Price Maintenance in the Distribution and Sale of Certain Household Appliances* (Ottawa, 1955).

[57] It is not clear from the *Report* whether this was a new policy or the continuation of a policy in effect before 1952.

[58] As a matter of interest, it may be added that the Restrictive Trade Practices Commission disagreed with the Company's position; it held that an attempt to control the advertised prices was necessarily an attempt to control resale prices. Hence, the Company's co-operative advertising arrangements constituted an attempt to circumvent Section 34. In a subsequent prosecution, the Company was found guilty of contravening Section 34, and was fined 500 dollars.

A related, but more explicit, criticism of the advertising of cut prices was that it contributed to the rise of 'retailing monopolies'. For example, the Canadian Electrical Manufacturers Association in its brief to the Standing Committee on Banking and Commerce advanced the following argument: 'Since 1952 we have seen the growth of retailing monopolies in the larger markets. These have been aided by the use of daily newspaper advertising which affects distribution far beyond the geographical limits of the advertiser's physical ability to serve. The result has been that more and more merchandise in the consumer goods field is reaching the public through fewer and fewer hands . . . smaller outlets stop purchasing or promoting his [the manufacturer's] goods because they cannot compete with the prices advertised by the larger outlets'.[59]

No information relating in a broad way to such alleged concentration of merchandising was made public, although reference was made to an unidentified market area in which two retailers, who in 1951 had accounted for about 10 per cent. of an appliance manufacturer's retail sales, had increased their share to about 70 per cent.[60] Thus the complaint in 1960 was not so much that so-called loss-leader selling had resulted in a decline in sales volume[61] – as had been the case in the 1952–4 inquiry – as that it had contributed to a serious concentration in the merchandising sector.

The insistence of both manufacturers and established distributors upon the desirability of maintaining uniformity of advertised prices whilst tolerating private price reductions to individual consumers is analogous to the more familiar oligopoly case in which manufacturers attempt to maintain closely similar list prices for like products but are prepared to grant secret discounts to commercial buyers when excess capacity develops. Open price reductions are delayed as long as possible to avoid 'disorganisation' of the trade. The chief difference between the two situations is that private price reductions to consumers of limited and varying bargaining skills on occasional purchases are less likely to become generalised than 'secret' discounts

[59] Standing Committee on Banking and Commerce, *Minutes of Proceedings and Evidence*, No. 3, 21 June 1960, pp. 177–8.

[60] *Ibid.*, p. 239.

[61] A statement was made by an industry representative that gross sales volume in the electrical manufacturing industry had increased from about $600 million in 1951 to about $1,200 million in 1959. *Ibid.*, p. 246. These figures apply, of course, to a wider range of products than electrical household appliances; r.p.m. also applied to a wider range of manufactured electrical products than appliances.

to commercial buyers who are skilled in using them to put pressure on other manufacturers for lower prices. And this, from the dynamic point of view, constitutes the major danger in permitting manufacturers and established dealers to eliminate cut-price advertising. Innovators in distribution who can operate profitably on a larger scale at a reduced margin will find entry much more difficult if they are unable to advertise their reduced prices.

That the 'regular' distributive margins were so generous as to make it attractive to retailers seeking volume turnover to offer selling prices substantially below the maintained, and, later, the 'suggested' retail prices, slowly impressed itself on the trade. For example, in a report in *Hardware and Metal and Electrical Dealer* (a trade association publication) of 18 July 1953, inquiring into the causes of the difficulties of appliance dealers following the ban on r.p.m., emphasis was placed on two factors: excessive numbers in the trade and excessive margins.[62] Nevertheless, reluctance to alter traditional margins has been strong, and the greater the incursion of cut-price dealers into the market with their increased power to put pressure on manufacturers, the more manufacturers attempt to protect themselves from such pressure by shoring up the position of the smaller dealers by protecting their margins and taking such steps as they (the manufacturers) can to eliminate the advertising of cut prices on specific brands.[63] Where the private interest of the manufacturers lies is fairly obvious, particularly if one assumes, as they tend to do, that

[62] One dealer is quoted as saying, 'I believe the only solution is to narrow the margin of profit to retailers by lowering the retail list prices so that merchants cannot afford to sell them for less or give premiums'.

At a meeting of 142 appliance dealers held in Toronto on 28 April 1954, dealing with conditions in the appliance trade, the following resolution was passed: '1. It is the opinion of the dealers present . . . that the manufacturers immediately adjust their suggested list so as to bring back to the buying public some semblance of value so that the cut-price dealers cannot show such a difference between the manufacturers' suggested list and their selling price'.

[63] That these attempts are enjoying some degree of success is indicated by an advertisement in the *Kingston Whig-Standard*, 7 August 1965, for the local unit of a 26-store chain of cut-price appliance stores. This advertisement listed cut prices for 17 different appliances, only two of which were identified by name. The others were referred to only as 'Brand new famous make 23″ television', 'Famous make fully automatic washers', 'Brand new 12 cu. ft. refrigerator', and so on. The defence against a charge of r.p.m. under Section 34 is obviously being used with considerable effect. In a 'flyer' distributed to householders, the same firm added the comment: ' No names . . . no lawsuits. Name withheld courtesy of the manufacturer!'

the demand for appliances is highly price-inelastic; where the public interest lies is in facilitating the entry of innovations in distribution.

The general attitude of firms in the jewellery and electric appliance industries with respect to the advertising of their products by retailers at cut prices was not reflected in anything like the same degree by suppliers in the field of grocery products, where monopolistic concentration in distribution is much greater. In a recent (1960) survey of such suppliers,[64] one question related to the use of the supplier's products as loss leaders. It should be noted that the definition of a loss leader employed by almost all the suppliers was a sale at less than the 'regular' or 'normal' shelf price; hence the answers refer to cut prices rather than to loss leaders in the strict sense. The replies are summarised as follows:

Q. – Please indicate whether your products are currently used as 'loss leaders'.

	'Yes'	*'No'*	*Total*
Firms which had practised r.p.m. before 1952	20	2	22
Firms which had not practised r.p.m. before 1952	10	11	21

The concentration of cut-price selling on former price-maintained products is obvious. The answers to a further question on the effect of loss-leader selling on sales did not all lend themselves to clear-cut classification, but the general sense of the replies could be summarised in the following manner: for firms that practised r.p.m. before 1952, three reported that their sales had been affected adversely by cut-price advertising and selling, whilst seven reported that their sales had been affected beneficially; for firms that did not practise r.p.m. before 1952, two firms reported an adverse effect on sales, and four a beneficial effect. The remaining firms either reported no significant effect or failed to answer the question.

Finally, it is of interest to note something of the sales record of the suppliers after 1951, as requested in the following question:

Q. – With sales in 1951 as 100, please indicate the level sales had reached in 1959.

[64] This survey was carried out under the author's supervision: Mary E. Arrow smith, *Some Aspects of Resale Price Maintenance in the Grocery Trade*, a thesis submitted in candidacy for the degree of Master of Arts, Queen's University, 1961; hereafter referred to as *Grocery Trade Survey*.

	PERCENTAGE VOLUME, 1959 (1951=100)			
	'200 or more'	*'200–150'*	*'150–100'*	*Total*
Firms which had practised r.p.m. before 1952	9	6	6	21
Firms which had not practised r.p.m. before 1952	3	7	5	15

Although, unfortunately, all fortythree firms did not reply to this question – the non-reporting firms being largely concentrated in the group which did not practise r.p.m. before 1952 – it is apparent that the larger sales increases were registered by the firms which formerly had practised r.p.m. In fact, the only firms, three in number, reporting 1959 sales as being over 300 per cent. of their 1951 sales were in this category. It is noteworthy that no firm in either group attributed its increase in sales (all reporting firms registered increases in sales) *in any large measure* solely to the ban on r.p.m. At the same time, the *Grocery Trade Survey* indicated that fewer than half the reporting firms that had previously practised r.p.m. would re-adopt the practice if the prohibition were repealed.[65] Among the rapid and fundamental changes accompanying the spread of supermarket chains and affiliated wholesale-retail groups in the grocery field, the high incidence of so-called loss-leader selling of formerly price-maintained products apparently assisted rather than hampered the process of adjustment for a considerable proportion, if not the majority, of firms that had practised r.p.m.

[65] A few firms explained the basis for their decisions. One, that would not re-adopt the practice, stated that as a result of dropping it, 'Increased competition at both the jobbers' level and the retail level has contributed significantly to increased efficiency and, in many cases, the consumer has benefited by lower retail prices'. A number of other firms in the same category stated that changes in retail distribution had been responsible for their changed point of view. One said, 'The growth of chains and their influence on sales makes resale price maintenance difficult to control and not desirable in merchandising in competitive fields'. Two others stated that the fixed shelf prices of price-maintained lines and the resulting inability of sellers to feature these items as 'specials' acted as a deterrent to potential volume. A number of firms that favoured a return to r.p.m. claimed that, since they distributed their products through a variety of outlets, they would prefer a system of 'orderly marketing'. A few others felt that the lack of r.p.m. jeopardised their position with independent grocers, a group they considered important in their system of distribution.

A supplementary issue in the concentration-of-merchandising thesis was the claim that some of the major chain department stores had elected to concentrate their sales efforts on private brands of electrical appliances because of the reduced margins available on national brands sold by the cut-price stores, thereby narrowing still further the number of outlets for manufacturers of the national brands. Such manufacturers, of course, supplied the so-called 'stencil lines' (private brands) to the department stores; but this was considered to weaken the position of the national brand manufacturers in maintaining and strengthening brand preference with consumers, as well as forcing them to bargain with strong buyers. In view of the high, and growing, power of brand names in today's economy, this development, assuming it to be real, would, on familiar grounds, have to be considered advantageous to the economy as a whole.

The issue of private brands and r.p.m. may not, however, necessarily develop along the lines suggested by the electrical appliance manufacturers. In the *Grocery Trade Survey*, one of the questions asked was whether the supplier's products had experienced an increased, decreased, or unchanged degree of competition from private brands since the banning of r.p.m. The 22 suppliers replying to this question were divided as follows: 'increased', 10; 'decreased', 2; 'unchanged', 10. In reply to a supplementary question, the suppliers, with one exception, stated that the banning of r.p.m. had not contributed to any of the reported changes in the competitive position of private brands. The single supplier who differed from this view suggested that if r.p.m. had not been banned, 'private labels would be bigger than ever', since a wider spread in price would have prevailed, thus making private brands more attractive to consumers. The remaining suppliers justified their views as to the position of private brands since 1951 by a wide variety of merchandising considerations.

In general, the views of the suppliers in the two fields, groceries and electrical appliances, are not necessarily in conflict. The economic settings of the two industries were, before 1951, so markedly different that the impact of the ban on r.p.m. could very well be expected to be different. The electrical appliance industry was, in essence, a tightly co-ordinated oligopoly behind a substantial tariff wall with a static system of distribution. The grocery industry covered a wide range of products characterised by varying degrees of competition but subject to an increasingly dynamic system of distribution.

Even where close oligopoly prevailed, as in the manufacture of soaps and detergents, one of the firms was strongly opposed to r.p.m. In other products, firms which practised r.p.m. were obliged in many cases to take account of the pressures of close competitors who did not. Thus, the grocery trade was, in general, flexible and adaptable. The electrical appliance trade, and certain other trades on which less information is available, were highly inflexible and structurally more capable of resisting change. The high-income economy of the post-war period, however, provided opportunities for imaginative innovators even in this field. The ban on r.p.m. undoubtedly facilitated the entry and expansion of such innovators, although resistance to their growth continues strong.

The Effect of Banning Resale Price Maintenance on Distributive Margins[66]

In attempting to assess the results of the abolition of r.p.m., one of the first indicators that suggests itself is the gross distributive margin for the individual trades affected, the reasoning being that if price maintenance tends to expand margins, its abolition should tend to narrow them. The converse can then be argued, that if the banning of r.p.m. does not result in a reduction of gross margins then the practice of price maintenance did not widen them and, hence, is not detrimental to the public interest.[67] In the author's view, this approach, as will be argued below, constitutes an undue oversimplification of the matters at issue. However, when properly qualified, information on the behaviour of gross margins is of some, proximate, evidential value, inadequate as it may be as any sort of definitive assessment.

In a section of their study, entitled 'The Great Illusion', Messrs Andrews and Friday undertook to demonstrate that the abolition of r.p.m. in Canada had not resulted in the reduction of retail gross

[66] The material in this section is taken largely from the author's article, 'The Abolition of Resale Price Maintenance: Some Notes on Canadian Experience', *Economica*, 31 (1964), pp. 260–9. Reprinted as 'Die Abschaffung der vertikalen Preisbindung – Einige Bemerkungen zu den kanadischen Einfahrungen', *Wirtschaft und Wettbewerb*, Heft 5 (1965), pp. 388–96; and as 'Concorrenza e prezzi imposti ai rivenditori', *Mercurio*, Anno VIII (1965), no. 3, pp. 1–6.

[67] This is essentially the position adopted by P.W.S.Andrews and Frank A. Friday in the statistical section of their study, *Fair Trade: Resale Price Maintenance Re-Examined* (1960), esp. pp. 35–9.

margins. The method employed was to compute a simple arithmetic average of the retail gross margins for both chains and independents (or for independents alone where chains were not involved in the trade in question) for thirteen retail trades at two periods of time: 1950–1 and 1956–7 in Canada and the United Kingdom. Since resale price maintenance was banned in Canada on 28 December 1951, this allowed a period of five to six years for the effects of abolition to work themselves out on retail margins.

It was found that over this period the average gross margin increased in Canada by about 1·9 per cent. of the retail price, and in the United Kingdom by about 1·7 per cent. Hence, the authors concluded: '. . . There is no evidence at all of a general downward pressure on gross margins after r.p.m. was prohibited in Canada . . . It is clear that the basic assumption of the opponents of r.p.m. that the practice raises gross margins is quite wrong. Therefore, much else of their analysis falls to the ground'.[68]

However, the technique employed is not directed to the point at issue: whether retail gross margins in price-maintained trades behaved differently from margins in non-price-maintained trades in Canada. In Canada, before 28 December 1951, r.p.m. was important, although in varying degree, in only five trades for which gross margin data are available: confectionery and tobacco, hardware, radio and electrical, drug-stores (chemists), and jewellery. If simple averages, as computed in the Andrews–Friday study, are calculated separately for the five 'price-maintained' trades and the eight 'non-price-maintained' trades, a different result is obtained. The average increase in the 'price-maintained' group amounts to 0·3 percentage point on an average gross margin (on the 1950–1 base) of 29·5 per cent., that is, an increase of about 1 per cent. The average increase in the 'non-price-maintained' group amounts to 2·4 percentage points on an average gross margin of about 25 per cent., or an increase of almost 10 per cent.

Clearly, the abolition of r.p.m. released competitive pressures in the former 'price-maintained' trades which, during a period of general upward movement of prices, held gross margins almost unchanged; whilst margins in the other group, where more effective competition apparently had previously prevailed, could not absorb the upward pressures and experienced a substantial rise.

The pressures released by the abolition of r.p.m. are not, however,

[68] *Ibid.*, pp. 38–9.

limited to the retail sector. It is one of the contentions of those who oppose the practice of r.p.m. that the competitive pressures released by its abolition will be passed back from retailers to wholesalers and, finally, to suppliers. No broadly based survey of suppliers has been undertaken, although it is clear from the discussion in the preceding section that manufacturers of electrical appliances are being subjected to more effective bargaining pressures, and the *Grocery Trade Survey* provides some limited evidence relating to the experience of suppliers in the food manufacturing industry.

Before reviewing that evidence, however, it will be appropriate to examine the behaviour of gross margins in the wholesale trades. The Dominion Bureau of Statistics publishes data on the operating results of a number of wholesale trades similar to those for the retail sector. A narrower range of types of wholesalers is covered than is the case with retailers: four trades in the former 'price-maintained' category, and five in the 'non-price-maintained' category. The average change in the wholesale gross margin for the former 'price-maintained' trades was −0·91 percentage point on an average gross margin of 15·3 per cent., or a reduction of about 5·9 per cent. For the 'non-price-maintained' group the average change was +0·38 percentage point on an average gross margin of 13·1 per cent., or an increase of about 2·9 per cent. The difference in the movement of the gross margins for the two groups must be regarded as being of substantial proportions, and it is consistent in direction with that postulated by the critics of r.p.m.

At the same time, the author would caution against regarding even this highly persuasive evidence as being final and conclusive on the price maintenance issue. This is so for a number of reasons. First, there is the technical point that a reduction in unit price following the abolition of r.p.m. may be fully offset by an increase in the number of units sold, so that gross dollar sales remain unchanged, gross margin in the aggregate may also remain substantially unchanged, but the cost of distribution *per unit* will have declined. In these circumstances, the gross distribution margin per dollar of sales would provide a misleading indicator. Second, the basic advantage to be anticipated from the banning of r.p.m. relates to the greater scope it offers for the play of competitive forces, especially those of a dynamic nature, at both the supplier and the distributor levels. These forces may, for example, encourage the development of new types of distributors straddling a number of traditional trades. The range of functions performed may change in significant degree: wholesalers may integrate with retailers, reducing some services, extending others, and even developing entirely new ones. Pressures on suppliers may result in changes in the number of product lines, a different mix of private brands and standard brands, in methods of distribution, and so on. Such developments are likely to take some time but there is serious doubt that they will, even then, be adequately reflected in changes in distributive margins. For example, the replacement of separate wholesaling and retailing firms by more efficient integrated retailers could show up as an *increase* in the recorded rate of retail gross margin, since it would include the formerly separate wholesale and retail margins. Shorter-run competitive pressures *may* show up in gross margin changes, thus indicating in a rough way what tendencies are beginning to develop; but the longer the period from the abolition of r.p.m., the more important it becomes to look behind the figures for evidence that the situations are genuinely comparable.

We now turn to the limited evidence available on changes in competitive pressures on manufacturers in the field of grocery products. Two questions were included in the *Grocery Trade Survey* which cast some light on this matter. First, the firms were asked whether the number of their competitors had changed since 1951. The replies are summarised as follows:

	'Increased'	*'Decreased'*	*'No Change'*	*Total*
Firms which had practised r.p.m. before 1951	14	2	6	22
Firms which had not practised r.p.m. before 1951	8	5	10	23

Approximately two-thirds of the firms that had practised price maintenance reported an increase in the number of their competitors since 1951, whereas only about one-third of the firms that had not practised price maintenance reported such an increase. No identification of the sources from which the 'new competitors' developed was offered, whether from new entrants, or from existing firms which became more effective competitors once the price-maintenance firms could no longer offer protected margins to distributors. Hence it is unprofitable to speculate about the causes of this development, or of that relating to decreases in the number of competitors (which is, in some respects, more surprising). The facts reported are merely recorded.

The second question was: 'Since 1951, has your firm experienced a significant change in either its production or distribution methods?' The replies are summarised as follows:

	Production Methods			*Distribution Methods*		
	'Yes'	*'No'*	*Total Answers*	*'Yes'*	*'No'*	*Total Answers*
Firms that did practise r.p.m. before 1952	15	2	17	16	2	18
Firms that did not practise r.p.m. before 1952	12	7	19	10	8	18

It is of interest that the factors emphasised by the firms as accounting for the changes were: the growth of chains of supermarkets, the increase in self-service in retailing, the development of affiliated wholesale-retail groups, and other merchandising changes. It is understandable that these dynamic changes which revolutionised grocery distribution should receive dominant attention from the firms caught up in the changes. At the same time, the fact that proportionately more of the firms which formerly had practised r.p.m. reported the necessity of making changes in both production and distribution methods suggests, at the least, that they were initially somewhat less adaptable and flexible than the other firms in meeting the changes as they occurred.

The Observance of 'Suggested' Resale Prices and Related Matters

It was pointed out above that the legislation dealing with r.p.m. neither specifically permits nor prohibits the use of suggested resale prices; the subject is simply not referred to. The Minister of Justice did, however, state that suggested resale prices would not be questioned if nothing were done to require or induce their observance. As was also observed above, it is characteristic of the legalistic framework within which combines matters are considered that it was implicitly assumed that if suggested prices were 'spontaneously' adopted in a trade, no problem of a price-maintenance character existed; whereas, in fact, the opposite is more likely to be the case.

In the early years following the abolition of r.p.m., it was the practice of most suppliers to qualify prices shown on a package or in the supplier's advertisement with a note indicating that the price was a suggested one only. This practice has now been almost completely discontinued and retail prices affixed to a product or advertised by the manufacturer are characteristically stated without qualification.

No general inquiry has been undertaken covering the retail trade to establish either the extent to which resale prices are suggested by the supplier, or the extent to which such suggested prices are observed. Some limited information is, however, available on a few trades. The spokesman for the Canadian Electrical Manufacturers Association, giving evidence before the Standing Committee on Banking and Commerce, testified that 'virtually all' electrical manufactured goods were assigned suggested resale prices by manufacturers. He also stated, 'with a fair degree of assurance', that taking account of all electrical goods sold through middlemen, 'between 60 per cent. and 75 per cent. of the electrical manufactured goods in Canada are being sold at prices that are suggested by the manufacturers'.[69] No specific percentage estimate was given for electrical household appliances, but it was implied that it was substantially below the over-all average cited.

In the *Grocery Trade Survey* a number of questions were directed to this matter. In response to a question as to whether the manufacturer currently suggested resale prices, 30 firms replied 'yes', and 16 'no'. These over-all totals were broken down as follows:

	'Yes'	*'No'*	*Total*
Firms which had practised r.p.m. before 1952	20	2	22
Firms which had not practised r.p.m. before 1952	10	14	24

The firms which had formerly practised r.p.m. were almost unanimous in adopting a suggested price policy in 1960. Most of the firms in the other group which suggested resale prices in 1960 had

[69] Standing Committee on Banking and Commerce, *Minutes of Proceedings and Evidence*, No. 3, 21 June 1960, p. 200.

also suggested such prices before 1952, although they had not attempted to maintain them. It is significant that six of these ten firms (which had *not* practised r.p.m. before 1952 but suggested resale prices in 1960) reported that 90 per cent. or more of the distributors 'currently' followed the suggested prices, whilst only six of the twenty firms (which had practised r.p.m. before 1952 and suggested resale prices in 1960) reported the same degree of observance of their suggested prices. Thus, eight years after the abolition of r.p.m., former price-maintained products apparently continued to offer advantages to distributors for use as 'cut-price specials'. The remaining eighteen firms which suggested resale prices in 1960 reported a wide range of observance of such prices by distributors, from 75 per cent. to a low of 10 per cent.

The manufacturers were also asked if they would continue to suggest resale prices if they were not observed by at least 50 per cent. of the distributors. Nineteen firms said they would and eleven firms that they would not. Most of the firms in the former group put forward the view that suggested prices offered a 'standard' for distributors which tended to reduce the severity of price-cutting. The majority of firms in the latter group offered some variant of the view that 'a continual reduced price from the suggested tends to cheapen the product in the consumer's eye', or, in some versions, that suggested prices that were not observed were regarded unfavourably by the distributors as an attempt 'to force prices by means of advertising'. The contrasting concepts of merchandising underlying these attitudes to the role of suggested resale prices are not, on the basis of available information, closely related to product differentiation or to the size of the firm *per se*. Firms which sold through a variety of channels – such as grocery outlets, drug-stores, and hardware stores – seemed to be convinced of the advantages of using suggested prices as a 'standard' to restrict price-cutting, as did *some* firms belonging to tight oligopolistic market structures. However, these are general impressions which, more than anything else, emphasise the need for research in this subject.

With respect to other trades, private inquiries establish that suggested resale prices are employed throughout the book trade and are accorded almost total observance. Innovations in merchandising in this field in Canada are not discernible. In drug-stores, proprietary medicines and toilet articles carry suggested resale prices without exception, and prescription drugs have been widely priced on the basis of formulae developed by professional associations of pharmacists. Recently, however, chains of cut-rate pharmacies have developed, which offer reduced prices on proprietaries, toilet articles and prescriptions,[70] whilst eliminating some services, such as telephone orders and delivery. These cut-rate pharmacies, otherwise, do not differ in scale or in organisation from the traditional pharmacies. The wide margins (33⅓ to 40 per cent.) on proprietaries and toilet goods and the formula-priced prescriptions apparently make it possible for the cut-rate stores to cut prices, trim costs, and still make attractive profits. This might be described as the 'limited' response to the abolition of r.p.m., in contrast to the 'broad and basic' response which involves innovations in matters of scale or of structural organisation of the trade.[71]

The two remaining trades in Canada in which r.p.m. was important before 1952 – hardware and jewellery – display, up to the present, no marked response, either 'limited' or 'basic', to the abolition of r.p.m., apart from the impact of the cut-price appliance stores on the hardware trade. Suggested resale prices continue to be the rule. It does not follow that the abolition of r.p.m. is without effect in these trades. The incubation period of the 'adjustment' or 'innovation' virus is by no means uniform from trade to trade, as the modest recent changes in the drug-store field make clear. The abolition of r.p.m. does not, of itself, cause change; it does remove one barrier to change.

[70] The president of Drug Trading Company Limited, a wholesale drug firm owned by retail druggists, in a letter to the owner-members, commented: 'At a meeting in a city in Western Ontario, our members admitted that in their opinion the three discount pharmacies in their area were filling a minimum of 300 prescriptions a day. I do not need to tell you what dollar volume this number of prescriptions means'. *The Kingston Whig-Standard*, 24 August 1964, p. 7. There is evidence that the Ontario College of Pharmacy (which has the power to discipline all pharmacists in the province and it should be added that only registered pharmacists can *own* drug-stores in Ontario) is seeking additional powers from the provincial legislature to enable it to fix minimum fees for prescriptions and to limit advertising by the cut-rate pharmacies. See 'Setting Drug Prices', *The Globe and Mail* (Toronto), 1 May 1965.

[71] *Cf.*, the following comment from the *Financial Times* (London) about Tesco Stores Ltd: 'Tesco is anxious to mount the new discount store venture on a large scale . . . but the restrictions of price-fixing legislation have held up the opportunities for marketing large consumer goods at cut prices. . . . The ending of price maintenance has radically changed the outlook'. *The Globe and Mail*, 7 July 1964.

Conclusion

It will not be profitable to review in detail all the varied aspects of Canadian experience with the abolition of r.p.m. which have been examined in this brief study. However, a few summary comments may serve to focus attention on some of the leading issues. First, the threat of loss-leader selling is so unsubstantial in the circumstances of modern merchandising that it cannot be regarded as a matter for concern.[72] Second, firms with strong brand names which have practised price maintenance are likely to be the leading beneficiaries of the abolition of price maintenance, in terms of increased volume of sales. Third, industries with tightly co-ordinated oligopolistic structures are likely to be strong supporters of r.p.m. and to offer the strongest opposition to the development of innovations in merchandising which emphasise scale economies and the rise of powerful distributors. Fourth, the abolition of r.p.m. does not *assure* the adoption or development of more efficient distribution or production methods, as some critics of the practice are inclined to argue. It does, however, appear to facilitate change in both sectors. Fifth, it is apparent that we know far too little about the dynamics of selective distribution, of which r.p.m. is only one aspect, particularly in the context of conservative, security-prone industries and trades such as are common in Canada. And, finally, the early tendencies in terms of the behaviour of retail and wholesale gross margins lend strong support to the view that the abolition of r.p.m. has promoted the public interest in Canada.

[72] Although no specific information is available on Canadian experience, it can be argued plausibly that in the 1920s and 30s, when units of strongly financed chains were competing with numbers of small independents, the use of loss leaders by the chains constituted an effective method of increasing sales. In more recent years, when powerful chains, corporate and voluntary, compete directly with one another, it seems clear that the loss leader has lost any effectiveness it may have possessed as a competitive merchandising technique.

Appendix: Provincial Legislation to Limit Retail and Wholesale Price-Cutting

In Canada, because of the division of powers under the constitution, federal legislation on combines and restrictive practices is dealt with under the criminal law. The provinces, on the other hand, have exclusive authority to deal with 'property and civil rights', and, under this arm of their powers, they can legislate on matters relating to the pricing of commodities within their respective boundaries. In the case of a conflict between a federal enactment under the criminal law prohibiting, say, resale price maintenance, and a provincial statute permitting resale price maintenance (under the property and civil rights clause), it is not clear which authority would prevail. In the beer merger case,[73] the trial judge argued that the provincial legislatures by statute had assumed 'direct control over the market', and, hence, removed certain actions by the breweries from the reach of the federal combines legislation. There is some doubt that this view is valid. The Attorney-General of the Province of Manitoba, in a letter to the author with respect to *The Food Products Minimum Loss Act* of that province, remarked: 'There is some opinion here that the Manitoba Statute may be *ultra vires*. This point has never been settled since there have been no cases to come before the courts'. Nor has the question of jurisdiction been determined for the other two provinces in which similar legislation has been enacted.

However, the question of jurisdiction aside, the provincial legislation falls into two categories: that dealing with so-called loss leaders, and that legalising r.p.m. In the former category three provinces have acts on the statute books. The British Columbia legislation[74] prohibits only the loss-leader selling of groceries. Section 3 of the Act states: 'No retailer shall offer for sale, sell or keep for sale in the Province any grocery product at a price less than five per centum above the costs of the same to the retailer'. 'Cost' is defined to include purchase price plus cost of transportation, sales tax, etc.

The Manitoba Act[75] applies to 'food products' and is similar to the British Columbia Act in that it prohibits the sale of such products at less than 5 per cent. above cost to the retailer. The Manitoba legislation qualifies this prohibition by permitting the offering by the

[73] *The Queen v. Canadian Breweries Limited*, C.R., vol. 33, 1960, pp. 1–33.

[74] *Commodities Minimum Loss Act*, R.S.B.C. 1960, c. 64.

[75] *The Food Products Minimum Loss Act*, R.S.M. 1954, c. 89.

retailer of 'specials' for a limited period of time, provided that the price reduction is originally made by the manufacturer or processor.

In Alberta, the Ministry of Industry and Development may formulate, under the Industry and Development Department Act,[76] codes 'setting up standards of ethics, practices and systems applicable to trades within the Province to effect an end to competitive practices that are in their nature detrimental either to the trade, persons employed therein, or to the public'. Codes have been formulated relating to both wholesale and retail trade. In their original form, these codes provided for a minimum mark-up over cost of 5 per cent. This provision was rescinded shortly after the Second World War, and the codes in their present form relate solely to such matters as hours and wages of employees, misleading advertising, and the like.

Inquiries directed to the attorneys-general of the three provinces involved indicate that no prosecutions have taken place under minimum mark-up legislation. The 5 per cent. mark-up requirement, of course, leaves substantial scope for the use of cut-price 'specials', even in the relatively low-margin food and grocery field. The chief danger in such legislation is that the minimum will be ratcheted upwards.

In the second category of legislation, that providing for the fixing of resale prices, only the Province of British Columbia has an act in force.[77] This is general legislation prohibiting the sale of commodities at retail 'at a price less than the cost of manufacture and sale'. The cost of manufacture and sale is deemed to be the retail price set by the producer or wholesaler. The producer or wholesaler may fix the retail price of a commodity by informing the retailer of the price at the time the goods are sold to him, by publishing the price in a newspaper, price list or catalogue, or by notice in writing to the Retail Merchants' Association of Canada, British Columbia Branch. It is difficult to assess the effectiveness of the legislation since producers or wholesalers who may take advantage of its terms are not required to report their action to any agency of government. However, in view of the number of complaints received by the Combines Branch about alleged loss-leader selling in Vancouver, there is ground for doubt that the legislation is widely employed.

[76] R.S.A. 1958, c. 30.

[77] *The Commodities Retail Sales Act*, R.S.B.C. 1960, c. 65.

The Province of Alberta did have an Act to legalise the fixing of resale prices for trade-marked goods, but it was repealed in 1939.

The limited range and effectiveness of provincial legislation dealing with minimum markups and with r.p.m. stand in sharp contrast to the widespread use of such types of legislation by the individual states in the United States. Although the explanation for this difference may lie partly in the political sphere, it seems probable that the generally effective enforcement of r.p.m. in Canada before 1952 by individual suppliers, supported and encouraged by certain trade associations, made resort to provincial legislation unnecessary. Doubts about the constitutional validity of such legislation in conflict with the federal combines legislation may also have been a factor.

3

UNITED STATES OF AMERICA

S. C. Hollander

Development of the Law

The avowed motive for adopting resale price maintenance in the United States was a claimed desire to protect the small retailers from predatory competitors. The legal concept expressed in the price maintenance laws has been protection of manufacturers' interests in the prices at which their products are resold. In these respects the development of r.p.m. in the United States has much in common with the development of the practice elsewhere. On the other hand, however, the political device of making r.p.m. a matter of state statutes and decisions seems to have been peculiar to the United States. This device was not what the 'fair trade' advocates wanted. Rather, it was the price that had to be paid to obtain any r.p.m. legislation at all. Since this unique state-by-state approach has seriously affected the conduct and results of price maintenance programmes, it is the appropriate point of departure for any discussion of American r.p.m.

As every reader of this book probably knows, the United States contains three types of major political subdivisions: (1) fifty quasi-sovereign states, each with its own constitution, legislature and judiciary; (2) a few less-autonomous overseas territories and possessions, not relevant to the present discussion; and (3) the District of Columbia, that is, the city of Washington, where the federal Congress serves as a local city council or legislative body. Under the national constitution, however, the federal government has primary jurisdiction over commerce between the states, so that state common and statutory law affecting interstate commerce is valid only in so far as it does not conflict with federal controls.

Nineteenth-century courts were divided on the question of whether the common law permitted r.p.m.[1] This question, however, became

[1] US Federal Trade Commission, *Report of the Federal Trade Commission on Resale Price Maintenance* (Washington, 1945), p. 15.

moot with the adoption of the national Sherman Anti-trust Act in 1890, which prohibited restraints on interstate commerce. In 1911 the US Supreme Court said that both this Act and the common law barred a system of so-called 'agency contracts' under which a manufacturer of proprietary medicines had been establishing resale prices with his wholesalers and retailers.[2] Some subsequent decisions wavered from that position, but over time the basic ruling held.

Various industry groups, dominated first by manufacturers of consumer goods and subsequently by pharmacy retailers, then waged increasingly vigorous campaigns for legislation to restore the acceptability of r.p.m. Between 1933 and 1937, the druggists, who possessed an amazingly effective political apparatus, obtained statutory authorisation for price maintenance in fourteen states. But national fair trade, or r.p.m. bills, which were introduced in every Congressional session from 1914 to 1936, were invariably defeated. Consequently each of the fourteen state acts merely authorised resale price control when the goods were manufactured, wholesaled and retailed completely within the state boundaries, a privilege of trivial economic significance.

By 1936–7, the fair-trade groups decided to try another tactic instead of pursuing the apparently hopeless quest for direct national authorisation. The latent 'states rights' sentiments that have always been present in Congress were at that time intensified by the reaction to the centralising tendencies of F.D.Roosevelt's New Deal economic programme. Taking advantage of this reaction, the fair traders then asked that the states be given an opportunity to determine for themselves if they wanted price maintenance. The change in approach attracted sufficient support to pass the Miller-Tydings Enabling Amendment in 1937. This legislation lifted the Sherman Act prohibition on vertical price control, even on goods that moved from one state to another, when and if the state in which the merchandise was finally retailed authorised r.p.m. Even so, the support was not strong enough to assure the fair traders that they could over-ride the anticipated presidential veto of the amendment. Therefore they used the parliamentary manoeuvre of attaching their bill as a rider to a crucial appropriation act in order to coerce presidential approval for r.p.m.

Most of the states then rushed to pass price maintenance laws, although Congress remained adamant in its basic opposition to r.p.m. and refused to adopt any legislation that would approve the practice within its own local jurisdiction, the District of Columbia.

[2] *Dr Miles Medical Co. v. Park & Sons Co.*, 220 US 373.

Many of the states simply adopted verbatim the California model statute which the National Association of Retail Druggists favoured.[3] This statute contained the crucial 'non-signers' clause' which provided that the manufacturer need conclude a price agreement with only one retailer to bind all other dealers within the same state. Thus, at first glance, it seemed as if the fair traders had gained as much as they would have derived from direct national authorisation. But actually several significant differences ensued from this complicated approach.

One was that some pockets of resistance remained. Missouri, Texas, Vermont, and, as noted, the District of Columbia rejected r.p.m. The existence of these non-fair-trade jurisdictions complicated manufacturers' and retailers' problems in using price maintenance in adjacent areas. The most severe competitive difficulties appeared in the Washington–Baltimore metropolitan area which embraces both the District (non-fair-trade) and substantial parts of Maryland and Virginia (fair-trade territory). Newspaper columnists, relying upon population and sales figures, are prone to claim that per capita liquor consumption in Washington grossly exceeds the national average; the fact is simply that Washington liquor retailers obtain a considerable share of their sales volume from thrifty Maryland and Virginia drinkers.

Second, although the question has not been fully adjudicated, the state-by-state approach seems to provide very limited support, at the most, for r.p.m. when the retail transaction itself is interstate commerce, that is, when the goods are sold to a consumer located in one state by a mail-order vendor located in another. In 1950 one US Circuit Court of Appeals (the level immediately below the Supreme Court) ruled firmly that the Miller-Tydings Amendment and the state laws did not exempt price maintenance on such transactions from the federal prohibitions against restraints of interstate trade.[4] Subsequent federal legislation (the McGuire Act, 1952) probably nullified this decision, however. But even more recently, two Circuit Courts have held that mail-order firms located in non-fair-trade territory cannot be bound by the minimum prices set for the fair-trade districts into which they sell.[5]

[3] See Federal Trade Commission, *Report* . . . (1945), chs III–V.

[4] *Sunbeam Corp. v. Wentling*, 185 F.2d 903 (CA-3, 1950).

[5] *Bissell Carpet Sweeper Co. v. Masters Mail Order Co. of Washington*, 240 F.2d 684 (CA-4, 1957); *General Electric Co. v. Masters Mail Order Co. of Washington*, 244 F.2d 681 (CA-2, 1957).

These rulings have not been particularly significant for the operations of the largest American mail-order firms such as Sears Roebuck and Montgomery Ward. Sears and Ward concentrate, to a great extent, on promoting their own private label (house brand) merchandise which, by its very nature, is immune to manufacturers' resale price control. Moreover, both firms obtain most of their sales volume from over-the-counter transactions in their stores and from consumer orders placed directly at catalogue order-desks in their stores and retail order offices. Consequently they would have very little interest in strictly mail-order promotion of manufacturers' brands at cut prices.[6] But there are other mail-order vendors, and still more would appear if market opportunities beckoned. Thus mail-order trading provides a potential limit on attempts to control resale prices for products, such as electrical appliances, which do not require demonstration and fitting, which are costly enough to warrant payment of ordering and shipping costs and trouble, and which are not needed with great urgency. In fact, even one or two attempts at developing reduced-priced mail-order services for filling medical prescriptions seemed likely to achieve considerable commercial success until they were stopped through pressure from state boards of pharmacy control.[7]

Finally, and most important, the state-by-state approach has meant that programmes of r.p.m. are subject to test in both state and federal courts, and that both state and federal criteria are applicable to such programmes. The trend of decisions in all courts was generally favourable to r.p.m. until the first Schwegmann case in 1951.[8] Then the US Supreme Court said that although the Miller-Tydings Amendment provided for the exception of vertical price-maintenance contracts from the prohibition of the Sherman Act, it could not be stretched, in the absence of specific language, to authorise the non-signers' clause which was an extreme departure from conventional American law. The McGuire Act of 1952 supplied the missing mandate, but the issuance of even one seriously adverse decision from the nation's highest court (plus some of the economic

[6] A.D.H.Kaplan, J.B.Dirlam, and R.B.Lanzillotti, *Pricing in Big Business* (Washington, 1958), pp. 196–7.

[7] See L.W.Stern, *An Economic Analysis of the Policy of Retail Price Maintenance from the Point of View of Consumers Goods Manufacturers* (unpublished Ph.D. dissertation, Northwestern University, 1962), pp. 110–1.

[8] *Schwegmann Brothers v. Calvert Corp.*, 341 US 384 (1951).

factors discussed below) seems to have stimulated second thoughts among the state judiciaries. Since 1951, Alabama, Montana, Utah and Wyoming courts have found that r.p.m. *in toto* violates their *state* constitutions. More significantly, since the group includes some of the more densely populated industrial states, approximately eighteen states now hold that the non-signers' clause deprives resellers of property rights without due process of law, constitutes an improper delegation of legislative power to private individuals, or in some other way offends state constitutional sanctions.[9] Moreover, some courts are interpreting the laws differently, and sometimes more strictly, than ever before. One instance of this arises out of the somewhat self-contradictory stipulation in the basic enabling act that manufacturers may apply resale price controls only to goods that are in 'free and open competition' with similar products. In the past this was generally considered to be a purely nominal requirement, although it was once invoked to stop r.p.m. by the country's then sole producer of colour camera film. More recently the Pennsylvania state courts have begun to give this proviso considerable weight. They now, for example, require manufacturers to make an affirmative showing that their goods are actually in 'free and open competition' before they can obtain restraining orders against price-cutting retailers.[10]

Even if economic forces were not operating, the constant change, adjudication and uncertainty as to what is permissible under the various state laws would undoubtedly increase many manufacturers' distaste for r.p.m. The adverse decisions also markedly increase the pockets of resistance and their competitive effects, as discussed above, as well as providing additional bases from which mail-order sellers can operate.

One further limitation, primarily federal in nature, is of interest. Since both the Miller-Tydings and McGuire Acts contain specific statements that their provisions do not legalise agreements *among* manufacturers, *among* wholesalers, or *among* retailers, federal and state courts and administrative agencies have ruled that vertically integrated firms may not establish resale prices for their competitor-

[9] See the tabulation of state decisions in *Commerce Clearing House Trade Regulation Reporter*, vol. 2, par. 6041 (loose-leaf).

[10] *Sinclair Refining Co. v. Schwartz*, 398 Pa. 60 (1959); *Gulf Oil Corp. v. Mays*, 401 Pa. 413 (1960); *Revlon, Inc. v. Kaufmann Furniture Co.*, 1961 Trade Cas. par. 70,161; *Mead Johnson & Co. v. Breggar and Breggar*, 410 Pa. 408 (1963).

customers. This prohibition has operated against a large drug wholesaler who also manufactured merchandise that was sold through other distributors as well as through its own establishments, and against gasoline refiners who sold to industrial users in competition with their service-station dealers.[11] Thus the current interest that many manufacturers have manifested towards forward integration also tends to curtail their ability to use r.p.m.

The Quality Brands Association of America (a manufacturer group, successor to the American Fair Trade Council) is currently mustering support for a proposed 'Quality Stabilisation Law', now pending before a Congressional committee. The proposed law makes no provision for quality standardisation, or really has anything to do with quality considerations except for its advocates' claim that a reduction in price pressures from price-cutting retailers will encourage manufacturers to maintain high standards of craftsmanship. Actually the bill is designed to supplement the present faltering r.p.m. system, by giving suppliers direct national authorisation to set retail prices anywhere in the country, although one version of the proposal excludes those states where the legislatures vote subsequent positive prohibitions on price maintenance. Instead of a non-signers' clause which says that every retailer in a state is bound by a contract that one has signed, the proposed bill says that every merchant who buys stocks of trade-marked articles enters into an implied contract to observe the manufacturer's resale price requirements. The distinction is a purely technical one, but at least some lawyers feel that the courts would find the new language much more acceptable.[12]

Some competent observers believe that the legislation has fairly good chances of adoption, particularly since the far more influential National Association of Retail Druggists, who formerly supported a rather different bill, have now joined ranks with the Quality Brands Association.[13] The Vice President of the United States, Mr

[11] *US v. McKesson & Robbins*, 351 US 305 (1956); *Esso Standard Oil Co. v. Secatore's*, 246 F.2d 17 (CA-1, 1957).

[12] The proposed legislation contains a number of features designed to deal with various limitations that fair trade has encountered in the courts. However, the probability of change in at least some of these elements when and if the bill is ever passed is so great that there is no point in discussing details here.

[13] G.E.Weston, 'Fair Trade, Alias "Quality Stabilisation" ', *American Bar Association Section of Antitrust Law*, 22 (1963), pp. 96–7.

Humphrey, was an ardent supporter of the bill when he was in the Senate. On the other hand, various federal agencies such as the Department of Justice and the Federal Trade Commission, consumer groups, academic economists, and the majority of anti-trust law scholars have joined in opposing it. In a case in which the basic issues were rather poorly joined, the US Supreme Court ruled that there was no conflict between the currently controlling federal enabling acts and a recent Ohio state law based on the same theory of an implied contract as in the proposed Quality Stabilisation Act.[14] Since the process by which the case came to the Supreme Court was defective, it was remanded to the state courts for the resolution of several still-outstanding issues.[15] However, the Court's opinion, as well as its willingness to take the case, seems to go beyond the specific question at hand in providing encouragement for the Quality Stabilisation advocates.[16]

Other Controls of Resale Prices

Another type of state control over retail pricing is found in the 'unfair practices' or 'anti loss-leader' laws. These statutes prohibit commodity resales at less than cost (usually defined as acquisition cost plus some minimum or stipulated cost of doing business) with intent (or effect) to divert trade or to harm competition (defined in various ways in the different states). Thirtyone states have laws of this sort of general applicability, although courts at different levels of authority have held five to be unconstitutional. Eleven more states

[14] *Hudson Distributors, Inc. v. Eli Lilly & Co., Hudson Distributors, Inc. v. The Upjohn Co.*, 377 US 386 (1964).

[15] See Mr Justice Harlan's dissent, criticising the Court for accepting the case in its defective condition.

[16] 'Congress, however, in the McGuire Act has approved state statutes sanctioning resale price maintenance schemes such as those invoked here. Whether it is good policy to permit such laws is a matter for Congress to decide. Where the statutory language and the legislative history clearly indicates the purpose of Congress, that purpose must be applied.' Majority opinion.

[Since the preparation of this chapter, the proposed Quality Stabilisation law cited above was defeated by committee vote in the Senate and by inaction in the House of Representatives committee to which it had been referred. Highly vocal opposition, expressed with an unusual degree of unanimity, on the part of the economics profession in the United States is believed to have been of major influence in defeating the proposal, at least for the time being. See 'Notes', *American Economic Review*, 55 (1965), p. 683.]

have similar laws applying to specific commodities, mainly cigarettes. Exceptions are usually created for clearances of damaged or obsolete merchandise, court-ordered sales, and similar transactions without significant competitive effect. Aside from these exceptions, however, the unfair practices acts supposedly apply to all (or all specified) commodity sales, unlike r.p.m., which operates only at the supplier's option. These laws also differ from the usual r.p.m. arrangement in that the government, as well as affected private individuals and firms, may act as the plaintiff in enforcement actions. The minimum cost-of-doing-business markups established by the state laws, often as low as 4 per cent., are considerably smaller than the minimum margins set under most traditional r.p.m. programmes.[17]

Much of the support for the unfair practices acts came from the grocery trade. American grocers, somewhat in contrast to many of their British counterparts, have tended to be unenthusiastic or ambivalent towards r.p.m. The grocers' doubts about r.p.m. have had several sources. One was a feeling that the thrust of competition in their trade could be controlled by other legislation, such as the unfair practices acts, the potentially serious taxes of the 1930s against chain stores, and the federal Robinson-Patman Act of 1936 which limited the chains' buying advantages. The grocers' assortment of goods for sale was another source of hesitancy towards r.p.m., since the trade in this country has handled a varying, but always significant, quantity of perishable and unbranded merchandise that is not susceptible to resale price control by suppliers. Moreover, even in the 1930s as today, chain store private brands were more firmly entrenched in the grocery trade than in drug-store lines. Although some national brands seemed relatively impervious to competition from private brands,[18] prescribed resale prices for other grocery products would have handicapped the independents in competing with the chains. Contrarily, the laws against loss leaders which applied to all merchandise, branded and unbranded, seemed to give the small grocer more comprehensive protection without destroying his traditional freedom in pricing.[19]

[17] G.M.Kiernan and J.Wilson, *Retailers' Manual of Laws and Regulations* (16th ed., New York, 1963), pp. 165–81.

[18] M.Adelman, *A & P: A Study in Price-Cost Behavior and Public Policy* (Cambridge, Mass., 1959), pp. 130–2.

[19] C.H.Fulda, 'Food Distribution in the United States', *University of Pennsylvania Law Review*, 99 (1951), pp. 1116–21.

To the extent that they work, these laws deal more directly and more comprehensively with aggressive loss-leader selling than fair trade does, even though this is the problem the advocates of r.p.m. often claim to be treating. Many analysts feel that the total extent and significance of that problem has been greatly exaggerated in the discussions of fair trade.[20] However, enforcement of these unfair practices acts does involve several difficulties, since the complainant usually has to go through the difficult process of proving that the alleged violations actually were below-cost sales. He may also be obliged to prove malicious intent, and he usually has to demonstrate injury to competition. Furthermore, local prosecuting authorities often have little interest in enforcing the acts.

Nevertheless, successful public and private suits in many states have been based on these statutes. The below-cost acts have also served on occasion as the nucleus for informal price maintenance activities by state officials and dealer associations, particularly in the food, gasoline and cigarette trades. During the 1930s, some grocery trade associations carried concerted enforcement efforts to the point of violating the federal anti-trust laws, and in some of these instances it appears that the state laws became mere subterfuges for the associations' activities. In the main, the unfair practices acts seem to have placed some actually, and many potentially, significant limits upon aggressive loss-leader selling.[21] In addition, the federal anti-trust laws place further limits upon the national chains' ability to use either loss leaders or geographical price discrimination as a competitive weapon.

The 21st amendment to the federal constitution, which in 1933 repealed the nation's 'noble experiment' in liquor prohibition, is

[20] See, for example, statement of A.Oxenfeldt in US House of Representatives, Committee on Interstate and Foreign Commerce, *Quality Stabilisation – 1963* (sub-committee hearings, Washington, 1963), pp. 285, 295–6. Unfortunately there has been no exhaustive and authoritative American study of loss-leader selling comparable to the inquiry of the Canadian Restrictive Trade Practices Commission.

[21] For a general discussion of these laws see D.G.Halper, *Public Policy in Marketing: Sales below Cost Prohibitions in the California Grocery Trade* (unpublished Ph.D. dissertation, Stanford University, 1958), *passim*; C.F.LaRue, 'Pitfalls for Price Competitors: State and Federal Restrictions on Below Cost or Unreasonably Low Prices', *Western Reserve Law Review*, 15 (1963), pp. 35–65; R.B.Jones, 'Regulation of Business: Sales-Below-Cost Statutes', *Michigan Law Review*, 58 (1960), pp. 905–19.

another example of legislation promulgated on a states' rights basis. Although most of the products move in interstate commerce, the states were given unusual powers over the liquor trade. Some, the so-called 'monopoly' states, chose to operate government beverage stores, usually at considerable profit to the state, with uniform resale prices established by the operating agency. (Price variations which might maximise the state's revenue would not be feasible politically.) A considerable number of the 'license' states in which private individuals and firms are permitted to conduct the trade have established special price maintenance rules. In the main these requirements include the specification of substantial minimum markups or requirements that national brand distillers and vintners use r.p.m. within the state. In many jurisdictions the prices so set are enforced not only by private lawsuits on the part of the suppliers but also by licence revocations and other disciplinary proceedings by the state control authority.

The ostensible reason for rigid price controls in this trade is the argument that high prices encourage sobriety, at least among the poor who presumably have less right than the wealthy to spend their money on liquor. The actual advocacy of r.p.m., however, comes mainly from the liquor store operators' associations.[22] (Interestingly enough, the representatives of these associations, who are very active in the state capitols, rarely testify in the perennial national congressional hearings on r.p.m.) Mandatory r.p.m. was recently abolished in New York, where a state investigating committee concluded that price controls had no impact on liquor consumption, drunkenness or alcoholism, but only on the pockets of consumers.[23]

The retail price of milk is also subject to state control in some communities. These milk marketing codes are part of a complex web of regulations that has emerged in the dairy industry in response to the interests of farmers, processors, deliverymen, and conventional retailers.[24]

It is likely that special treatment for prescription pharmaceuticals

[22] J.E.Diamond, 'State Monopoly and Price-Fixing in Retail Liquor Distribution', *Wisconsin Law Review* (1962), pp. 454 ff.

[23] New York State Moreland Commission on the Alcoholic Beverage Control Laws, *Report and Recommendations No. 3* (New York, 1964); H.L.Wattel, *Moreland Commission Study Paper No. 5* (New York, 1963).

[24] A.Phillips, *Market Structure, Organisation and Performance* (Cambridge, Mass., 1962), pp. 80–90.

may be a part of *future* legislation on r.p.m. One version of the proposed national price maintenance bill now being urged on the Congress, discussed above, specifically excludes prescription items from its sanction of retail price control. The justification for this is that pharmaceutical products are not sold in 'free and open' competition with each other, since the consumer cannot instruct the druggist to substitute other brands for the physician's selection. This exclusion avoids associating the proposed bill with the cost of medicine, a tender subject in the minds of consumers and legislators since the 1960 Kefauver investigation of the drug industry. In any event, manufacturers of prescription items have less interest in price maintenance, and are less responsive to dealer pressure, than the manufacturers of patent (over-the-counter) drugs and beauty aids.[25]

Manufacturers may control resale prices in a few other ways besides using r.p.m. Bona-fide consignment selling, in which the supplier retains ownership of the goods and the retailers act only as agents, provides a clear-cut and apparently lawful means of controlling prices in all states. But the courts generally insist on rigorous tests to determine whether transactions are actually on consignment terms and not outright sales. The supplier must absorb all merchandising risks, insurance costs and personal property taxes on the goods, and he cannot require or expect payment from the dealer until the merchandise has been re-sold. These requirements are costly and cumbersome, tend to limit the number of outlets that can be used, and become especially burdensome if the manufacturer distributes his products through wholesalers. Consequently consignment selling is usually used only when some basic marketing problem, such as reluctance of dealers to carry adequate inventories, makes it unavoidable. However, resale prices of a few products, including electric light bulbs and some appliances, have been controlled by consignment arrangements.[26] Consignment selling has also been used in the gasoline trade at times, particularly during local price wars.[27] Its

[25] G.C.Sawyer, 'Profiles of the Future: The Ethical Drug Industry', *Business Horizons*, 7 (Fall, 1964), pp. 11–12.

[26] See 'Agency System of Price Maintenance', *Iowa Law Review*, 43 (1958), p. 603; J.E.Baker, 'Agency and Consignment Selling', *Antitrust Bulletin*, 9 (1964), pp. 299–312.

[27] M.G. de Chazeau and A.E.Kahn, *Integration and Competition in the Petroleum Industry* (New Haven, 1959), p. 410.

future use in that trade probably will be limited by a recent Supreme Court decision that a 'consignment device . . . used to cover a vast gasoline distribution system, fixing prices through many retail outlets', was an unreasonable restraint of trade.[28]

Even if the manufacturer sells his merchandise outright, rather than on consignment, he may *suggest* appropriate resale prices and he may mark or pre-ticket those prices on his goods or their containers. But recently the Federal Trade Commission has ruled that pre-ticketing with prices *above* those at which dealers customarily resell is an unfair method of competition since it tends to give consumers an erroneous impression of the value of the merchandise. Consequently a price-marking programme is likely to imply unfair competition if the suggested prices are not enforced, and unreasonable restraint of trade if they are.[29] Nevertheless price suggestions are frequently used, particularly in apparel lines. During the 1962 Senate hearings on r.p.m., Senator Monroney commented on the extent to which suggested prices were observed in Washington, DC (non-fair-trade territory), and a small survey of merchants in one Texas town (also non-fair-trade) found fortyseven out of fiftyseven respondents reporting that they sold at least some merchandise at prices nominated by the manufacturer. Thirtyeight out of the fifty-seven replied that they never sold below suggested prices.[30]

Obviously mere suggestion will not support prices if the dealers wish to reduce them. Consequently some manufacturers reinforce their price suggestions by a policy of selecting only those dealers who would be extremely unlikely to sell below suggested, list or customary prices. In practice, this policy is feasible only when the manufacturer sells directly to the retail trade and only where he requires a limited number of outlets. It is, however, a permissible policy since American law requires only a few special types of firms, such as hotels and public utilities, to supply all would-be purchasers. Dealer selection may reach its extreme form under the various arrangements called 'franchising', which have recently become very popular in the service

[28] *Simpson v. Union Oil Co. of California*, 373 US 901, 83 S. Ct. 1290, 12 L. Ed (2d) 98 at 105 (1964).

[29] A.R.Kidston, 'Preticketing and List Prices', *Antitrust Bulletin*, 8 (1963), pp. 427–46.

[30] US Senate, Committee on Commerce, *Quality Stabilisation* (sub-committee hearings, Washington, 1962), p. 169; H.N.Lackshin, 'Refusal to Sell: A Means of Achieving Resale Price Maintenance in Non-Fair Trade States', *Texas Law Review*, 36 (1958), pp. 808–11.

and inexpensive restaurant trades, where the supplier may control the design and appearance of the retail facilities, the advertising and promotional practices, and elements of the service-mix. Franchising, which really is a very elastic term and covers many degrees of control, is also used in the distribution of automobiles, farm equipment, television sets and gasoline.[31]

But while the choice of dealers is a valid and frequently exercised right, any step beyond mere choosing is likely to be an illegal restraint of trade. Practices that may put the supplier over the boundaries of the anti-trust laws include: *requiring* dealers to agree to maintain prices (outside of r.p.m.) rather than merely hoping they will do so, requiring or asking *wholesalers* to select only 'full-price' dealers, establishing systems for the surveillance of dealer prices, providing advertising allowances or merchandising support only to dealers who maintain prices, or agreeing to cut off supplies from cut-price stores at the behest of full-price competitors.[32] Undoubtedly all of these things are done at times, perhaps quite often, but at the very least they press close to the somewhat hazy limits of antitrust.

Extent of Resale Price Maintenance

The fraction of retail sales subject to r.p.m. is difficult to define for several reasons. Unlike some other countries, such as Germany, that permit r.p.m., the American laws make no provision for a register or file of price agreements. With the minor exceptions of some state requirements in the liquor trade, and a list once maintained by the Utah Trade Commission, there are no official (and no comprehensive unofficial) lists of individual fair-trade agreements. Moreover, at least some manufacturers have found it politic to declare themselves as advocates and users of r.p.m. even though their intentions have not included serious enforcement of their announced resale prices. In this respect the extent of actual price maintenance has been considerably less than that of ostensible price control. On the other hand, the amount of actual, rather than ostensible, r.p.m. has been

[31] L.W.Stern, 'Approaches to Achieving Retail Price Stability', *Business Horizons*, 7 (1964), pp. 78–80. Of course, many franchising arrangements provide the dealer with considerable pricing freedom, and some, as in the automobile trades, may give him more encouragement towards vigorous price competition than he really welcomes.

[32] See, for example, *US v. Parke, Davis & Co.*, 362 US 29 (1960).

increased by the indeterminate extent to which informal or extra-legal price maintenance has been utilised.[33]

Estimates of the fraction of total retail sales subject to fair-trade agreements have ranged from 4 per cent. to 20 per cent.[34] The most accurate estimate available is generally considered to be Herman's calculation that goods produced by approximately 900 manufacturers and amounting to 7 per cent. of total retail sales were subject to r.p.m. in 1954.[35] Although 7 per cent. is probably considerably higher than the present rate of use, it marked a substantial decline from the 1950–2 peak period in which the American Fair Trade Council claimed almost 1,600 manufacturer-users of r.p.m.[36]

Pharmacists' items, such as drugs and medicines, druggists' sundries, cosmetics and perfumes, accounted for approximately 42 per cent. of the r.p.m. sales volume covered in the Herman study. Tobacco products and accessories, cameras and photographic supplies, and clocks and watches, which are also sold in part through drug-stores, constituted another 14 per cent. of the total. The

[33] Fair-trade advocates, who usually seek to minimise statements of the extent to which their technique of r.p.m. is used, frequently claim that the total figure for price-controlled merchandise should include the volume of merchandise sold either through manufacturer-owned outlets or under dealers' private brands. These two methods of retailing, however, do not seem analogous to r.p.m., since in neither case is the price-setter usually obliged to determine margins that will attract or please independent dealers.

[34] Cited by S.M.Lee in US Senate, *Quality Stabilisation* (1962), p. 302.

[35] E.S.Herman, 'A Statistical Note on Fair Trade', *Antitrust Bulletin*, 4 (1959), pp. 583–92. Herman derived this estimate from an analysis of returns to a questionnaire distributed by a US Senate sub-committee in 1956. The questionnaire was sent to a list of slightly over 1,400 manufacturers which, the sub-committee believed, included all fair-trade-using firms in the country. Only 514, out of 836 respondents, indicated current use of r.p.m. Assuming a similar rate of use among the non-respondents, Herman estimated a total population of 893 fair-trading firms. He then determined the total retail value of price-maintained goods sold by a sample of 175 respondent-users by adding the appropriate industry-average distributive margins (taken from Barger's study of distribution costs) to the value of sales at the manufacturing level. This figure was multiplied by 5·1 (893/175) to derive the retail value of price-maintained sales for the entire 893-firm population. Two assumptions, that the original list exhausted the roster of fair-trading firms and that r.p.m. goods were only subject to average distributive margins, probably caused some under-statement in the final figure. This was probably off-set, at least in part, by the assumption that price maintenance behaviour among the non-respondents was similar to that among the respondents.

[36] US House of Representatives, Committee on the Judiciary, *Resale Price Maintenance* (sub-committee hearings, Washington, 1952), p. 731.

remainder consisted of electrical appliances (14 per cent.), alcoholic beverages (10 per cent.), boats, outboard motors, firearms, ammunition, automotive supplies, clothing, shoes, hardware, books, hosiery, and other miscellaneous items. Approximately 11 per cent. of the manufacturers accounted for over 60 per cent. of the volume.[37] The conclusion that large manufacturers tend to be the major suppliers of price-maintained merchandise is more or less corroborated by Bowman's report that, in 1950, fifty of America's 100 largest advertisers applied r.p.m. to some portion of their output.[38]

The Decline of Resale Price Maintenance

The decline in the use of r.p.m. since 1950 is due, in part, to the increasing number of adverse, critical or limiting decisions issued in many jurisdictions, as discussed above. However, dynamic marketing forces seem to provide even more fundamental motives for the increasing abandonment of r.p.m. The legal and the economic influences are intertwined. As noted, judicial and legislative curtailments and restraints on fair trade in some states tend to increase price competition even in the remaining areas. The spread of this competition in turn has seemed to make the courts somewhat more aware of, and somewhat less sympathetic to, the limits on competition imposed through r.p.m.

Even without legislative or judicial attack, the American type of r.p.m. works best when everyone involved, including both manufacturers and retailers, wants to avoid price competition. The basic means of enforcement are weak and individualistic. Collective enforcement by groups of manufacturers, through joint black lists or stop lists, is supposedly, and apparently actually, unavailable. Organised dealer efforts have, at times, forced the use of fair-trade pricing on reluctant manufacturers, particularly in the drug, cosmetic and liquor trades.[39] Even in such instances the manufacturer may try to thwart the dealers' aims through equivocation and procrastination in the actual control of price-cutters, unless he is subjected to constant pressure. The public authorities do not enforce the prices

[37] Herman, *op. cit.*, pp. 586–9.

[38] W.S.Bowman, 'Prerequisites and Effects of Resale Price Maintenance', *University of Chicago Law Journal*, 22 (1955), p. 834.

[39] US Senate, Select Committee on Small Business, *Discount House Operations* (sub-committee hearings, Washington, 1958), p. 264.

on their own initiative, outside of the liquor trade, and private legal action by groups of full-price retailers has generally proven impractical.[40] Consequently the critical element in each programme of price maintenance is the extent to which the manufacturer is willing, or can be induced, to police and litigate his resale prices. The direct costs of a strong enforcement programme, including lawyers' fees, court charges and shopping-service expenses, can be prohibitive when the products are sold through large numbers of restless dealers. For example, during the 1953–5 period the W.A.Shaeffer Pen Company (fountain pens) reportedly spent up to 4 per cent. of annual sales on an ultimately fruitless price maintenance campaign.[41] But even more fundamental to the problem of enforcement is the question of the extent to which the manufacturer wants to cut himself off from what may be some of the most vigorous and important outlets in the market.

Some manufacturers of such lines as cosmetics and liquor may be concerned about the possibility of the backward-sloping demand curve, that is, a tendency in consumers to use the price, rather than the intrinsic merits of the product, as an indicator of its quality. In this situation it is claimed that retail price reductions will ruin the product's 'image' even though they do not affect its inherent quality. But, on the other hand, the backward-sloping demand curve is not based upon the price that the consumer *pays*. Instead, it results from what he or she *perceives* to be the 'normal' or 'regular' price of the product. Maximum consumer appeal often results when the buyer feels that he is somehow able to purchase a normally high-priced item for less than the going rate. Consequently even manufacturers whose products are supposedly subject to evaluation by consumers on the basis of price often find that they too are concerned with the question of how to reach the price-conscious segment of the market.

Today this question is often expressed in terms of whether the manufacturer wants distribution through discount outlets. But the post-war manifestations of discount selling are really simply another expression of deep-seated tendencies in American retailing. Merchants who use price appeals to attract customers have always played an important, even if varying, role in the country's distribution

[40] 'The Enforcement of Resale Price Maintenance', *Yale Law Journal*, 69 (1959), pp. 172–7.

[41] *Advertising Age*, 26 (12 December 1955), pp. 1, 8; S.M.Lee, 'Problems of Resale Price Maintenance', *Journal of Marketing*, 23 (1959), pp. 278–9.

system, and most important new types of retailing, such as chains, mail order houses and department stores, first appeared, at least in part, as low-price outlets. The druggists' campaign for r.p.m. during the 1920s and 30s to provide protection from high-volume, low-price competitors is itself demonstration of the significance of pre-war price competition.

Electrical Appliances: The extension of r.p.m. to such products as electrical appliances, cameras, fountain pens and phonograph records seems to have taken it into fields in which discount selling was bound to become particularly significant to both the manufacturers and the consumers. Price maintenance has always been difficult in such lines as major electrical appliances, where the dealers can manipulate trade-in allowances to the customer's advantage and where the amount of money involved is likely to lead the consumer to invest considerable shopping effort in the purchase. Recently even the Magnavox Company, which has long been regarded as one of the staunchest (and perhaps only) adherents of r.p.m. in the television-set industry, franchised two large discount firms in New York and Chicago as dealers because its full-price outlets could not provide satisfactory sales volume in those cities.[42]

Discount selling appeared in small electrical appliances long before the war. However, much of this discounting consisted of informal bargaining and personal price concessions, particularly in the small neighbourhood shops. Another portion consisted of semi-surreptitious purchases made by consumers through conventional and pseudo-wholesalers, employee buying plans, discount catalogue arrangements, and other such 'irregular' or unorthodox agencies. Many department-store operators found this discount competition especially vexatious, since even the most half-hearted adherents to r.p.m. among the suppliers of price-maintained merchandise usually had to forbid the use of the department store's major competitive weapon, widespread newspaper advertising of price cuts. At the same time many department-store merchants, through their attempts to obtain full markups on all appliances, furniture and other hard goods, undoubtedly helped provide opportunity and room for the growth of discount houses. Consequently an extremely uneasy *modus vivendi* prevailed in the pre-war appliance trade.[43]

[42] 'What's Really Up at Magnavox?', *Forbes*, 95 (15 March 1965), p. 29.

[43] S.C.Hollander, 'The "One-Price" System, Fact or Fiction?', *Journal of Retailing*, 31 (1955), pp. 127–44.

The timing of the post-war upsurge in the discount selling of appliances is somewhat surprising since it occurred during a decade or so that was generally quite prosperous. Apparently consumers, who were avidly building up their personal inventories of durable goods, exchanged more and more information about potential sources of supply. In any event, increasing numbers of people seemed to become aware of discounting dealers, obtained access to them, and patronised them. The process became cumulative in that the increased willingness to buy from discount retailers attracted more such vendors whose availability, in turn, intensified consumer reluctance to pay full list price. Discussions of the growth of discounting appearing in newspapers and popular magazines helped the process along.

Some of the discount retailers displayed considerable ingenuity and persistence in obtaining their supplies of price-maintained merchandise through complicated and unorthodox channels, such as the trans-shipment of goods from one retailer to another. The supply of goods available for trans-shipment resulted, at least in part, from manufacturer practices that tended to overstock the full-price dealers. The use of dealer sales-quotas, dealer sales-contests with luxurious vacation trips as prizes, sharply-stepped quantity discounts and rebates, and frequent model changes, encouraged the conventional wholesalers and dealers to order stocks, part of which eventually had to be liquidated through cut-price stores.[44] However, it is clear that many manufacturers and wholesalers, particularly in the post-war period, made their products more directly available to the discount sellers.

Most manufacturers of appliances appear to feel that both the individual brand and the total industry demand curves are fairly elastic. Purchases of appliances are usually postponable, and, in the case of gift purchases, are subject to the possible substitution of alternative products. The dollar amount involved warrants shopping effort on the consumer's part. The servicing, demonstration and persuasive tasks involved in selling small appliances are not great, and are often absorbed by the manufacturer, so that the consumer in many instances is not attached to a particular retail outlet. At the same time, many consumers regard the leading brands and some private brands as substitutable for each other, with the result that the individual manufacturer's monopoly power is quite limited.

[44] F.Meissner, 'American Discount Houses', *Weltwirtschaftliches Archiv*, 84 (1960), pp. 78–9.

There seems to be room for one or two firms to undertake the role of the small retailer's friend, rather successfully, by insisting on rigorous resale price enforcement. But most of the producers, including some of the largest, do not want to let their competitors be the only suppliers to the price-conscious market served by the discount stores. Moreover, many of the suppliers have been quite eager for the extra volume that these stores can provide.[45]

The combined effects of aggressive retailing and manufacturer support for discounting resulted in a complete breakdown of r.p.m. in the appliance trade. With one or two exceptions, r.p.m. was virtually eliminated in major appliances, where it had always been weak and vulnerable, in the early 1950s. By 1958 practically all the producers of small electrical appliances had followed suit in abandoning price maintenance. In general, the manufacturers and wholesalers have, rather willingly, given up the role of retail price-setters, although some apparently will intervene in an informal way if they think retail price-cutting is getting out of hand.[46] In an attempt to have the best of both possible worlds, some firms are producing two lines, one of which is confined by various means to full-price stores while the other is allowed to move freely throughout the market.[47] History suggests, of course, that it can only be a matter of time before at least some cut-price stores obtain supplies of the supposedly price-maintained prestige lines.

The prevailing retail margins on many lines have dropped to 20 or 25 per cent. (of selling price), a sharp decline from the r.p.m. levels of 35 to 40 per cent.[48] Consequently, electrical goods and

[45] 'Who Pays List Price?', *Fortune*, 45 (June 1952), p. 106; C. I. Kanter and S. G. Rosenblum, 'Operation of Fair Trade Programmes', *Harvard Law Review*, 69 (1955), p. 317.

[46] For examples of a mild interventionist policy, see Stern, 'Approaches to Achieving Retail Price Stability', *op. cit.*, pp. 78, 81; A.R.Oxenfeldt, *Marketing Practices in the TV Set Industry* (New York, 1964), pp. 158–60.

[47] For example, Stern, *ibid.*, p. 82; L.M.Hughes, 'Sunbeam's "In" is Innovation', *Sales Management*, 4 September 1964, p. 40; 'Pricing Paradox', *ibid.*, 17 July 1964, p. 14. A combination of formal and informal price maintenance and the production of dual lines seems to have been very rewarding for the country's largest manufacturer of luggage: see 'Samsonite: On Land, In the Air, On the Sea', *Business Week*, 27 February 1965, pp. 98–104.

[48] For evidence of sharp declines in appliance prices with the elimination of r.p.m. see W.A.Sandridge, *The Effects of Fair Trade on Retail Prices of Electric Housewares in Washington, Baltimore and Richmond, 1952–9* (unpublished Ph.D. dissertation, University of Virginia, 1960).

'hard lines' in general (with the exception of toys) are of considerably less interest today to many of the discount-house operators, who now have difficulty in offering the drastic price savings needed to attract the volume their stores require. As a result, some of the old and many of the new entrants into discount retailing are now featuring clothing and other textile lines in a new type of discount house which is really a large, well-located, popular-price, self-service junior department store. Meanwhile, the conventional department stores have reacted to the change in the appliance business in various ways. Some have discarded major appliances entirely. Others, with surprising success in some cases, have developed private brands. Many have learned to operate on narrower margins, in part through the use of self-service, warehouse sales and other promotional techniques. (One of the by-products of the discount trade in hard goods was considerable discussion among department-store merchants of new accounting and control methods, such as merchandise management accounting, that would encourage flexible pricing tactics instead of emphasising departmental average percentage costs as the basic factor in determining markups.)

In short, the changes in the retailing of electrical housewares have been largely movements towards an equilibrium in margins, although at a level considerably below the r.p.m. margins. It has become almost a cliché to note that the discount stores have traded up, moved to more attractive and convenient buildings, and adopted department-store features while the department stores have learned to use some of the discount-house tactics. Interestingly enough, the Sunbeam Corporation, which was the best-known ardent exponent of fair trade in the small appliance business, and which always claimed that even sporadic price-cutting was harmful, now enjoys about twice the sales volume, through about one-third more outlets, than it had in 1950, at the height of r.p.m.[49]

Current pricing practices in the typewriter, fountain pen, camera and watch trades are roughly similar to those used for small electrical appliances. Although most of the major suppliers in those trades once used r.p.m., with varying degrees of sincerity, almost all have now abandoned it. Some firms employ selective distribution and informal persuasion to preserve some elements of control over retail prices, but most manufacturers in these lines are now trying, often

[49] Hughes, 'Sunbeam's "In" is Innovation', *op. cit.*

with considerable success, to obtain increased sales volume through a mixture of full-price and discount outlets.[50]

Meanwhile self-service discount stores have become particularly important outlets for toys. A number of new suppliers have come to prominence in the toy industry in recent years, mainly through intensive television advertising directed primarily at the child-consumer rather than the parent-buyer. The suburban locations (which lead to shopping visits in family groups), open massed displays and aggressive pricing policies of the discount stores have combined to sell these advertised toy lines in truly remarkable quantities.[51]

Phonograph Records: The breakdown of price maintenance in phonograph records is also somewhat analogous to that in electrical appliances, except that a single, identifiable innovator appears to have sparked much of the change in the pricing of records. Record pricing has also been complicated by the development of manufacturers' record clubs, which essentially are cut-price mail-order subscription offers analogous to the well-known book clubs. Before 1950 the typical retailer of records offered extensive demonstration services, often providing a series of sound-proof booths in which customers could play their selections and make their choices, usually sold his merchandise without any return privilege, and did a low-volume business on a high margin. About 1949, at a time when technological developments had disrupted the historic standardisation of records and playing instruments, Sam Goody, a dealer in New York, began aggressively promoting long-playing classical records at deeply cut prices. He advertised extensively, featuring a 30 per cent. discount from list prices. A considerable portion of his business was conducted by mail order, contrary to the usual industry practice. All of his records were sold, over-the-counter as well as by mail, in sealed envelopes without demonstration, but with liberal return privileges. His sales grew from $500,000 in 1949 to about $3,000,000 in 1953. In short, although he sold only classical and semi-classical long-playing items, Goody at that time accounted for somewhat over 1 per cent. of all phonograph record sales at retail

[50] See Stern, *An Economic Analysis . . . , op. cit.*, pp. 145–62; J.S.DeLeeuw, *Fair Trade Developments: 1951–61* (unpublished Ph.D. dissertation, The University of Oklahoma, 1962), pp. 225–53; J.G.Plunkett, 'The Fair Trade Pendulum', *Sales Management*, 92 (5 June 1964), p. 27.

[51] 'Marketing: The Toy Industry: Going Big Time', *Printers' Ink*, 289 (20 November 1964), pp. 41–2.

in the country. The manufacturers dragged their heels at invoking legal sanctions against his price-cutting; the hiatus in r.p.m. from the first Schwegmann (non-signers') decision to the passage of the McGuire Act, the first rulings on the inapplicability of state r.p.m. legislation to mail-order sales, and the Korean War price controls provided excuses for their procrastination.[52] Goody was, of course, followed by imitators, and for a time his business suffered reverses. The net result has been to end mandatory margins and to encourage flexibility in retail pricing in the record trade.

Books: American book dealers have not received special legal treatment similar to the approval given to r.p.m. in the British book trade by the Restrictive Practices Court. American booksellers complain bitterly about the retail price competition that has developed, particularly in some of the larger cities, but this is in fact only one of several difficulties they face. Although bookmen differ in their diagnoses of the industry's ills and in their recommended prescriptions, they seem generally to agree that the US book distribution system is poorly designed for the functions it should perform. Fundamentally, the bookstore operator's problem (which is not necessarily the same thing as the book industry's problem) is partly one of having access to only a limited share of the total book market, and partly one of being a rather inadequate instrument to serve even that share.

Textbook sales account for about one-third of the total dollar volume of book sales in the country. This market is almost entirely foreclosed to the conventional ('trade') bookstores. Elementary and secondary school systems usually lend their pupils texts that are purchased in quantity directly from publishers and wholesale outlets. On the other hand, college and university students usually do buy their own texts. However, locational considerations, problems of adjusting to frequent changes in syllabus, the relatively narrow retail margins (20 to 25 per cent. of selling price) allowed on new copies of textbooks, and the special problems of handling the profitable trade in used textbooks have encouraged the development of specialised academic bookstores operated either by the institutions themselves or by private entrepreneurs. Consequently the conventional general bookstore usually does not participate in the textbook market. Also,

[52] M.J.Racusin, 'Record Industry Watching Suit Seeking to Continue Cut Prices', *New York Herald Tribune*, 17 August 1952, sec. 4, p. 2; 'Fair Trade: The War's Not Over', *Business Week*, 7 November 1953, p. 44.

American libraries purchase almost all of their holdings from the publishers or from specialised library contractors, so that library sales are not available to subsidise or supplement book retailing in general.

Very substantial portions of the rest of the business in books (other than the textbook and library business) move through mail-order sales, house-to-house solicitation, and other channels rather than the conventional bookstore. These portions include the lion's share of the encyclopedia trade, the sale of professional reference sets such as law reports and medical books, practically all the book-club volume (perhaps 10 per cent. of total book sales), inexpensive 'mass' paperbacks sold through magazine distribution channels (separate from the book business in the United States), children's inexpensive books sold in supermarkets, and, in recent years, an increasing number of market-oriented subscription series and 'coffee-table' books, that is, oversize, elaborately illustrated art and history books. These channels are used for expensive books and sets because more aggressive selling practices than the bookstores can provide are needed to develop profitable sales volume. Mail-order solicitation for subsequent delivery also allows the publishers to gauge demand in advance of printing, or even before final commitment to undertake the projects, an important consideration in the case of the coffee-table books. The inexpensive paperbacks and children's books require much more exposure to potential customers, many of whom never visit a conventional bookstore, than the regular book dealers can offer. In addition to these categories that move mainly or entirely outside the bookstore, American publishers generally will accept a direct individual consumer order for a single copy of almost any book in their catalogue. In fact, most publishers attract orders from academics, an important category of book buyers, with a 10 or 15 per cent. (net, after postage) discount off the announced retail prices for their books.

These limitations on market opportunities are partially off-set by the very substantial trade discounts off list price (40 to 50 per cent.) and the extremely liberal return privileges that the bookshops are allowed on 'trade' books. The retailers' problems in handling these books arise out of the large number of titles added to the lists each year, and out of the small number of sales that the typical title enjoys. The number of new book titles each year (including, of course, many that do not go through bookstores) has been estimated at from

15,000 to 20,000. Perhaps five to ten times as many titles are available in publishers' backlists. Yet the typical novel will sell less than 5,000 copies, or less than an average of three copies per bookstore in the United States.[53]

Under these circumstances, a book dealer cannot maintain a large, well-rounded stock, regardless of the available percentage margins, unless he has a very large clientele of book-buying consumers to draw upon. Even the largest retailers can carry only a fraction of the available titles, and have to use cumbersome special order procedures for the remainder. In effect only large metropolitan areas, well-developed high-income suburbs and cultural centres can support bookstores whose assortment extends much beyond current best-sellers, bibles, cook-books, dictionaries and recreational manuals. Yet urban booksellers who concentrate on the popular titles and who enjoy a high volume business can operate profitably on considerably less than the standard margins. This situation naturally leads to cut-price, or discount selling, both in department stores and in specialised discount bookshops. Mail-order booksellers, who offer to supply any non-text title in print at 20 to 25 per cent. off list, now advertise regularly in the leading literary and book review journals.

Other problems, such as the difficulty of securing knowledgeable salespeople willing to work for low wages, must be added to the list of apparent handicaps that the conventional bookseller faces. Yet, in spite of this, trade sources report that the number of regular book outlets is actually increasing. To some extent the stores are becoming less 'bookish' and are devoting more of their space to phonograph records, gifts, greeting cards and stationery. To some extent they are profiting from a significant increase in the total amount of book-buying in the country. But the past few years seem to have demonstrated that full-price booksellers who serve large markets and who maintain full stocks can operate quite successfully in the face of cut-price competition. A few years ago the president of New York's largest (full-price) bookstore predicted ruination as a result of discount competition. The current situation in the book trade is illustrated by the recent announcement by the same man of plans

[53] Much of the data cited above appeared in *Daedulus*, 92 (Winter 1963) and has been reprinted in R.H.Smith, ed., *The American Reading Public* (New York, 1963). Also see H.B.Schaffer, 'Reading Boom: Books and Magazines', *Editorial Research Reports* (1961), pp. 917–34.

to add additional selling space to his main store.[54] At the same time, one of his strongest cut-price competitors has apparently raised its prices and is now allowing 20 to 25 per cent., rather than 40 per cent., off list.[55]

Drugs, cosmetics and toiletries: The most important area of application for fair trade has been and remains in the sale of health and beauty items. A distinction should be noted here between prescription or 'ethical' merchandise on one hand, and proprietary or over-the-counter goods on the other. The prescription items are sold under conditions that are largely inimical to price shopping and favourable to price maintenance. Pharmacy regulations in some states forbid any sort of prescription price advertising. Consumers, except for hospital patients and one or two other groups, can only obtain their supplies from registered retail pharmacists, a strongly cohesive group with rigorous controls over the entry of competition. Pharmacists usually retain prescriptions in their own files, so that consumers find it extremely difficult to shop different stores even when they make repeated purchases of the same items. Physicians, who do not pay the bills, control the choice of items, and even of brands, since they frequently write prescriptions in terms of the trade or individual manufacturers' brand names, rather than the generic names, for the drugs they recommend. The physicians' control over the consumers' choice of prescription items does reduce the pharmacists' influence over their suppliers' price policies except in so far as the same manufacturers are involved in the production of proprietary items. On the whole, however, manufacturers of prescription pharmaceuticals have little incentive to encourage retail price cutting. Yet in spite of all these conditions, discount prescription services have appeared in a number of cities and seem likely to spread elsewhere in time.[56]

The sale of non-prescription merchandise is a rather different story. Some state pharmacy control boards have managed to give the pharmacies within their jurisdiction exclusive selling rights for some packaged, non-prescription remedies, such as aspirin, Epsom

[54] 'ARPC Proposals to Expand Prime Market', *Publishers Weekly*, 185 (22 June 1964), p. 52.

[55] 'American Booksellers Association', *Publishers Weekly*, 185 (20 January 1964), p. 93.

[56] See Sawyer, 'Profiles of the Future', *op. cit.*; Stern, *An Economic Analysis . . .*, *op. cit.*, pp. 84–114.

salts and milk of magnesia. However, almost all packaged cosmetics, grooming aids, shaving supplies, dentifrices, and most patent medicines have been free of any such restrictions. Consequently the relatively high percentage and dollar markups established for these products as they moved through drug-store channels attracted considerable interest among supermarket operators. The grocery-store operators discovered, in effect, that the tasks of selling bottled salad-oil and bottled hair-oil were relatively similar, and that the latter was likely to yield many more cents and percentage points of markup per bottle. Consequently, increasing portions of the total volume of popular, high-turnover packaged items have been moving through grocery channels. The manufacturers of these items have also gained from their increased exposure to consumers as their products moved into the supermarkets.

In 1955 Professor Bowman published a detailed analysis of the toothpaste purchases recorded for 1951 and 1952 by a group of consumer-panel members, consisting of 313 families in Texas and Missouri (non-fair-trade) and 324 families in Alabama, Louisiana, Oklahoma and Minnesota (fair trade).[57] Months in which the non-signers' clause was, and was not, valid were both included, as the study period extended from about five months before the first Schwegmann decision to about six months after the passage of the McGuire Act. Bowman reported a high degree of non-compliance with fair-trade minima, since about half of the sales in non-fair-trade states and about a third of those in fair-trade states occurred at below-minimum prices. Interestingly enough, the prices paid in food stores were somewhat higher than the prices paid in traditional drugstores. Later Oakes made an even more intensive study of the prices a similar group of families in Chicago (fair trade) paid for toothpastes, headache remedies and sanitary napkins.[58] Oakes went behind the tabulations obtained from the research service that maintained the panels, and laboriously checked the panel members' original diary reports and the data cards prepared from those reports. As a result of this examination, he concluded that a great many of the apparent instances of retail sales below fair-trade minima were actually cases of reporting or clerical errors. His final conclusion was

[57] W.S.Bowman, Jr, 'The Prerequisites and Effects of Resale Price Maintenance', *op. cit.*, pp. 852–73.

[58] R.H.Oakes, 'Resale Price Maintenance in Chicago, 1953–5, A Study of Three Products', *Journal of Business*, 30 (1957), pp. 109–30.

that the manufacturers' price stipulations for these three commodities were well observed during the period of his study, at least in Chicago, in both drug and food stores.

Other sources agree that, until fairly recently, the food-store operators tended to adhere to fair-trade prices for health and beauty aids.[59] The grocers clearly did not want to disturb the markups that had attracted them to the drug and cosmetic business in the first place. This policy not surprisingly provided an umbrella for the growth of drug departments in discount houses and the recent spread of specialised discount drug-stores, somewhat similar to the low markup, rapid-turnover 'pineboards' (which did not provide prescription services) of the 1930s. Some of the supermarket and drugstore managements have revised their pricing policies as a result of this new competition, and there is a growing tendency to depart from fair-trade minima.[60] None of this seems to have disturbed the drug and cosmetic manufacturing industry, which is enjoying record sales and profits.[61]

The Effects of Resale Price Maintenance

The record to date rather definitely indicates that, at least during a period of prosperity, manufacturers seldom need r.p.m. to achieve marketing success. In some instances, assurances of a guaranteed margin may conceivably help persuade dealers to render demonstration or other special services that a manufacturer happens to desire.[62] The advocates of 'quality stabilisation' claim that resale price control eliminates backward pressure on their own prices, although this argument would seem to hold only when all significant competitive suppliers stabilise retail prices and relative shares of the dealer market at some mutually satisfactory level.[63] Some manufacturers say that another reason for liking r.p.m. is its effects in hampering

[59] C.H.Fulda, 'Resale Price Maintenance', *The University of Chicago Law Review*, 21 (1954), p. 192; G.Snyder, 'New Frontiers for Health and Beauty Aids: Discounting, Friend or Foe?', *Progressive Grocer*, 42 (August 1963), pp. 68 ff.

[60] Snyder, *ibid.*; S.Freedgood, 'The Reluctant Dragon of the Drug Industry', *Fortune*, 66 (November 1962), p. 224.

[61] 'P. I. Editors Give the Marketing Slant', *Printers' Ink*, 290 (8 January 1965), p. 53.

[62] L.G.Telser, 'Why Should Manufacturers Want Fair Trade', *Journal of Law and Economics*, 3 (1960), pp. 86–105.

[63] See Telser's discussion of the value of resale price control to inter-firm price stability during the electric light bulb (patent-licensing) agreement, *ibid.*, pp. 99–104.

the development of countervailing power in the retailing sector.[64] This argument, which is another version of the claim that r.p.m. eliminates backward pressure, also falls unless competitive forces, such as conflicting desires for shares of representation in the large outlets and the impact of private brands, are pretty well neutralised. But in any event the recent history of the industries noted above seems to be filled with instances of manufacturers who said they needed r.p.m., yet who have reached new sales and profit levels since price maintenance disintegrated. Their current success has, of course, resulted from economic forces far more fundamental than the collapse of fair trade. Nevertheless, it is also clear that the collapse has not been a barrier to success.

Congressional hearings on proposed legislation on r.p.m. during the 1950s usually received tabulations of some sort concerning business failures or bankruptcy rates. A typical analysis of this type, presented during the 1959 hearings, showed that the percentage increase in retail failures from 1953 to 1959 was greater in non-fair-trade than in fair-trade states.[65] Since so many factors besides price maintenance determine the retail failure rate, and since there was no particular reason for computing change rates on a 1953 base, these figures were not helpful. Moreover, recent government tabulations show that the annual failure rate per 10,000 listed businesses has been consistently higher, from 1946 through 1962, in fair-trade states than in the other states.[66] While these new computations also demonstrate very little about the effects of r.p.m., they do underline the irrelevance of the older data. An extremely interesting analysis, prepared by Professor Stewart Lee, shows that from 1939 to 1958 the ratio of number of stores to population was substantially the same in fair-trade states as in the non-fair-trade states. He reported also that total retail sales, number of drug-stores, drug-store sales, retail failures and drug-store failures by states were closely related to population.[67] Thus there seems to be little evidence that r.p.m. reduces retail failure rates.[68]

[64] Stern, 'Approaches to Achieving Price Stability', *op. cit.*

[65] Testimony of Senator William Proxmire and of M.Mermey in US Senate, Committee on Interstate and Foreign Commerce, *National Fair Trade Legislation – 1959* (sub-committee hearings, Washington, 1959), pp. 36–7, 400.

[66] US Senate, Committee on Commerce, *Quality Stabilisation* (sub-committee hearings, Washington, 1964), pp. 10, 247 ff., 426.

[67] S.M.Lee, 'Problems of Resale Price Maintenance', *op. cit.*, pp. 687–8.

[68] The advance retail trade report of the 1963 business census, which became

A completely rigorous study of the relationships between r.p.m. and the prices that consumers pay would require (1) selection of two study areas or localities which were identical in all relevant demographic, social, economic and commercial characteristics; (2) introduction and exclusion of r.p.m. in the test and control areas respectively, while all other independent factors were held identical and while the effects of the testing process itself were somehow neutralised; and (3) observation of all prices paid by representative samples of consumers in the two areas. Even merely stating these requirements indicates the impossibility of entirely fulfilling them. Consequently none of the many empirical studies of fair-trade prices is totally free of reservations or immune to criticism.[69] Nevertheless, the data now available strongly demonstrate that fair trade reduces the range of price options available to consumers on price-maintained merchandise, and rather clearly indicate that it raises average prices of the price-maintained items.

A few analyses, mainly those commissioned or conducted by advocates of fair trade, report that price maintenance raises prices insignificantly or not at all. The study conducted by Ostlund and Vickland in 1940 is probably the best known of this group.[70] Its conclusion, that prices for fifty drug products *fell* 0·9 per cent. after the introduction of fair trade in various states, is still cited today by fair-trade supporters, in spite of the many methodological criticisms to which the study is susceptible.[71] Space here is inadequate

available just at the time of writing, shows approximately a 22 per cent. increase in retail dollar sales, a 6 per cent. increase in the total number of non-owner retail employees, a 27 per cent. increase in retail employee pay-rolls, and a 5 per cent. decrease in the number of retail establishments (i.e. stores, not firms) over the period 1958–63, a time when r.p.m. was losing effectiveness in this country. However, considerable analysis is needed to determine what portions of the reductions in the number of stores are due to chain-store policies favouring the operation of fewer, larger units, to the variety of factors that affect the retail entry rate, to population re-distributions, to intensification of price competition, and to other factors.

[69] M.Frankel, 'The Effects of Fair Trade: Fact and Fiction in the Statistical Findings', *Journal of Business*, 28 (1955), pp. 182–94.

[70] H.J.Ostlund and C.R.Vickland, *Fair Trade and the Retail Drug Store* (Chicago, 1940).

[71] For example, the study is cited in material submitted by a drug-trade group in US House of Representatives, *Quality Stabilisation – 1963*, *op. cit.*, p. 153. For detailed criticisms see Frankel, *op. cit.*, pp. 186–90.

to itemise all the weaknesses of the study. Perhaps it is sufficient to note that the findings were based upon unverified non-random replies (at about a 27 per cent. response rate) to a mail questionnaire in which retail druggists were called upon to recall the prices they had charged for the 50 items at various times over periods ranging up to two or three years previously, depending upon the dates on which r.p.m. was introduced in their states. A contemporary trade press programme that used the slogan 'cast a vote for fair trade' to urge the druggists to complete their questionnaires probably did not improve the validity of the study.

The A.C.Nielsen Company, which operates marketing research and information services based upon panels of selected retail stores throughout the country, conducted a potentially more useful study in 1952. Nielsen compared prices reported for 24 packaged remedies and grooming aids in 1949 and 1951 in stores in fair-trade and non-fair-trade states, and concluded that consumers in fair-trade jurisdictions were, on the average, charged somewhat less than those in non-fair-trade states. The same firm prepared a somewhat similar report in 1958, but for some reason limited the comparison to fifteen items. However, in response to inquiries from the Department of Justice, Nielsen indicated that its data were inadequate for comparison of comparable regions, for example, fair-trade and non-fair-trade states of roughly equal degrees of industrialisation; that it would not supply information about its sampling or weighting techniques or identify the respondent stores; and that it could not submit the original price reports for verification. Interestingly enough, it did note that chain-store prices were lower in non-fair-trade jurisdictions than in fair-trade ones, so that consumers in the former tended to have available much wider ranges of prices.[72]

As against the results reported in these and a few other studies, government, academic and consumer-group analysts have almost invariably reported that fair trade raises prices. The Federal Trade Commission concluded in its massive, but in some ways poorly co-ordinated, report of 1945: 'The essence of resale price maintenance is control of price competition . . . The net result in enhancement and maintenance of high living costs is no less real because it is concealed in the prices at which goods reach the consumer in such a way that it is not subject to direct measurement.'[73] According to

[72] US Senate, *National Fair Trade Legislation – 1959*, pp. 300, 615–28.
[73] US Federal Trade Commission, *Report . . .*, *op. cit.*, p. LXI.

the Commission, fair trade forced particularly sharp price increases among mass distributors, such as the chain stores.[74]

Numerous other studies have involved comparisons between market-place prices and fair-trade minima (in a sense measuring what happens when and if fair trade is actually enforced), or between prices before and after the imposition of fair trade, or between prices in fair-trade and non-fair-trade jurisdictions. Some of the best known of these comparisons were made by Grether (1936, drug prices before and after r.p.m.), Wolff and Holthausen (1938, fifty drug items before and after r.p.m.), Cassady (1939, advertised branded drugs compared with non-price-maintained generic counterparts), Gault (1939, cut-rate drug-stores' advertised prices compared with fair-trade minima), Lewis (1939, drug prices before and after fair trade, and advertised v. minimum prices), Seelye (1941, drug prices in two adjacent cities, one with and one without r.p.m.), Bowman (1955, prices consumers paid for toothpaste in fair-trade and non-fair-trade states), McEwen, Smith and Scully (1956, photographic flashbulbs in two cities, one with and one without r.p.m.), US Department of Justice (1956, actual prices for 132 drug, toiletry, photographic, appliance and miscellaneous items in non-fair-trade cities compared with fair-trade minima), and Sandridge (1960, an exhaustive analysis of advertised prices for electric appliances in non-fair-trade territory and in fair-trade territory both before and after the elimination of controls).[75]

McEwen, Smith and Scully found that dealers in both Washington (non-fair-trade) and Boston (fair-trade) generally observed the

[74] *Ibid.*, pp. LIX, LX. Frankel feels that the F.T.C.'s only 'reasonably conclusive' finding was that 'chain and department stores raised their prices in fair-trade areas on fair-trade items' after they had been placed under r.p.m. Frankel, 'The Effects of Fair Trade . . .', *op. cit.*

[75] E.T.Grether, 'Experience in California with Fair Trade Legislation', *California Law Review*, 24 (1936), pp. 640–70; R.P.Wolff and D.Holthausen, 'The Control of Retail Prices under the Fair Trade Laws', *Dun's Review*, 46 (July 1938), pp. 15–22; R.Cassady, Jr, 'Maintenance of Resale Prices by Manufacturers', *Quarterly Journal of Economics*, 53 (1939), pp. 454–64; E.H.Gault, *Fair Trade* (Michigan Business Studies, vol. 9, Ann Arbor, 1939); C.W.Lewis, 'Economic Effects of Price Maintenance in Knoxville, Tennessee', *Journal of Marketing*, 4 (1939), pp. 139–46; A.L.Seelye, 'Drug Prices in Cities With and Without a Fair Trade Law', *Journal of Marketing*, 6 (1941), pp. 16–21; Bowman, 'Prerequisites and Effects of Resale Price Maintenance', *op. cit.*, pp. 852–9; Rev. R.J.McEwen, W.J.Smith and C.J.Scully, 'Fair Trade Prices', *The Boston College Guidepost*, 9 (October 1956), pp. 6–15; US Senate, *National Fair Trade Legislation – 1959*, pp. 300–10; Sandridge, *The Effects of Fair Trade . . .*, *op. cit.*

manufacturers' suggested prices foı flashbulbs. Lewis noted no substantial or significant effect from the imposition of r.p.m. on the great majority of prices in conventional, full-price drug-stores, although there was a $1\frac{1}{2}$ per cent. decline on the items shopped. However, prices rose materially in cut-price stores. Grether also noted a slight decrease in prices in full-price stores, off-set by substantial increases in prices in cut-price outlets. The other studies report significantly higher, and in many instances very substantially higher, prices under r.p.m.

Although many of these studies were quite rigorous, they are all subject to possible attack under the allegation of selectivity. It is sometimes claimed that prices charged for branded items, and particularly advertised prices for them, are not representative of the prices charged for all the goods sold in cut-price stores. According to this argument, the supposedly cut-price dealers recoup their losses on the cut items through over-charges for non-advertised and non-branded lines. The studies cited above cannot, by their very nature, throw any light on the claim that price reductions on the cut lines are in fact counterbalanced by price increases on the other lines. However, this claim could not be applicable to price-cutting by specialised discount record and book dealers, who have little to offer for sale except the general lines on which they offer reductions, or to the discount appliance dealers who have demonstrated that they can operate on less than r.p.m. minimum margins. Moreover, since many states confine their liquor retailing licences to specialised dealers who can have little opportunity for recoupment through over-charges, and since the cut-price liquor dealers in other states are specialists, particular significance attaches to the New York State Moreland Commission finding that a system of rigorously enforced price maintenance raises liquor prices.[76] It may be noted, finally, that so far as the author knows no systematic attempt has been made to compare the resale prices, in fair-trade and in other states, of goods which are not subject to r.p.m. in either set of states. There is no convincing evidence to support the recoupment theory.

[76] Wattel, *op. cit.*, p. 30; New York State Moreland Commission, *Report No. 3*, *op. cit.*, pp. 1–8, 40–1.

The Commission concurred in its economic advisers' estimates that the leading brands of whisky, which retailed in New York at prices ranging from $4.50 to $7.09 per standard fifth gallon bottle, were about $1.00 higher than they would have been without mandatory r.p.m.

Changes in Dealer Margins under Resale Price Maintenance

A common hypothesis concerning r.p.m. is that manufacturers who use the practice are likely over time to increase the retail margins they allow to dealers. This hypothesis rests on the belief that the desire to win the favour of retailers is one of the main reasons – if not the only one – for the adoption of r.p.m. by manufacturers. Since retailers' attitudes are considered to be important, manufacturers, having instituted r.p.m., are then likely to compete for the support of retailers by raising margins.

There has been relatively little empirical investigation of the behaviour over time of retail margins under r.p.m.[77] The available studies for the United States indicate no uniform tendency, which suggests that the wish or need to satisfy or please dealers is no more than one of several factors considered by manufacturers in formulating their marketing strategies. Individual manufacturers, operating from different strategic positions, evaluate differently both the wishes of dealers and other considerations.

One study assembled fragmentary information of retail margins under r.p.m. for twenty-five brands of toothpaste and headache remedies over the period 1950–61. The average retail margins, indicated by the relationship between published wholesale and minimum resale prices, actually decreased for slightly less than one-sixth of the brands, increased for about two-fifths, and remained substantially constant for the others. A somewhat similar lack of uniformity, but with a fairly strong tendency towards increased allowances on large purchases, appears in trade discount policies announced by book publishers during the period 1947–62. The decreases seem to have been important in toothpaste, where vigorous retail competition by low-margin grocery outlets had become increasingly important, and for purchases of books in small lots, where the retailers probably were unable to exert much bargaining pressure.[78] The data in this and other similar studies do not, of

[77] See S.C.Hollander, 'Dealer Margins under Resale Price Maintenance', *Quarterly Review of Economics and Business*, 3 (1963), pp. 25–33, for discussion of the studies that have been made.

[78] For details, see Hollander, *ibid.*

The margins actually available on any brand of toothpaste or headache remedy differed from the margin reported in the study for that brand to the extent (1) that an average weighted by the relative sales of each item in the brand line would have differed from the unweighted average used in the study, and (2)

course, shed light on the question whether or not, without r.p.m., the decreases might have been greater (and the increases smaller) than they actually were.

Conclusion

The United States experience with r.p.m. demonstrates the complexity and difficulty of trying to regulate interstate commerce on a state-by-state basis. But more fundamentally it seems to demonstrate something about r.p.m. itself. Almost thirty years' use of price maintenance, with varying degrees of enforcement, shows it to be little more than a futile and costly barrier to change and competition in marketing. Resale price control certainly has not been essential to manufacturers' marketing success. The record is replete with cases of manufacturers, even in the commodity fields where price maintenance was supposedly significant, who developed successful brand strategies without regard to r.p.m. or after r.p.m. had withered away. Price maintenance seems to have played little or no role in assuring retailer survival.

What it does seem to have done was temporarily to bottle up some economic forces, thereby disadvantaging the consumer, until discounting and private branding ultimately and painfully induced its collapse. The basic lesson apparently is that r.p.m. can be imposed upon a dynamic economy only if it is accompanied by a set of more restrictive practices, such as barriers to entry, prohibitions on private branding, stop lists, and cartelisation. There have been traces of some such practices, particularly in the distribution of alcoholic beverages and drug-store products. The results clearly have been undesirable from the point of view of consumers and of the economy as a whole.

that the prices retailers actually paid differed from the manufacturer's published wholesale list. The lack of item-weights probably did not warp the results greatly since many of the firms announced uniform margins for each relevant item within a brand line. But the second condition probably was a more serious source of error, because of the widespread use in the trade of various types of special offers and quantity discounts that varied or may have varied from time to time.

4

SWEDEN

U. af Trolle

Resale price maintenance was allowed to develop perfectly freely in Sweden right up to the year 1954, when the law of 1953 against restrictive trade practices came into force. The main purpose of the 1953 legislation – with later modifications and additions – was not to prohibit restrictive trade practices as such, but primarily to remove any possible injurious effects of such practices by means of a system of negotiation. In two instances, nevertheless, certain types of restrictive trade practices were expressly prohibited. The more important of these is that any form of r.p.m. which interfered with the liberty of the retailer to reduce his prices was made illegal. The law does not, on the other hand, prevent the supplier from fixing a maximum resale price below which (but not above which) the retailer may sell, or from suggesting a 'target' price which the retailer may disregard in either direction. Moreover, the legislation provides for the granting of exemptions from the general prohibition of r.p.m.

Thus neither horizontal price agreements nor vertical price maintenance in the form of the prescription of target resale prices is prohibited. These practices may, however, be made the subject of negotiation in accordance with the basic principle of the law if they are found to have injurious effects. In 1965 the Swedish government appointed a committee to consider whether the prohibition of r.p.m. should be extended to include all types of price agreements, that is, also horizontal price agreements and the vertical target price system.

The Development of Resale Price Maintenance

As will be more fully explained in the following section, only one comprehensive investigation of r.p.m. has been carried out in Sweden. A report on it was published in 1951 and contains, among other things, estimates of the prevalence of r.p.m. in Sweden around the period 1948–50, when the system may be considered to have reached its peak.[1] Two types of estimate were made.

The first estimate was based primarily on information obtained from 245 industrial undertakings in the consumer-goods sector and from a large number of trade associations in trade and industry. The material also included information obtained by systematic examination of the contents of the cartel register for cases in which r.p.m. was combined with other agreements having the effect of restricting competition. The estimate was intended to show the prevalence of r.p.m. in various branches of trade and industry.

The second estimate was based on the household budget investigation carried out by the National Social Welfare Board in 1948. For this, detailed information had been provided by some thousand households about their total expenditure during one complete year. The expenditure was classified under 180 headings. Foodstuffs, which appeared in this investigation as a single item, were subdivided into some seventy subsidiary headings in an investigation undertaken in 1949. From this basic material for these investigations a hundred household budgets were selected at random, and these were subjected to a detailed analysis on a basis of separating expenditures subject to r.p.m. from the remainder. This approach also made it possible to estimate the importance of r.p.m. for families in different income groups.

It was also considered whether a similar investigation should be carried out on the basis of an earlier budget investigation for the year 1938. The basic material proved, however, not to be sufficiently detailed for this purpose. The change, over a period of time, in the extent of r.p.m. could therefore only be established from the information obtained from firms in the first inquiry referred to above. In this inquiry information was also obtained about the date of the introduction of r.p.m. in various branches of trade. Some further information was also obtained by studying a number of price catalogues made available by various wholesale and retail firms in the food trade going back as far as the end of the 1920s.

All the information given in the following pages about the forms and development of r.p.m. is taken from these investigations, with the exception of certain information about the tobacco trade which

[1] U. af Trolle, *Bruttoprissystemet. En Problemanalys*, in Government Report SOU 1951: 28 (Stockholm, 1951).

is taken from an investigation into competitive conditions in this trade published in 1965.[2]

By far the most widespread form of r.p.m. in Sweden was that in which the supplier – normally the producer – determines fixed prices which the retailer must neither exceed nor fall below. Other forms of r.p.m. had achieved so little importance up to 1954 that, with one exception, they are not worth mentioning in this brief account.

If a system of r.p.m. is to be enforceable, it is necessary that the goods sold should somehow be capable of identification throughout the whole of the distribution process. This condition is most easily fulfilled in the case of branded goods, which explains why formerly, particularly in the German literature, the system of branding goods and the system of r.p.m. were frequently treated as being identical. The same necessary condition can, however, also be fulfilled in the case of non-branded goods, even of staple commodities such as nails and electric cable, if all the producers join together to determine and enforce the prices at which their products are to be retailed. Such combinations of producers' price cartels and r.p.m. became common in Sweden as r.p.m. became more widespread.

As was said above, the most usual form of r.p.m. was that in which the *supplier* determined the prices at which his goods were to be retailed, even if this determination was often done after negotiations with the retailers. There was, however, another type of r.p.m., in which the retailers joined together in a horizontal price cartel to determine the prices at which goods were to be retailed, while the suppliers undertook by agreement with the retailers to ensure that the prices thus determined were respected, if necessary by withholding supplies. Such systems functioned in all other respects in exactly the same way as the ordinary r.p.m. systems with the supplier as the price-determining party. They have consequently been treated in the surveys carried out as ordinary systems of r.p.m.

In Sweden, as in other European countries, the system of r.p.m. was first applied to books and although it is uncertain when this application first began there is evidence that it was in operation already by the middle of the nineteenth century.

The system of branded goods was introduced in Sweden about the

[2] U. af Trolle, 'Femtio År av Monopol och Konkurrens', in the anniversary volume, *Om Tobak i Sverige* (Stockholm, 1965).

turn of the century, but it was a long time before any attempts were made to apply r.p.m. to anything other than books. When the practice first came to be extended beyond the book trade, it was done in a way that was probably unique to Sweden, namely by means of a law enforcing r.p.m. This was in 1915, when the Swedish tobacco industry was nationalised and about sixty undertakings were absorbed into the tobacco monopoly that was then founded.

When the bill for nationalising the tobacco industry was first drafted, nothing was said about r.p.m. for tobacco products. It was assumed that these would continue to be sold freely as before by the retailers at prices determined by themselves. During the process of redrafting at the relevant ministry, however, a clause was added under which it was made illegal for the individual retailer to sell tobacco goods at prices other than those set by the state monopoly. There was no public statement to explain this change. From records made available by the Swedish Tobacco Company it would appear, however, to have been the result of skilful lobbying on the part of the leaders of the tobacco dealers' trade association. Certainly, no one concerned in carrying out the nationalisation had put forward any such suggestion. When the bill was under discussion in the Riksdag, no interest at all was shown in the clause about r.p.m. in spite of the fact that its introduction represented a startling innovation.

No one had any interest in trying to introduce r.p.m. in the years that followed (up to 1920), when prices were moving upwards in an inflationary situation, but interest arose with the sharp fall in prices after the war. It seems, however, that only in one trade did it prove possible to draw up an effective resale price agreement before 1925, namely in the wholesale trade in sugar. This took place as early as 1921. For a number of years the wholesalers had been trying to establish horizontal price agreements, but these had always broken under the pressure of competition. In 1921 they succeeded in obtaining the promise of the producers to support the price cartel by withholding supplies from such wholesalers as tried to under-cut the agreed prices. The producers, who merged by stages to form a single firm, were in return given a voice in the price-fixing by the wholesalers.

The problem of how to control fixed prices effectively proved the worst stumbling-block in the way of those producers who wished to introduce r.p.m. In a number of cases producers in various branches of industry, mainly manufacturers of chemists' goods, tried to introduce r.p.m. during the 1920s but were never able to reach any firm agreement on account of the difficulties of individual enforcement. The most successful was Colgate-Palmolive, which drew up formal agreements with its customers about fixed prices on the American pattern. In time the firm accumulated no less than some 30,000 agreements which were enforceable in a court of law.

In general it proved impossible to ensure effective individual enforcement of resale prices – Colgate-Palmolive with its vast resources was an exception. It was an obvious step then to try to establish a joint board for the control of resale prices of branded goods. The first initiative in this direction was taken in 1926 by a number of wholesalers with common interests. The initiative was supported by the wholesalers' trade associations, and a certain number of retailers' associations also appealed to their members to uphold the work of the board. The suppliers who joined the board undertook collectively to withhold supplies from retailers guilty of under-cutting. Trade competition, however, was too strong, and interest in co-operation too weak for the attempt to succeed. The board closed down after a couple of years.

About the year 1930 the position seems to have been that a few suppliers such as Colgate-Palmolive had succeeded in building up effective individually enforced systems of r.p.m., and that most of the others who adopted r.p.m. were unable to enforce compliance with their resale prices, so that effective r.p.m. by and large was practically unknown.

The year 1931 has been selected here as a dividing line between a first period of groping attempts and a second in which r.p.m. developed rapidly. The reason for this is as follows. In 1931 a new law was brought in against what was called 'unfair competition'. Hopes had been entertained in trade circles that this law would include prohibitions against 'unfair price competition'. At the same time the trade associations had asked the Government also to introduce control of new business establishments in the form of the prescription by law of qualifications for the right to run a business. All hopes of a prohibition of 'unfair price competition' were dashed when the bill was published, while the representations about legal control of the establishment of new businesses were also rejected. The minister responsible for the legislation implied, however, that the field now lay open for efforts on the part of industry itself. The depression had also made conditions more favourable for control.

Developments now followed rapidly. In 1934 seven of the major Swedish manufacturers of cosmetic products set up their control board for the purpose of ensuring that their prescribed resale prices were adhered to. The mere fact of the board's establishment and presence had a markedly stabilising effect even in other branches of trade. Although there are no figures to support this statement, all the available material seems to indicate that, by the outbreak of war, practically all branded goods of importance were sold under r.p.m. There were, however, a few notable exceptions, such as flour and sugar, which were subject to r.p.m. in the wholesale but not in the retail trade. Resale price control was, however, not yet fully effective, particularly in the larger towns where price competition must still have been considerable.

Side by side with this development towards firmer vertical price agreements, a system of private control of new business establishments grew up in most sectors of wholesale and retail trade. These controls were mostly run in co-operation between manufacturers', wholesalers' and retailers' organisations. Any person who wished, for example, to open a new shop, had to apply to the appropriate control organisation, which then decided whether there was a need for a new shop. All the suppliers connected with the organisation undertook not to supply goods to those whose applications were rejected. Control was gradually extended to cover not merely new firms but also new branches of established firms and even extensions of the type of goods stocked. This latter measure made it possible to an increasing extent to keep the different branches of trade 'clean'.

The Second World War in many respects proved to be a great help in the efforts to regulate distribution.

Government price control was appreciably facilitated by the existence of r.p.m., which among other things meant uniform prices. The price control authorities consequently were very much interested in the further extension of r.p.m. to include spheres in which it had not previously operated, for example because branded goods did not occur in them. New systems were now introduced, as in the clothing trade, on the basis of compulsory marking of goods with the manufacturer's name. The price control authorities also took an active part in the creation of price cartels for standardised 'anonymous' goods, so that r.p.m. could be introduced for them.

Thanks to government price control, consumers soon grew accustomed to the idea that prices should be uniform, and it gradually faded from their consciousness, and from that of the distributors, that anything else could ever be contemplated. In these circumstances, and with the additional shortage of goods, difficulties in the way of controlling the fixed resale prices soon evaporated.

In anticipation of a post-war revival of competition, a new and still more effective organ for supervising fixed resale prices, known as the Uniform Price Board, was set up in 1945. All trade associations of any importance engaged in r.p.m. were represented on this board. Its task was, however, an easy one. The number of cases in which supplies had to be withheld from retailers because of undercutting was very small; the many years of government price control had, as was mentioned above, accustomed both consumer and retailer to the idea that prices should be uniform. It is characteristic of the attitude of the time that it was actually a Riksdag motion demanding the introduction of uniform prices in one of the few spheres in which r.p.m. did not yet apply which, paradoxically, eventually brought about the abolition of r.p.m.

The clearest idea of the extent of r.p.m. towards the end of the 1940s can be obtained from the budget investigation referred to previously. This showed that approximately 29 per cent. of consumers' purchases in the retail trade were subject to r.p.m. (Alcoholic beverages were not included in this estimate. See footnote 10.) The percentage varied systematically for consumers in the different income groups. It was highest (approximately 32 per cent.) for the lowest income groups and lowest (approximately 27 per cent.) for the highest income groups. The reason for this difference is so obvious that no explanation is called for.

The investigation also included estimates of the extent of r.p.m. with reference to different classes of goods. It would, however, take us too far afield to discuss the results here, more particularly as this would involve a number of supplementary explanations about the structure of retail trade and the investigation procedure. The following particulars must suffice. It may be said, as was stated above, that in principle r.p.m. was applied to practically all branded goods, regardless of the class of goods. This meant that classes of goods of which a high percentage was branded, automatically contained a high proportion of goods sold subject to r.p.m. As examples of classes of goods with at least 80 per cent. coverage by r.p.m. in retailing to the consumer may be mentioned chemists' goods, cosmetics, musical instruments, glass and china, photographic equipment, books and stationery, tobacco products, motor cars and fuel, cycles, and so on. In the food trade approximately 35 to 45 per cent. of retail sales seems to have been under r.p.m. Furniture and fabrics were among the classes of which only a small proportion came under r.p.m.

The Development of Public Policy

The official attitude towards r.p.m. may be inferred from reports of government committees, Riksdag debates, and legislation.

During the 1920s and 1930s a number of investigations were carried out in connection with questions of competition. It was not, however, until 1940 that r.p.m. was first mentioned in a published report.[3] Even then the reference was only incidental, and implied that the branding of goods and r.p.m. were inextricably associated. In so far as the report contained any analysis of advantages and disadvantages, it drew no distinction between the system of branded goods and r.p.m. Only one conclusion could be drawn. The system of branded goods had to be regarded as an inevitable, integral part of the modern economy.

A few years later r.p.m. was discussed in the Riksdag in connection with a bill for regulating tobacco distribution.[4] As we have seen, r.p.m. had been applied to tobacco goods ever since the creation of the tobacco monopoly in 1915. On the other hand, in the 1930s there was no control of the establishment of new businesses in the tobacco trade, unlike in most other branches of retail trade. The reason for this was obvious. It was the tobacco monopoly that decided what trade customers it wished to have, and the legislation then in force did not allow the Company to prevent financially sound retailers from buying its products. This combination of r.p.m. and free entry into the trade had naturally resulted in a steadily increasing number of tobacco retailers. Even though their margins were raised

[3] *Organiserad Samverkan inom Svenskt Näringsliv*, Government Report SOU 1940: 35 (Stockholm, 1940).

[4] U. af Trolle, 'Femtio År . . .', *op. cit.*

periodically, the increase in the number of retailers was considered to have involved a deterioration of their financial position.

In 1938 a committee was appointed to consider primarily what could be done to improve the financial position of tobacconists. As it regarded r.p.m. as an inevitable condition, its conclusion was also inevitable: control of new establishments must be introduced. In the Riksdag debate in 1943 on the Committee's proposals, the idea was hinted at in one or two of the speeches that it might possibly have been more to the point to question the retention of r.p.m. But no one dared put forward such a revolutionary idea in a formal proposal. They restricted themselves to Platonic declarations in favour of free competition, and then voted for the introduction of the control of new establishments.

The next phase of the official attitude towards r.p.m. found expression in a complete lack of interest in the system or of understanding of what it meant. During the first half of the 1940s a series of investigations was carried out into the state of the Swedish economy in preparation for the post-war period. In these, questions of competition were also dealt with. The investigations led to a law of 1946 under which *agreements* restricting competition had in certain circumstances to be registered with the authorities. Resale price maintenance was simply never mentioned in these investigations. The law was so formulated that resale price agreements were not affected by the obligation to register unless they formed part in any way of other agreements restricting competition, as was sometimes the case.

As a final expression of the indifference or even the favourable attitude of the authorities towards r.p.m. may be mentioned a proposal put forward in the government inquiry into the furniture trade, the report of which was published in 1947.[5] The furniture trade was one of the few consumer-goods trades in which r.p.m. had not been adopted to any significant extent. The Committee then suggested as one of the solutions to the problems of the furniture industry that it should introduce r.p.m. It considered that this would enable the industry to achieve a system of price-fixing which would be satisfactory both to the producer and to the retailer and the consumer.

A major change in attitude took place during the immediately succeeding years.

During the years 1945 and 1946 the author of this chapter undertook two assignments connected with r.p.m., both of which resulted

[5] *Möbler*, Government Report SOU 1947: 52 (Stockholm, 1952).

in reports published in 1948. The first of these assignments involved the drawing up of a 'correct' price-fixing system for the leather trade, which would include r.p.m. What it really meant was, by 'objective' methods, to find a solution to a conflict between the leather manufacturing industry and the distributive trade. The second assignment originated in a Riksdag motion and was concerned with the distribution of sugar. As has been stated above, r.p.m. had been applied in the wholesale trade in sugar since 1921, but never in the retail trade. The Riksdag motion now demanded uniform prices for sugar to the consumer. The task of investigating this question devolved upon the author, by way of various government departments and the Swedish Sugar Company.

In both these investigations a great deal of material was assembled about costs and prices. Both investigations led to one and the same conclusion. It would be impossible to construct a r.p.m. system with fixed prices which would at the same time satisfy the demand for 'justice' for all parties and also provide a suitable price-fixing system in a dynamic economy. The investigation into the leather trade involved an extensive theoretical analysis.[6] The investigation into the sugar trade resulted in the concrete proposal that, instead of introducing the r.p.m. system into the retail trade in sugar, it should be dropped from the wholesale trade.[7] It may be mentioned here that the Sugar Company, after negotiations with the wholesalers and authorities, followed this advice and as early as 1951 abolished all vertical price agreements.

At the same time as this was going on, a government committee had been at work since 1946 on a general inquiry into the effects of restrictive trade practices. The terms of reference had originally covered the control of new establishments only, some aspects of which had been attracting attention; but it had soon been extended to include every form of restrictive trade practice. By 1948 and 1949 the Committee had reached the point of agreement in principle to putting forward a proposal under which a new government authority would be set up with powers to examine individual restrictive trade practices and which would endeavour to eliminate from case to case any injurious effects. For some reason unknown to the author, the Committee had not yet included r.p.m. in its deliberations.

[6] U. af Trolle, *Från Producent till Konsument. En Studie av Läder-distributionen* (Stockholm, 1947).

[7] U. af Trolle, *Om Enhetliga Priser på Socker* (Malmö, 1947).

The two above-mentioned reports attacking r.p.m. and some subsequent articles on the subject caused a vehement discussion. Many voices were raised in defence of the system. As a natural outcome of this discussion, the Committee in session felt it ought to take up r.p.m. for detailed consideration. Having established, however, that time would not allow it to draw up its own report on the subject, the Committee decided to incorporate a survey of the author's two reports in its own general report. The author, who had at the same time been made a member of the Committee, was given the opportunity to make the estimate of the extent and development of r.p.m. in Sweden referred to in the preceding section. When the Committee's recommendations were published in 1951, the report thus included as one of its appendices an analysis of r.p.m.[8]

The author had come to the conclusion that the system was harmful, and the Committee shared this view in principle. It was not, however, prepared to recommend anything so drastic as a prohibition of r.p.m., but thought more along the lines of treating the system in the same way as other restrictive trade practices, that is, on a case-to-case basis. The author contested this attitude, pointing out that in the matter of r.p.m. one had to adopt a definite attitude in one direction or the other. It was, in the author's view, the system as such that was harmful, not its application in individual cases. One could never achieve any real results by trying to eliminate the system in individual cases, apart altogether from the difficulty of explaining satisfactorily why one intervened in one case and not in another.

During the ensuing discussion of the Committee's proposals at the Ministry of Trade, the authorities came to the conclusion that r.p.m. should be forbidden (as also another form of restrictive trade practice which is of no interest in the present connection). In the meantime a remarkable change of heart had taken place in industry. Some of the most zealous supporters of the system had changed their minds in various ways. During negotiations between the Ministry and representatives of industrial organisations an agreement was accordingly reached under which industry accepted the prohibition of r.p.m. in return for the abandonment by the authorities of another clause in the original bill which had aroused violent indignation. This was the clause relating to what was called the 'inverted burden of proof', that is, that it should devolve upon the party supporting a restrictive trade practice to show that it did *not* have

[8] U. af Trolle, *Bruttoprissystemet . . . , op. cit.*

harmful effects. It may be mentioned here that the author strongly supported this construction, which was borrowed from American legislation, on the grounds that it is easier for those who introduced and practised a restrictive practice to show that it is not harmful (when it is not harmful) than it is for the authorities to do the opposite (when it is harmful). The construction was, however, considered unanimously by a body of legal experts to involve something new and inappropriate for Swedish law. The inverted burden of proof was abandoned as part of the compact. (It may be mentioned here that the change proved to have no practical significance. Since the general construction of the law is such that in the final analysis it is the subjective view of the authorities that determines whether a restrictive trade practice is to be regarded as harmful or not, it is of no significance as to where the burden of proof rests.)

The Riksdag in 1953 approved the compromise thus reached, though not without serious reservations as to the manner in which the compromise had been reached. Since the authorities had negotiated directly with industry, the Riksdag had been confronted with a *fait accompli.*

As early as 1956 the restrictive trade practices law was tightened up as the result of another government investigation and another agreement with industry.[9] In this agreement industry accepted a tightening-up of the law in return for the abandonment by the Government of the last remains of official price control. The tightening-up did not directly affect the prohibition of r.p.m. but indirectly created better conditions for its enforcement. In the account of the law given below, it is considered in the form it took after the changes of 1956.

After the statute of 1953 came into force in 1954, r.p.m. remained operative only for tobacco products and in some exempted trades which are considered in a later section.[10] It was obvious, however, that the situation could not persist in which deviations from fixed prices for tobacco were criminal offences, while at the same time r.p.m. for most other goods was regarded as an offence. A government commission inquiring into the tobacco trade came to this self-

[9] *Konkurrens och Priser*, Government Report SOU 1955: 45 (Stockholm, 1955).

[10] Alcoholic drinks are still sold at uniform prices all over the country, but this is not a question of r.p.m. in the proper sense. There are no independent retailers in the retailing of alcoholic drinks, which is done through the state monopoly's own shops.

evident conclusion in its report.[11] It was not, however, until 1 January 1960 that tobacco was set free from resale price-fixing, and was replaced by the 'target' price system in order to allow retailers time for re-adjustment. At the same time the control of new establishments in the tobacco trade was abolished, as were also to all intents and purposes the monopoly rights of the State Tobacco Company. As will be noted below, the control of new establishments had already been abolished in all other trades as a result of enactment of the law of 1953.

The Economic Basis for the Prohibition of Resale Price Maintenance

The prohibition of r.p.m. was based on the opinion the authorities formed from the material laid before them in the report published in 1951. A detailed survey of the investigations would take us too far afield; a brief account must suffice, showing, first, the form the investigation took and, second, the main considerations which led to the final decision.

It is not possible to give an answer that will be completely satisfactory, from a scientific point of view, to the question of whether or not a system of r.p.m. is harmful. The possibilities of objective analysis have to be set within narrow limits, as can best be shown by a quotation from the report of the investigation carried out:[12]

> The present investigation has as its mainspring the question: Is the distribution of income brought about by resale price maintenance more or less desirable from a socio-economic point of view than that which would prevail under free price competition? This is the question that seems now to be generally implied when the problem of resale price maintenance is discussed.
>
> The question is not peculiar to resale price maintenance but is common to all types of restrictive trade practice. Just as with other types of restrictive trade practice, it can only to a limited extent be made the subject of an objective, unbiased analysis. The final decision must be largely based on a balancing of purely personal evaluations of phenomena that cannot be measured. It is important to draw a clear distinction between the possibilities of objective

[11] *Tobakshandelsregleringen*, Government Report SOU 1955: 38 (Stockholm, 1955).

[12] U. af Trolle, *Bruttoprissystemet . . .*, *op. cit.*

analysis and the personal evaluations which play an essential part in any judgment of the problem.

First as regards the direct effect on the distribution of income, an objective analysis can do no more than indicate the conditions of income formation under resale price maintenance as compared with those under the free formation of prices. It cannot, on the other hand, indicate which distribution of income is to be preferred. This is a political question involving the conflicting interests of different social groups.

An analysis of the effects of resale price maintenance on the structure of the distributive trades may be carried somewhat further. The analysis will then comprise the following successive stages:

1. A *theoretical* discussion of the effects of resale price maintenance with the object of clarifying the problem and establishing in which direction it tends to work in various respects.

2. An attempt to *measure* the effects which resale price maintenance may be assumed to have in various respects, in the light of the theoretical discussion.

3. A *consideration from the socio-economic point of view* of the results obtained under the two above headings, in so far as this is possible on objective, generally accepted premises.

It will be convenient to consider the third point first. What is a socially desirable structure of distribution? Without attempting to enter here into a discussion of the various attempts to answer this question which have been made within the framework of the welfare economy, it may be said quite briefly that in the present investigation the following standards have been adopted:

If a given activity of production-plus-distribution can be carried out with less expenditure of productive factors, this is desirable from society's point of view. This simple rule, however, is not always enough. Problems arise where a change in the method of price-fixing not merely affects the expenditure of productive factors, but also alters the character of the end-product which the distributor offers the consumer. As an example may be mentioned the fact that resale price maintenance involves a restriction of the consumer's choice between various combinations of price and service. Is this a disadvantage, and if so, how is it to be evaluated? The effects of resale price maintenance on the structure of distribution in this and other respects may be defined, but there is no yardstick which enables us to measure objectively their socio-economic effects. It may be said here quite briefly that an objective evaluation of the effects of resale price maintenance from a social point of view would only seem possible in so far as the end-product to the consumer remained unchanged. This is a considerable limitation of the field.

We return then to the first two points, i.e. to an analysis with the object of establishing in which direction the system tends to work and of measuring the strength of the tendencies.

The measurement of the strength of these tendencies presents great difficulties. Occasionally it is possible to elaborate methods by which reliable measurement would be feasible, but it often proves that the cost would exceed available financial resources. Often it is not even theoretically conceivable to measure the strength of a tendency. Measurements cannot therefore attain the same systematic character as the theoretical analysis of the problems posed, but must always be subject to gaps.

What practical importance this has depends to some extent on the object of the investigation. If all tendencies run in the same direction, no measurement is necessary for one to be able to express an opinion on the effects of the system from a socio-economic point of view. Moreover the difficulties become less important if one is aiming at achieving the sort of solution in which one would counteract harmful tendencies in the system while trying to encourage beneficial tendencies. Things are different if one is considering an extreme solution: either to allow the system to remain intact or to prohibit it altogether. In this case what is needed is a comprehensive judgment, and then one has to try to balance advantages against disadvantages in numerical terms.

The author has not been able to carry out investigations of such a nature that he can with absolute certainty give a comprehensive judgment on the effects of resale price maintenance, quite apart from the difficulty of keeping such a judgment free of subjective evaluations. In many cases statistics are lacking which might indicate the importance of a particular aspect, and one has to be content with an estimate – at times possibly merely a feeling, based on experience, that a particular factor is important or not important.

The theoretical analysis, together with the factual investigations carried out, seems, however, in the author's opinion to provide very strong reasons for the conclusion that resale price maintenance has had a predominantly harmful influence on the structure of distribution.

It should therefore be strongly emphasised that the law against r.p.m. was based mainly on logically constructed hypotheses, which it was not possible to verify by means of scientifically satisfactory investigations or experiments. To obtain ideas for hypotheses, firms and organisations were questioned, in the inquiry described above, as to their reasons for and against adopting r.p.m. For obvious reasons, arguments in favour of the system predominated. These were examined carefully to see whether they could be regarded as reasonable hypotheses for further investigation. In the final judgment of the effects of the system, however, main emphasis came to be laid on effects which were presumed or observed, but which were not normally mentioned in the general discussion of the system.

Some of the arguments for and against the system, as put forward in the investigation, follow. The view taken of them by the authorities is also given. First we will consider the arguments normally put forward in defence of the system.

Anyone studying this analysis now, fifteen years after it was carried out, will certainly wonder at the amount of effort the author spent on certain arguments in favour of the system, which later developments have completely exploded. If these arguments were then considered so carefully, the reader should bear in mind that the investigation was carried out at a time when price competition in trade in Sweden was regarded as a more-or-less unsound but fortunately extinct phenomenon. A few examples of such arguments may be given.

1. The main argument given by the producers in favour of r.p.m. was that it prevented their – 'well-known' – branded goods being used, as they said, as footballs in the competitive market with such depressed margins that retailers completely lost interest in them. After an analysis of the whole procedure of r.p.m. in trade and of known cases of under-cutting, the author came to the conclusion that the individual producer need run no such risk under free resale pricing, given two conditions. One condition was that no competitor was able to use r.p.m. as a competitive weapon, that is, that everyone was treated equally. The other was that it should be possible to

prevent organised boycotts of individual producers by retailers. Developments since the prohibition have proved the soundness of this conclusion. Right up to 1965 the author has not come across a single case in which even obvious loss-leader pricing in the retail trade involved any drop in sales for the producer, except in a few early cases of boycotts, which were quickly stopped.

2. Another basic argument was that if the producer cannot quote a *fixed* resale price in advertising, then he cannot make any use of price as a competitive weapon in advertising. This argument was thoroughly investigated, including a quantitative analysis of the part played by price in competitive advertising. Here again, experience since the prohibition has shown the correctness of the conclusion that the argument was of no importance.

3. One frequently heard argument was that the consumer would lose confidence in an article that was sold at a low price, that is, that price and quality were connected in the consumer's mind. The conclusion here was that this would not apply in any case in the event of price competition between different retailers for one and the same article. Experience since the prohibition has proved the correctness of this conclusion.

4. An argument frequently brought forward in certain trades was that r.p.m. had the effect of acting as a *maximum* price control, which manufacturers were anxious to preserve. This argument was taken more seriously. As will be seen below, it has often been repeated in later analyses. It was considered, however, that the same effect could be achieved equally well by a 'target' price system, and this has proved to be the case. Even if retailers could in principle exceed a target price, this has generally been prevented by competition. This fact became increasingly clear as more price competition became the normal condition.

5. An argument brought forward particularly frequently in the fashion-goods industry was that r.p.m. provided better conditions for facilitating long production-runs in manufacturing. If retailers were free to set their own prices, the producer would be obliged to prepare special collections for each of the categories of retailers differentiated according to their chosen level of service and therefore of price. The author could find no basis for a reasonable hypothesis relating to this question, which was therefore left open. It has been found since then that this is one of the few really significant problems connected with r.p.m.

6. Resale price maintenance was considered in the retail trade to save a good deal of work in the pricing of goods. According to the investigation, the same effect could, however, be achieved in the main by a target price system. It was also found during the investigation that the quantitative importance of this argument should not be exaggerated. So far as the author knows, no complaints have ever been raised about the amount of labour involved in pricing since the prohibition of r.p.m.

7. Arguments were often put forward by both producers and distributors that r.p.m. was necessary in order to guarantee a certain level of quality of service in the trade, in particular in cases where it was difficult for the consumer to judge the level of quality, for example in repairs to radio sets. The lack of logic in this argument is immediately obvious. What was there in such cases to prevent the distributor reducing the level of quality and thus increasing his profit? The weakness of the argument was, in fact, dramatically illustrated by an experiment carried out by a well-known trade journal. In this a radio set was used which had been found under expert examination to be completely faultless. All details in the set were checked, and then one small point put out of order. The set was then left at fifteen radio shops in turn for repair. Each time it was returned, the set was carefully examined. The result was shattering. In six cases the account given was correct; the others ran the whole gamut up to qualified fraud. Even though the choice was not made at random and the result was therefore only representative of the fifteen radio shops which undertook this particular repair, it nevertheless dealt a deathblow to any attempt to equate r.p.m. with a guarantee of quality of service.

8. One of the arguments perhaps most frequently heard in favour of the system was that it made it possible to fix a fair price both for consumer and for retailer. To the consumer r.p.m. meant uniform prices, that is, that every consumer had to pay the same price, which was considered to be fair. In the case of the retailer, r.p.m., and the negotiations with the producer about the size of his margin which was often involved with it, were considered to give him the same rights as are enjoyed by workers and employees generally to negotiate for a fair income for themselves. It would appear unnecessary to point out the shortcomings of this argument. Suffice it to say that it was easy to demonstrate, on the basis of comprehensive cost and price material, that it was not possible to achieve anything that could

be characterised as fair prices *even* at a given moment, leaving aside complications caused by the dynamics of change.

It might be mentioned in this connection that the supporters of r.p.m. made much of the fact that the general public had declared itself in favour of the system in an opinion poll. But the question had been so framed in this inquiry that the result was a foregone conclusion. It was shown by practical experiment that, by making minor alterations in the wording of the question, the replies could be made to support any opinion whatever, even two diametrically opposed views in one and the same interview.

Much weight was also attached to the fact that consumers in a number of inquiries gave price as a minor factor among their reasons for choosing a particular source of supply. This result, however, was obvious, since price was practically always the same everywhere.

With regard to both the preceding arguments in favour of the system, a general point of view was put forward, which was also developed in the analysis of a number of other arguments, and which acquired a certain importance in the final decision, but above all in the tightening-up of the law which took place in 1956. The author maintained that one must base all argument on a general and logically consistent philosophy of competition. If, for example, one maintained – as was done in industry and trade – that government price control should be abandoned, one could not at the same time allow the desire of the retailers to ensure by negotiation a fair income for themselves to carry any weight. The manufacturers could not be regarded as suitable partners in negotiation when it was a question of safeguarding the interests of the consumers in the 'fair-price' equation. If the retailers demanded the right to determine 'fair' prices for themselves in this way, then the consumers must be allowed the right to appear as participants in negotiation through the medium of government price control.

The same idea appeared in another form in the analysis of the frequently propounded argument that r.p.m. was necessary in order to prevent unintelligent consumers from wearing out several shillings' worth of shoe leather in order to save a few pennies on prices. This argument was particularly grotesque when it was put forward perfectly seriously in a well-known journal which ran a leader in the same number inveighing against the view that the consumer stood in need of protection against misleading advertising, and asserting that he was perfectly capable of deciding whether advertising statements were correct or not. One must at least take a consistent view of the consumer's qualifications as purchaser. The author's own view was that, in so far as the consumer showed shortcomings as a purchaser, these should be removed by consumer information and not by attempts at control.

A number of other arguments in favour of r.p.m. were analysed in the same way. This analysis led in the main to the conclusion that the arguments generally put forward in favour of r.p.m. were untenable. It should be pointed out once again, however, that the analysis with few exceptions could only bear fruit in the shape of hypotheses which could not at that time be verified. One can only say that developments since the prohibition of r.p.m. have not in the main revealed any error in the conclusions.

It was not, however, this analysis of the arguments most frequently put forward in the popular debate that decided the question.

As has been shown above, the analysis summarised here of the arguments usually brought forward *in favour of* r.p.m. was considered to have shown that no importance could ordinarily be attached to these in judging the effects of the system. On the other hand, the analysis had not shown any important adverse effects on the economy. In so far as this aspect had been touched upon, the answer was uncertain (with regard, for example, to the effects of r.p.m. on the length of production-runs).

The major part of the investigation was devoted to the socio-economic effects of the system. Various means of measuring the effects were first discussed at some length in the report. It was decided that it would not be possible to draw any significant conclusions from comparisons between prices and margins for goods sold subject to r.p.m. and those for goods not sold under this system; the same applied to comparisons between prices and margins in different geographical areas, respectively with and without r.p.m.

A completely different method of investigation was necessary. This consisted in the setting up of hypotheses to elucidate various possible effects. All of these were based on a common assumption, which at the same time indicated the direction of the analysis, namely that the traders were aiming at maximum profits. The question might be formulated as follows: What effects can r.p.m. be expected to have in view of the efforts of traders always to try to promote and protect their financial interests?

This method made it possible in a number of cases to work out hypotheses which, even if they could not be verified by means of formal experiments, could still be so thoroughly checked against the material assembled that it sufficed to convince the authorities concerned of their validity. A number of such hypotheses are discussed here.

1. It seemed a reasonable hypothesis that competition between manufacturers under r.p.m. would take the form of competition in the granting of discounts, which would steadily increase resellers' margins, except where this could be prevented by agreement among the manufacturers. It was easy to find examples of such developments in practically every branch of trade. It was particularly instructive to study the motives for the agreements on discounts frequently entered into by manufacturers.

2. It seemed a reasonable hypothesis that discount competition in combination with r.p.m. must result in such a flood of new businesses into distribution that control of new business establishments would become inevitable. One control leads to another. The intimate connection between r.p.m. systematically applied and the demand for the control of new distributive establishments seemed to be confirmed by the actual developments during the 1930s described in an earlier section. In considering the effects of r.p.m. it was therefore reasonable to consider also the effects of the control of new establishments.

3. It seemed a reasonable hypothesis that fixed prices in retail shops must lead to an excessive use of costly weapons of competition such as service in various forms. This hypothesis, too, could not be verified in a scientifically satisfactory manner, but it was easy to find striking examples. In the final decision on the system, particular importance was attached to the fact that it must inevitably lead to a levelling-up of services, which in turn was considered to reduce the consumer's freedom of choice in an undesirable manner. It was considered to be extremely important that the consumer should be able to choose freely between various combinations of services and price.

4. It was considered to be a reasonable hypothesis that r.p.m. must involve serious risks of distortion in the structure of wholesale distribution. This came about because the manufacturer in choosing between different channels of distribution could only compare his own costs of direct distribution to the retailer with the margins set by himself for the wholesaler, but not with the margins which would

be applied by a rationally conducted wholesaling undertaking in conditions of free pricing. Some very convincing examples were available on this point, which in some cases provided a basis for estimates of the possible loss to the economy. It may be mentioned that it was this particular analysis which undoubtedly prompted the wholesalers' organisations to support the abolition of r.p.m.

5. It seemed reasonable to suppose that the rarity in Sweden of forms of distribution with demonstrably lower costs than others must be attributable to the fact that they could not allow their lower costs to be reflected in the form of lower prices. As examples of this may be mentioned the severely limited success achieved earlier by self-service retailing and mail-order trading.

6. Perhaps the most important aspect of the investigation was that concerning the effects of r.p.m. and the control of new establishments on the structure of retail trade. It was shown by means of analytical models of various kinds that the resulting trade structure must contain a large number of different 'distortions', distortions in the sense of higher costs than were necessary for certain activities in distribution or of obstacles to low-price channels of distribution which were considered desirable. In some cases it was possible to estimate the additional costs which resulted from the controls. At this point the investigation gave rise to a number of hypotheses concerning the future development of retail trade if r.p.m. were to be abolished. Wherever later developments have deviated from the predictions made, it has always been because developments have proved to be considerably more dynamic than had been expected. This does not, of course, prove even in retrospect that the hypotheses developed were well-founded. Here again it must suffice to say that they convinced the authorities responsible for the decision.

The above account has dealt with what were, in the author's opinion, the most important of the hypotheses to which the investigation gave rise. Of the remaining ones it need only be said that the summary and conclusion were considerably facilitated by the fact that the hypotheses which in the author's opinion were reasonable all seemed to point in the same direction. Thus the author could not find any hypothesis of importance from which it seemed to follow that r.p.m. in general had beneficial effects for the consumer. The conclusion as to the injurious effects of the system therefore was self-evident.

In the main the reasonableness of the hypotheses still stands, even after the experience of the past ten or so years of freedom of pricing by resellers. On some points the author might now wish in retrospect that he had covered himself better. Some of these will be dealt with in a later section.

The Law Against Restraint of Competition

The deliberations and negotiations resulted in r.p.m. in its earlier predominant form, namely, with fixed resale prices from which no deviations are allowed, being made a criminal offence from 1 July 1954. The law, however, allows exemption from the prohibition in certain circumstances.

The prohibition of r.p.m. is included in the more general 'Act to counteract Restraint of Competition in Business in Certain Instances'.[13] The sections regarding r.p.m. are quite distinct from the rest of the statute, in form as well as in legal construction. Practical experience has shown, however, that there is a close relation between the prohibition of r.p.m. and the general stipulations, which have been used to a great extent to uphold the prohibition of r.p.m.

In the following discussion all the sections regarding r.p.m. are presented and commented upon. Their close relation to the more general stipulations of the law has made it necessary to give some idea of the main contents of the latter also. By way of introduction therefore, the essential general sections of the statute are considered. The account of the law in this section is intended to do no more than explain its construction and general meaning. Its application will be dealt with in a later section.

The purpose of the general stipulations and their general construction can be read from Section 1 of the law: 'For the purpose of promoting competition in business such as is desirable in the public interest, it is provided hereunder that certain types of restraint of competition shall be prohibited, and in addition that it shall be the duty of the Freedom of Commerce Board to endeavour through negotiations to eliminate the harmful effects of restraints on competition submitted for its consideration'. In Section 5 the expression 'harmful effects' is further explained: 'Harmful effects are such caused by a restraint on competition which influences pricing,

[13] The translation of the Act used here is that in the OECD *Guide to Legislation on Restrictive Business Practices.*

hampers the activity of industry and commerce, or obstructs or impedes another enterprise in its business, provided that such effect or effects are incompatible with the public interest'.

The foregoing 'explanation' clearly shows the subjectivity of the law; when the law was written it was believed that after a few years there would be a number of legal precedents which would show the more exact meaning of all the terms in Section 5 for the guidance of business. It is true that there now are a number of precedents, but the precise meaning of the law is still largely obscure. Strangely enough, this is often looked upon as one of the positive qualities of the law. The fact that business men do not know precisely how to interpret the law is believed to create a tendency for them to be more cautious in attempting to restrict competition than would otherwise have been the case. It should be noted that the Freedom of Commerce Board is only empowered to negotiate. It has no direct means of enforcing its wishes. In Section 21, however, provision is made for two indirect means: 'If the negotiations are completed without it being possible to eliminate the harmful effects of the restraint of competition, the Board shall, if the matter is deemed to be of major importance, so inform His Majesty. If the harmful effect is manifested by a particular price being obviously too high with regard to costs and other circumstances, and if the matter is found to be of public importance, His Majesty, on the request of the Freedom of Commerce Board, may specify a certain maximum price which may not be exceeded by an entrepreneur without permission of the Board. Such a decision by His Majesty shall relate to a specific period of time, which shall not exceed one year.'

It may be mentioned – perhaps as a sign of the efficacy of the law – that up to May 1965 it has never been deemed necessary to apply Section 21. It might, however, be necessary to apply the first part of this section during 1965, as the negotiations in a case involving refusal to sell a certain brand of furniture have broken down. (This might incidentally lead to a more rigorous statute.)

Indeed, very few cases go as far as the stage of negotiation. In most cases the possible harmful effects of a restraint of competition are eliminated by the time the matter is taken up by the Commissioner for Freedom of Commerce, an official who is appointed by the Crown according to Section 14 of the Act. The Commissioner may on his own initiative or on application by a business man or an association of consumers or employees initiate negotiations with the

Freedom of Commerce Board. The Commissioner's decision to bring a matter before the Board usually results in the abandonment of the restraint considered to have the harmful effects. In this connection it should be mentioned that 'if in a certain case the Commissioner decides not to initiate negotiations, an entrepreneur who is directly affected by the restraint of competition in question, or an association of consumers or employees may apply for the institution of negotiations' (Section 16).

The general part of the statute also contains a number of sections regarding, for example, the composition of the Board, the procedures to be followed in negotiations, the extension of the law to various types of areas and commodities, the definition of 'entrepreneur', and so on.

The prohibition of r.p.m. is to be found in Section 2 of the Act: 'Unless otherwise provided by the law, no one engaged in business (entrepreneur) may, without permission of the Freedom of Commerce Board, require a reseller to maintain a specific minimum price when reselling a commodity in Sweden, or otherwise specify a price as a guidance to the establishment of resale prices in Sweden unless it is clearly stated that a price lower than that price may be charged'. It has been generally accepted that the last-mentioned condition is fulfilled if the term 'suggested price' ('riktpris') is used.

In Section 4 the exemption from the prohibition is explained: 'The permission specified in Sections 2 and 3 may be granted only if the restraint on competition can be expected to result in lower costs, accruing substantially to the benefit of consumers, or otherwise to form part of a system which is expedient from a public point of view, or if there are other special reasons for granting such permission. The Freedom of Commerce Board may withdraw a permission once granted in the event of abuse, or if the circumstances under which it was granted have materially changed.'

It will be shown below how Section 4 has recently lost all practical importance.

There are also provisions for penalties in Section 29: 'Any person who intentionally violates the provisions of Section 2 . . . shall be liable to daily fines, or, if the violation is grave, to imprisonment for not more than one year, or daily fines'. If there is a violation of the prohibition of r.p.m., this is not handled by the Freedom of Commerce Board but by the general court system. In Section 31 it is stated, however, that proceedings in such cases 'may be instituted by the public prosecutor only at the request of, or with the approval of the Commissioner for Freedom of Commerce'.

From this brief account of the law against restraint of competition, it should be clear that the efficacy of the law, to a large extent, depends on the Commissioner for Freedom of Commerce. His judgment and decisions are of extreme importance. The fact that the Swedish law, despite all its formal deficiencies, has generally been regarded as a success is in the author's opinion due mainly to the good judgment and great skill shown by the two persons who have been Commissioners.

Application of the Law Against Restraint of Competition

Although only a few paragraphs of the law directly mention r.p.m., much of the practical application of the general provisions has turned out to have some bearing on this pricing practice. It will be shown that the general stipulations have been used mainly in order to prevent evasions of the prohibition in all cases where the necessary conditions for prosecution for outright violations have not been met.

The following account of the application of the law first deals with exemptions from the prohibition, then with cases of outright violations, and finally with attempts to counteract evasions of the prohibition. As a general background it should be noted that all restrictions on entry into various lines of business ceased very soon after the Act was passed, either on the initiative of business itself or after negotiations before the Board.

An exemption from the prohibition of r.p.m. may be granted, as has been seen, by the Freedom of Commerce Board 'only if the restraint on competition can be expected to result in lower costs, accruing substantially to the benefit of consumers, or otherwise to form part of a system which is expedient from a public point of view, or if there are other special reasons for granting such permission'.

During the first few years of the operation of the law quite a number of hopeful firms, or organisations representing all the firms in a particular line of business, applied for permission to use r.p.m. Although the law gives the individual firm a right to apply for an exemption, it seemed reasonably sure from the outset that such applications would invariably be rejected, since any individual firm granted an exemption not extended to its competitors would have been given a discriminatory advantage. Only exemptions to an entire industry would be seriously considered.

As a rule, however, applications by industries have not fared much better than applications by individual firms. From the wording of the law it can be seen that the claim for exemption must be supported by something stronger than the general hoary arguments for r.p.m. which could be advanced in every case. Acceptable reasons were given in a few cases where r.p.m. was found to tie in with some particular government regulations, and also, at least for some time, in the case of the book trade (including the publishing of music books). Only the latter case is of general interest. As a matter of fact, when the provision for exemption from the prohibition was written into the law, the legislators had the book trade mainly in mind. Temporary permission to continue with r.p.m. was granted immediately, pending a study of the special problems of the book trade.

The present author was asked by the Freedom of Commerce Board to direct this special study into the effects of abolition of r.p.m. in the book trade. The study was carried out by Lennart Myrén, then an assistant to the author, and published in 1958 in conjunction with a special analysis and recommendation made by the author.[14] It may be mentioned that the author would have preferred to stop at the analysis, and not let his study appear as a recommendation, as this would necessarily be subjective. The Board, however, specifically asked for a definite recommendation to be made to it.

Some special features of the organisation of the Swedish book trade should be noted. In addition to r.p.m. on books, the so-called stockholding booksellers (of whom there were about 300 in 1965) had, in principle, the sole right to sell books (other than cheap books), and the publishers collectively controlled the establishment of new stockholding bookselling establishments. Moreover, the consignment system operated: stockholding booksellers were obliged to take copies of all new books on consignment terms, so that copies of all

[14] L.Myrén, *Bruttoprissättningen inom Bokhandeln* (Gothenburg, 1958); U. af Trolle, *Utlåtende Rörande Bruttoprissättningen inom Bokhandeln* (Gothenburg, 1958).

new books were available in the bookshops. (Publishers did not always choose to exercise their rights in respect of all titles.)

Myrén and the author both came to the conclusion that retail margins on books would on average be lower if r.p.m. were prohibited (unless this effect were offset by a steady, high rate of inflation in the economy). The reduction in average margins would be brought about by several factors: these included the spread of the trade in best-sellers to low-cost distributors who had not previously been allowed to sell books; avoidance by the ordinary book trade of the slowest-selling titles; and the concentration of trade in a smaller number of bookshops. However, in the author's view there would also have been adverse effects from the abolition of r.p.m., damaging to the cultural life of the country. Although the publication and sale of best-sellers in the widest sense would be helped by abolition and the improvement in distribution, the publication and sale of slow-selling books would be prejudiced. The stocking of such books would suffer because the consignment system would break down and, further, the stockholding bookshops would not to the same extent be earning 'surplus' on their sales of faster-selling books. The author concluded that the harmful effects of abolition would be likely to outweigh the disadvantages of r.p.m., and that provided the rigour of r.p.m. could be reduced, the system itself should be allowed to continue.

The Freedom of Commerce Board followed this recommendation, and permission to continue r.p.m. was granted for four years from 1 January 1959. The book trade accepted the modifications proposed by the author. These included the following: the raising of the retail price at which books ceased to qualify as 'cheap books' from 8 to 10 kronor (roughly, from 11s. to 14s.), with provision for subsequent increases should prices continue to rise; the liberalisation of the control of entry into the book trade; and the introduction of the right of booksellers to give discounts to customers buying more than a certain value of books. The working of r.p.m. was further modified by certain concessions to the largest local government authorities, and by allowing university students to buy prescribed books (other than *belles-lettres*) at a discount of 10 per cent. for cash.

In 1962 the industry applied for renewal of the permission granted to it. Again, temporary permission was granted pending a final decision. The Price and Cartel Office (Statens Pris- och Kartellnämnd), an organisation especially set up to conduct research into the economic effects of restraints on competition, was entrusted with the task of collecting pertinent information. The author was once again asked to make an independent analysis and to put forward a recommendation. The Office published a series of penetrating studies during the years 1962 and 1963.[15] The author's study was published at the end of 1963 as one of a series of studies in the philosophy and legal aspects of competition.[16]

The author made the same final evaluation as in 1958. He recommended the retention of r.p.m. subject to further modifications. When making his report, the author paid special attention to the steady inflation which now seems to be an inevitable feature of the Swedish economy. After more than a year of deliberations, the Freedom of Commerce Board decided not to accept the recommendations, but to order the termination of r.p.m. subject to a rather short transitional period of up to five years.

In view of the fact that slow-selling but culturally valuable books (primarily Swedish works of *belles-lettres*) were a vital consideration in the matter of exempting the book trade from the general prohibition of r.p.m., the Board tried to determine the economic importance of the sales of such works. The Price and Cartel Office conducted an inquiry into the sales of Swedish *belles-lettres* of the slow-selling type (defined for this purpose as titles with editions of under 3,000 copies). Rough estimates suggested that the sales of these books accounted for no more than 4 per cent. of all book sales in bookshops (or just over 2 per cent. if the sale of school books and foreign-language books was included). The Board attached great significance to these calculations, which were interpreted to show that at worst the prohibition of r.p.m. would place in jeopardy only a very small segment of culturally valuable literature, and that the outcome of prohibition could be judged more optimistically than it had been previously.

When the decision was made public, it naturally provoked some comment that the Board had not followed the advice of 'its own

[15] H.Fischerström and T.Arvidsson, Statens Pris- och Kartellnämnd, *Den Svenska Bokmarknaden År 1961* (Stockholm, 1962); *Den Ekonomiska Betydelsen av Försäljningen av s.k. Bestsellers i Bokbranschen År 1961* (Stockholm, 1963); *Leveransutvecklingen för 1958 Års Böcker under 1958–62* (Stockholm, 1963); *Undersökningar Rörande Kommisionslagrets Sammansättning m.m. Hos Vissa Bokhandelsföretag* (Stockholm, 1963).

[16] U. af Trolle, *Studier i Konkurrensfilosofi och Konkurrenslagstiftning* (Gothenburg, 1963).

expert'. There is, however, nothing astonishing in this. First, it should be emphasised that any decision, to a great extent, must be based upon subjective judgments and evaluations. Second, during the last few years there has been a general sharpening of the attitude of the authorities against restraint on competition, as is evinced, for instance, in the appointment of the new committee mentioned in the introduction to this chapter.

The refusal to permit r.p.m. in the book trade in practice means that the paragraph about exemptions from the prohibition now may be regarded as virtually inoperative.[17]

As has been mentioned, the manufacturer is not forbidden to suggest a resale price provided that it is clearly stated in one form or another that the price may be cut. This is usually done by using the term 'suggested price' (riktpris) on invoices, in advertising, and so on. It constitutes an outright violation of the prohibition for a manufacturer to advertise a resale price without stating that it may be cut, or to put any pressure to bear on a retailer to make him refrain from cutting prices, for instance by threatening to stop deliveries if he does not comply with the suggested prices. If such violations should be considered to be 'intentional', all conditions for a prosecution would be present.

It is not surprising to find that only a couple of cases have been brought to the courts in the more than ten years of the operation of the law. It has happened now and then that a firm in its advertising has forgotten to state that the prices may be cut; but as the offender has immediately apologised and made amends when approached by the Commissioner, cases of this kind have never been taken to court. In the early cases actually brought to the courts, there was no doubt about the intentions of the offenders. Anyone who seeks to evade the prohibition today knows better than to do it by outright violation of the law.

Lately a new phenomenon has appeared to tease the legal experts. Several of the big chain stores, mostly in the food trade, have found

[17] One of the minor exemptions is in respect of Baltic herrings, as part of governmental regulation in support of the fishing industry. The exemption is to terminate in 1966. The other exemption concerns medicines sold only by druggists holding a special government licence. In this case the exemption does not include the right to enforce resale prices, but only the right to state resale prices without adding that they are no more than *suggested* resale prices.

it to be more convenient to have their own resale prices marked on the packages by the various manufacturers. They have also proved to be large enough customers to force the manufacturers to comply with these requests. As long as the chains do not ask for the same prices to be marked on the packages, this practice does not constitute a violation of the prohibition. But how should it be looked upon if – by agreement or just by chance – they should ask for the same prices to be marked on their packages? If it should happen, it would amount to much the same thing as if the manufacturer himself maintained the price. The consequences of a more general adoption of this practice have been one of the factors behind the decision to appoint the new committee mentioned above.

Quite apart from any possible wish to refuse to sell to a price-cutter, a seller often has sound commercial reasons for restricting his sales to fewer customers than he might attain. There is a great variety of commonly recognised and sound reasons for 'selective' selling. A few examples will illustrate this. (1) The most common kind of restriction has to do with the customers' ability to pay their debts. There are many ways of using credit terms systematically as a basis for selective selling, for example, by only selling to customers paying in ten days or by refusing to accept bills of exchange. (2) In many lines of business there are firms which sell only to wholesalers and who consequently refuse to sell directly to retailers. (3) In many lines of business, especially in the fashion trades, it has often been found that it increases total sales if the manufacturer has only one or a few customers in smaller towns. (4) Some types of articles are sold in connection with a rather complicated service, for example, motor cars. This has long been regarded as a legitimate reason for the restriction of sales to 'authorised' outlets. (5) In order to keep down the costs of selling, many firms refuse to deliver quantities under a minimum size or to customers buying less than a fixed minimum sum per year.

Examples could easily be multiplied. The new law, of course, does not generally try to stop selective selling. On the other hand, it is obvious that selective selling might very well be a means of re-introducing r.p.m. by the back door. Any intelligent seller wanting to maintain resale prices on his goods would naturally not do it by refusing to sell to a price-cutter while openly admitting that the price-cutting was the reason for his refusal. He would, instead, try to build up some kind of 'selective system' having the same effect, but having the appearance of a bona fide system which is not aimed at the price-cutter. If the price-cutter happens to have a shortage of capital – perhaps because of very rapid expansion – he might be cut off by a general tightening of the terms of credit. If the price-cutter is a small firm, it might be worth while to sacrifice some other small customers by introducing a minimum limit for the size of customer. If the price-cutter happens to be a mail-order firm, the seller might at least attempt to adopt a system of selling only through open shops; and so on.

In fact most of the cases reported to the Commissioner or brought by him to the Board concern 'selective selling'. Several hundred cases of this kind have been brought to the attention of the Commissioner during the operation of the statute. In most cases the legal problem has been to decide whether there was a legitimate bona fide reason for the selective selling or whether it was just an attempt to evade the prohibition of r.p.m. To date the law has not been completely clarified, partly because of the efficiency of the Commissioners. As has been mentioned earlier, the mere fact that the Commissioner has decided to bring a case to the Board has usually been enough to make the supposed offender give up the practice.

In summary, it can be said with some confidence that any selective system resulting in the refusal to sell to low-price distributors is regarded with great suspicion by the authorities. There must be strong and obvious reasons for this kind of selectivity if it is to be regarded by the Board as not being against the interests of consumers.[18]

Some Changes in the Structure of Distribution since 1954

The year 1954 marked the beginning of a series of dramatic changes in the structure of Swedish distribution. Although it cannot be proved conclusively, there does not seem to be any doubt that most of these changes would not have taken place without the abolition

[18] U. af Trolle, *Studier i Konkurrensfilosofi . . . , op. cit.*; U. af Trolle, *Om Lagstiftning mot Prisdiskriminering* (Uddevalla, 1950); Å.Ahlberg and U.Öjeman, *Diskriminering. Att Gynna eller Missgynna*, Rygaards Småskrifter 4 (Stockholm, 1956); L.Lidén and B.E.Holmberg, *Prisdifferentiering inom Handeln* (Uppsala, 1960); U.Bernitz, *Swedish Anti-Trust Law and Resale Price Maintenance* (Stockholm, 1964).

of r.p.m. (in its earlier form of rigidly fixed prices) and of the restrictions on entry of new firms. The changes have to such a great extent manifested themselves in the development of new types of retail outlets in conjunction with price competition on branded articles that it seems safe to assume a cause-and-effect relationship. As far as the author is aware, no one seriously contends that these changes would have taken place if the restrictions had not come to an end.

This, however, does not necessarily mean that the changes in structure have been due, wholly or even mainly, to the law against restraint of competition. It has been argued that the restrictions would in any event have disappeared by themselves without any legislation, simply as a result of dynamic forces inherent in distribution. It has thus been observed that r.p.m. had been abandoned for certain commodities in the years 1951 to 1953, in some cases even before the law was formally proposed. This is true. But there was no evidence of any coming change in the attitude of business men in the study relating to the years 1949 and 1950. In support of a more sceptical opinion, it may be mentioned that the first examples of the abandonment of r.p.m. occurred as part of a deal with the price control authorities after the publication of the critical report of 1951: government price control was then dropped on some commodities in exchange for the termination of r.p.m.

It does not seem to be very important, however, whether the restrictions were dropped as a result of the law or as a result of the inherent dynamic forces in business. Suffice it to say that restrictions were abolished, and that dynamic changes in the structure of distribution for some reason began to occur simultaneously. A short account is given of the main changes. Unfortunately there is no comprehensive factual material available to illustrate the changes. A distribution census was taken in 1951, and another in 1964; but the results of the latter are not yet available for comparison at the moment of writing. The tendencies, however, are clear. (The account given here is based on information in the 1965 edition of the author's textbook on marketing.)

The structure of Swedish distribution in the early 1950s and the tendencies of change prevailing at that time are made clear by distribution censuses for 1946 and 1951.

In 1951 there were some 80,000 retail shops. About 63,000 of these belonged to firms having only one retail outlet, the remaining 17,000 being divided among about 3,900 multiple-shop firms. Apart from Consumer Co-operation (Konsumtions-föreningar) there were virtually no important multiple-shop firms. In over 70 per cent. of all shops no more than three people were employed. Approximately 11,000 of the shops were general stores of the kind to be found everywhere in the rural districts. In the towns and cities there had long been a tendency to greater specialisation. This was apparent in every field of retailing, as for instance in food distribution. Dry groceries, meat, fish, dairy products and fruit and vegetables were as a rule sold in different stores. There were fixed and apparently stable boundaries between the various specialised lines of business.

Self-service had just recently been introduced in food retailing in 1951, but the number of self-service stores was still only a few hundred. There were no supermarkets and no discount-houses of any kind. Mail-order houses and department stores were of little importance, the former having less than 1 per cent. and the latter about 3 to 4 per cent. of the total retail trade.

Consumer Co-operation had been gaining very much ground since 1931, when the first census of distribution was taken. In 1951 it handled about 15 per cent. of the total retail volume and 25 per cent. of the food retailing. In his study of r.p.m. the author had come to the much-disputed conclusion that Consumer Co-operation had been greatly helped by r.p.m.; this practice had throttled the flexibility which would otherwise have been the best weapon of the independents with whom they were in competition.

The same picture of specialisation and small-scale business was also to be found in wholesaling. There was no self-service in the form of cash-and-carry operations, very little mechanisation, and in many lines of business rather gloomy prospects, for instance in food distribution. There was a pronounced tendency towards more direct distribution from manufacturers to retailers.

The structural changes started in the food trade. Special homage should be paid to a new and unique type of retail undertaking which started in 1954 in direct connection with the introduction of the prohibition of r.p.m., namely, AB Hemköp in Stockholm. Although this firm has never attained any important market share, it initiated many changes and was undoubtedly in the van for some time.

The founder of AB Hemköp based his initial policy on the fact that during the period of r.p.m. retail margins on standard branded food products and chemists' goods had grown out of all proportion to the costs of handling these articles. This was due to a combination of poor knowledge of costs in retailing and of competition among the manufacturers. For most commodities the retailers' sensitivity to increases in margins had naturally been much greater than the consumers' awareness of the corresponding increases in prices. (This is natural, since, for instance, a 5 per cent. increase in price to the consumer generally corresponds to a 20 to 25 per cent. increase in the retailers' gross income, and perhaps to a doubling of his net income.)

Hemköp concentrated on some 200 standard items, which were then sold at a considerable discount from the suggested resale prices. Orders were given by telephone or sent in by mail. The goods were delivered directly to the home of the customer. ('Hemköp' means 'buying at home'.) There was naturally a minimum limit to the size of the delivery. The size of the discount was based on the size of the order. Hemköp quickly managed to grow so large that it could buy directly from most manufacturers, getting the support of the Commissioner and in some cases of the Freedom of Commerce Board in its attempts to obtain the necessary supplies.

Subsequently Hemköp has had to change its policy rather radically in order to keep abreast of the general progress in retailing. Its assortment has grown very much. It has also had to change over to a 'net price' policy in order to meet price competition. Its importance today is rather limited, but, in the opinion of the author, the structural changes would not have got off to such a flying start had it not been for Hemköp. The initiative was soon taken over by the 'open' shops which had adjusted their prices more closely to the costs of handling the various articles.

The other changes in the food trade can be summarised briefly:

(1) It was soon apparent that 'complete food' stores could offer lower prices, and the more specialised food stores have greatly decreased in number.

(2) A further widening of the assortment to include standard articles from various other lines of business yielded further economies and offered the consumer 'one-stop shopping' in the bargain.

(3) Both these tendencies were closely connected with conversion to self-service. The number of self-service shops has increased very rapidly, to about 8,500 in the middle of 1965, handling about 70 to 80 per cent. of food retailing.

(4) All three tendencies have been connected with a significant growth in the size of and decrease in the number of shops. For several years now a (net) average of five food stores a day have gone out of business. In 1965 there are approximately 400 stores in the food business which may be called supermarkets, having a combined turnover approaching 15 per cent. of total food retailing.

(5) There has been a pronounced growth in importance of the big chain stores, who own most of the supermarkets. Independents in the aggregate, however, still have a preponderant market share.

There are several ways of illustrating these changes. In the following this is done by comparing the characteristics of the food stores of Consumer Co-operation in 1954 and in 1963. (There are, as we have seen, no up-to-date figures for all Swedish retailing.)

Type of shop	*Number of stores*		*Change*
	end of 1954	*end of 1963*	
Self-service stores having complete food line	1,140	3,176	+2,036
General shops, not self-service ...	2,570	479	−2,091
Grocery shops, not self-service ...	1,011	276	− 735
Butcher shops	856	115	− 741
Dairy product shops	1,334	334	−1,000
Fish shops	118	60	− 58
Total	7,029	4,440	−2,589

There is no reason to believe that the tendencies have been different in the 'private' sector of retailing. Incidentally, it may be mentioned that the market share of Consumer Co-operation for several years ceased to grow; only lately has there been a new tendency for it to increase slightly.

The changes in food distribution have had a direct impact on the structure of some other branches of retailing. This is a natural result of the growth of the assortment stocked by food stores to include standard articles from a number of other fields, as for instance textiles, paint and varnish, household goods and perfumery. A great many small shops selling these types of articles in residential areas have now disappeared. There is a general tendency towards a retail structure composed of 'one-stop shopping' supermarkets in the residential areas and more specialised shops only in the centres of towns and cities.

The structural changes in the food trade have probably also had an indirect effect on other branches of retailing. The obvious success of low-cost low-price distributors in the food trade seems to have been one of the earliest sources of inspiration to the new types of low-cost low-price distributors that today can be found in almost every field of distribution. It would lead us too far to attempt any detailed description; one example will be enough to illustrate the magnitude of the changes.

Ten years ago it was taken for granted that furniture shops must be clustered together in the centres of towns and cities. Today, *one* store in a small village (Ikea in Älmhult) far from any big town sells as much as 10 per cent. of all the furniture sold in Sweden. It has customers coming from every part of the country. Part of its sales are made on a mail-order basis. Its main method of competition is its low prices. Today, there is a general tendency for furniture stores to move outside the towns and also to adopt self-service methods in order to decrease their costs and enable them to meet the formidable competition.

Self-service has generally increased in all fields. It has been forecast that in the middle of the 1970s as much as 80 per cent. of all Swedish retail distribution might be handled in some sort of self-service operation.

The total number of shops has decreased in other fields as well as in food retailing. It is estimated that in 1965 the total number has decreased to about 60,000 (from the 80,000 in 1951), and the forecasts for 1970 hover around 50,000.

A summary of changes in retail structure should also include some notes on mail-order business and department stores.

Mail-order business started to grow very quickly in 1954. Up to the end of 1964 the annual growth has been between 15 and 30 per cent. Mail-order firms which did not exist ten years ago are today among the biggest outlets in Swedish retailing. The market share of mail-order business has increased to somewhere around 3 to 4 per cent. of total retailing. In 1965 there was a set-back, whether temporary or permanent cannot yet be said.

In 1951 there were some 50 department stores. In 1965 the three biggest chains of department stores alone have a total of more than

260 stores with more than 10 per cent. of the total national retail trade. These chains have used low prices as one of their main means of competition. It has been forecast that they will reach about 20 per cent. of total retail trade in the 1970s. Lately a new type of low-price department store – a mixture of gigantic supermarket and discount-house – has enjoyed much success.

There have been corresponding structural changes in wholesaling. The tendency towards large-scale operation has been even more pronounced, which in its turn has resulted in a streamlining and mechanisation of operations. In the food trade cash-and-carry operations become increasingly important. Wholesale firms have generally fared much better than was expected, having probably gained in market share as sellers to retailers. The strengthening of the position of wholesalers has been especially pronounced in food distribution, where concentration in the hands of fewer and bigger firms has gone far. In this field, as in some others, there are today, as a result of growth and merger, gigantic firms (by Swedish standards) where ten years ago there were virtually only small-scale operators.

No one has attempted to make a quantitative evaluation of the consequences of these structural changes for consumers. The reason seems to be simple. This question has not been an issue. While it has been discussed whether the changes have been due to the law or not, it seems to have been taken for granted universally that they have been favourable for consumers.

In every field of retailing consumers today may choose between a variety of combinations of service and price, in contrast to the uniformity before 1954. This may in itself be regarded as an achievement. It cannot be 'proved' that the costs of distribution on the whole are lower today than they would have been without the structural changes. The rapid inflation has in any case made meaningful measurement and comparison almost impossible. Suffice it to say that low-cost distributors today operate on low margins which were unheard of in the early 1950s.

Possible Changes in the Law

Manufacturers are not forbidden to suggest resale prices, provided that it is clearly stated that these prices may be cut. Moreover, neither manufacturers nor distributors are forbidden to make horizontal price agreements. Both these types of restrictions may, however, be looked into by the authorities and be subjected to negotiation in accordance with the main provision of the Act against restrictions on competition.

As has been mentioned in the introduction to this chapter, the Government in 1965 appointed a committee to study the effects both of resale prices suggested by manufacturers and of horizontal price agreements. In distribution these price agreements take the form of universal price lists established by trade associations. Such price lists are in no way binding on the members. It should also be stressed that they are never used by distributors outside the associations like Consumer Co-operation, the department stores, mail-order houses and, generally, the low-price distributors.

Two main reasons have been put forward for the appointment of this committee. (1) Where resale prices are not suggested by the manufacturers, the associations to an increasing extent work out their own price lists. There is also a pronounced tendency for distributors in the associations to prefer their own price lists to the vertically suggested prices. In some lines of business the distributors have waged formal campaigns against the meddling of manufacturers in their pricing, pointing out that manufacturers have no competence in this. (2) A number of studies made by the Price and Cartel Office have shown that adherence to the suggested prices or list prices is high, sometimes as high as 70 to 90 per cent. of the number of quoted prices examined. There is no doubt some remaining rigidity in retail prices, although in every field there are low-price distributors who deviate widely from the general pattern.

Both these tendencies (in combination with other less comprehensive phenomena, as for example the price-marking by manufacturers on behalf of the big chains) have been regarded as possible threats to the interests of the consumer. At the same time it has been felt that the present statute is not designed for coping with general restrictions of these kinds. They should be judged as a whole and not individually from case to case.

There are several possible outcomes of the work of the committee. The main ones seem to be the following. (1) The committee may find everything to be perfect as it is and propose no changes. (2) The committee may propose that the Freedom of Commerce Board should be given greater power in its negotiations, as for example the right to issue cease-and-desist orders. Violations of these should then be considered to be criminal offences and handled by the courts. (3) The committee may propose that vertically suggested prices and/or horizontal price lists should be prohibited.

It is too early to make any accurate prediction of the outcome of the studies and deliberations of the committee. The author can only make a strictly personal guess. In his opinion, alternative (3), the most radical one, is out of the question for several reasons. It is quite unrealistic to expect pricing in retailing to resemble a wavy sea with constant deviations and changes. Even an adherence to suggested prices or list prices of as much as 80 to 90 per cent. does not mean that competition cannot be efficient with regard to the interests of the consumer. The really important factor is that there are no obstacles to anyone who wants to cut prices or to enter a new field. In this respect the horizontal price lists are even less dangerous than vertically suggested prices. Their coverage is much smaller, as they do not apply in shops belonging to firms outside the associations. While a manufacturer may at least conceivably cut off supplies from a price-cutter, the associations have no means at their disposal for disciplining their members, let alone non-members.

It may be true that the publication of suggested prices or list prices may actually *increase* competition, by making price-cutting more obvious to the consumer. Again, it has been demonstrated in some cases that a system of vertically suggested prices may in fact tend to *reduce* margins. One such case should be mentioned. In 1960 r.p.m. was abolished in tobacco distribution, but a system of suggested prices was introduced. After a year, the management of the Swedish Tobacco Company in its firm belief in the dynamics of free competition – shared by the author as its adviser – abolished this system of suggested resale prices. Resale prices were left completely free by the Company. Trade associations quickly issued guiding list prices. The result of the liberation has been astonishing. By May 1965 the retail margins were double those of 1962, and had reached an incredible level, making tobacco one of the most profitable products in Swedish retailing. In fact, consumers then paid about as much for the retail distribution of a standard package of cigarettes as they did in total for the growing of the tobacco, and its subsequent manipulation, handling, transportation, manufacturing, packing and selling until the arrival of the package at the retail shop.

It would take too long to analyse the process of agreement and price leadership that has led to this development. Suffice it to say that a situation of this kind will not last for any length of time.[19] It must be regarded as an unfortunate exception. The author is of the opinion that in general price competition in Swedish distribution must be regarded as severe, despite the prevalence of systems of suggested prices of various kinds.

Examples of the kind mentioned above also seem to make it highly unlikely that the government committee will find everything to be perfect and propose no changes. The present law with its restricted authority for the Freedom of Commerce Board has not been able to cope with price restrictions on a large scale.

This reasoning leaves alternative (2) as the probable line to be taken by the committee: as for example, in a re-inforcement of the law probably along the lines mentioned earlier. Even if the law generally seems to have been efficacious up to the present time, the respect on which the efficacy has been built will eventually wear off and re-inforcement become necessary. In 1961 the author frankly would not have believed that business men would have dared to carry through increases in margins of the order which have in fact taken place in tobacco distribution since that date.

It may be mentioned here that there are many business men who would welcome a re-inforcement of the law. A manufacturer being told by the Freedom of Commerce Board to sell to a price-cutter would certainly be in a better position with regard to his other customers if he could show that he had been forced to do so by a compulsory order and not as a result of voluntary negotiation.[20]

[19] U. af Trolle, 'Femtio År . . . ', *op. cit.*

[20] Postscript, December 1965: In the autumn of 1965 there were further developments in the case of a manufacturer's refusal to sell a certain brand of furniture (noted on p. 126 above). The manufacturer refused to follow the recommendation of the Freedom of Commerce Board to continue to sell to a low-price distributor. The Board informed His Majesty. This isolated case was followed by an announcement by the Government of its intention to amend the law to make it more rigorous. The announcement was made independently of the work of the committee. The proposed amendment corresponds in principle to the second of the predicted alternative outcomes (set out on p. 142) of the work of the committee. It now remains to be seen whether the committee will be satisfied with this change or will feel that it should go a step further. In any event the position now is not the same as it was when the author wrote the concluding pages of this chapter six months ago.

5

DENMARK

H. Kjølby

Introduction

In Denmark, as in many other countries, cartel legislation includes rules directed against resale price maintenance as practised in trade and industry. The general prohibition of r.p.m. is laid down in the Monopolies and Restrictive Practices Control Act of 1955 as amended (short title: The Monopolies Control Act, 1955), and makes it unlawful for suppliers to enforce observance of stipulated prices in subsequent resale stages. Consequently, resale prices prescribed by suppliers are merely recommended prices, except where specific exemption has been granted from the general ban. As such exemptions have been granted in a few instances only, the predominant rule is that the prices charged in Danish shops are freely determined by retailers without vertical control by their suppliers.

While the distinction between collective and individual r.p.m., which is important in some other countries, is of no special consequence in Denmark, great importance is attached to the distinction between *binding* and *recommended* resale prices. Recommended prices may be defined as resale prices recommended or suggested to distributors by the supplier, compliance with the recommendation being voluntary. In the case of binding resale prices, on the other hand, the suppliers can enforce their observance by means of the cutting-off of supplies or other economic sanctions against the reseller. This distinction is clear in principle; in practice, however, it often becomes blurred at the edges. It sometimes happens that suppliers, although in principle they are only recommending resale prices, nevertheless discontinue supplies where, for instance, goods usually sold at recommended prices are sold below such prices, or where goods are sold at extremely low prices. The fact that many resale prices which are said to be no more than recommended prices are being adhered to widely is a matter of much significance when one considers the Danish prohibition of r.p.m.

According to Danish usage, the word *bruttopriser* (that is, resale prices) covers both binding and recommended resale prices; and in accordance with this terminology, only part of what is generally understood in Denmark by the term r.p.m. is outlawed by the legislation of 1955.

This chapter should be read against the background of the fact that Denmark is a small country with a population of about 4·7 million and that the economy is greatly influenced by an extensive foreign trade. Denmark is no longer primarily an agricultural country. A marked industrialisation has taken place, and over the last 25 years the share of industrial exports in total exports has doubled. The sectors in which the practice of r.p.m. plays or played an important part have expanded much more than agriculture. In 1963, 42 per cent. of the gross national product was in industry, 44 per cent. in 'other activities' including trade and services, while only 14 per cent. was in agriculture.

There is no full account available of the problems concerning r.p.m. in Denmark. The material used in this chapter has been gathered from many and mostly Danish sources to which reference is made in the footnotes.[1] The opinions expressed are, of course, the author's own and do not necessarily coincide with those held by the Danish cartel authorities.

Developments up to 1955

When manufacturers began to become interested in expanding their sales to new groups of customers spread over wider areas, the prices charged in subsequent resale stages gradually acquired significance as a feature of sales policy. This happened early in the book trade. Already from 1837 books were sold to consumers at prices prescribed by the publishers. In their advertisements the publishers made use of the sales-promoting fact that the prices advertised were those charged by all booksellers in the country. A contributory cause of this development was the customary commission-sales system, in which the books remained the property of the publishers until they were sold by the booksellers to the final consumers.

[1] Reference may be made to the following sources in English pertaining to the subject: Søren Gammelgaard, *Resale Price Maintenance* (OECD, Paris, 1958); and *Guide to Legislation on Restrictive Business Practices*, vol. II, Denmark (OECD, Paris, 1964).

Later, in the 1870s and 80s, some manufacturers of perfumes and toilet preparations became interested in fixing minimum resale prices. As the production costs of these articles were relatively small, and as it was difficult for consumers to judge the quality of the goods, advertising and the fixing of resale prices were used in sales promotion. During the same period r.p.m. came to be adopted for other goods such as chocolate, tobacco and spirits.

Although r.p.m. was initiated by manufacturers, many retailers soon saw that the practice had special advantages for them. As competition grew keener, some retailers could not resist the temptation to undersell, and the other retailers reacted by refusing to stock the articles in question until the so-called 'unfair cut-throat competition' had been brought to an end. In this way the retailers exerted pressure on manufacturers, and in their trade organisations began to proclaim the advantages of fixed price systems. Sometimes the retail trade organisations were anxious to secure the manufacturers' co-operation in the fixing of gross profit margins, for in this way the system became more effective from their point of view. Their work in connectionwith r.p.m. and the prevention of various forms of 'unfair' competition tended to strengthen the influence of the trade organisations. Thus the initiative to operate r.p.m. passed from the manufacturers to the retailers and their organisations; and by the beginning of this century this development was reflected in legislation to such a marked degree that for a period the law required that fixed resale prices should be observed by resellers.

The further spread of r.p.m. was a direct result of the development of large-scale production and the ensuing widespread appearance of branded goods. New sales methods developed where the manufacturer's ability to influence subsequent resale stages was seen as a pre-requisite for large-scale production. At the same time, branding brought the individual manufacturer into closer contact with the distribution of his goods, and made him more interested in following them through the various resale stages to the final consumer. There was a resulting tendency for retail prices and production costs to diverge from each other because of rising selling costs and because, under the system of r.p.m., retail gross profit margins often rose under the influence of the competitive efforts of rival manufacturers to stimulate or retain the retail trade's interest in their respective brands.

Freedom of contract is a fundamental principle of Danish judicial practice. Any person is free to contract with any other person and on any terms he may choose. For a long time the fixing of resale prices was viewed favourably in the light of this principle.[2] It was not until the 1930s that the question first arose of limiting the freedom of contract on socio-economic grounds, the main consideration being that freedom of trade may be curbed harmfully by monopolistic tendencies and restrictive practices in trade and industry. In the 1950s, this development resulted, *inter alia*, in the prohibition of the enforcement of resale prices.

In accordance with the principle of the freedom to contract, the earlier situation was that, as a general rule, the prescription of binding resale prices was legally valid in respect of fully fledged price systems which were clearly formulated and uniformly implemented by the parties concerned. Such situations were found especially where the retailers were bound by specific obligations to observe certain terms and conditions, including prices, stipulated by the suppliers. These obligations could be imposed separately by the individual supplier in his contracts with the various dealers, or they could be imposed collectively by several suppliers. Sometimes such arrangements were combined with agreements between the retail trade associations and the suppliers' organisations on concerted action to be taken against price-cutting resellers.

On the initiative of the retail trade and its organisations a provision was embodied in the Competition Act of 1912 to the effect that the price-cutting of articles marked with resale prices was unlawful and punishable. In support of this provision it was argued, *inter alia*, that when an article was subject to price-cutting, 'the other shopkeepers in the district, in order to keep their customers, are forced also to cut its price – and even to break their contracts with their suppliers – or they may have to give up carrying the article altogether'.

This provision was changed in 1918. There was evidence of extraordinarily high profits on the resale of some goods. Moreover, general economic policy during the war required some change. The new provision was to the effect that r.p.m. was to enjoy legislative support only where the resale price did not allow a higher gross profit to the dealer than 25 per cent. of the purchase price. The amended provision remained in force until 1926. In the changed

[2] Detailed accounts of judicial practice until the beginning of the 1930s are found in Povl Bang-Jensen, *Mindstepris og Undersalg* (Copenhagen, 1934), and Johannes Hansen, *Aftaler om Detailpriser* (Copenhagen, 1934).

economic conditions it was particularly desirable to ensure that the decline in world-market prices was transmitted to, and reflected in, prices in the home market. The repeal of the statutory ban on the price-cutting of price-maintained branded goods reflected this dominant aim of economic policy.

Some rulings of the Supreme Court on cases of the price-cutting of price-maintained goods may serve to illustrate the legal position after the legislative ban had been repealed (that is, after price-cutting had ceased to be a statutory offence). A retailer had removed from a consignment of soap the control numbers assigned to it by the main distributor so as to be able to trace its movement through its various resale stages. Finding that the retailer had sold below the prescribed prices and had refused to reveal the name of his supplier, the Supreme Court ruled, in 1929, that his sales procedure was improper because the dealer had not complied with the conditions laid down by the supplier. In another Supreme Court ruling, in 1930, it was held that a retailer who had bought soap in the free market should not have sold it below the fixed price. In order to escape the r.p.m. arrangement in operation, the retailer had bought the soap through middlemen. He was nevertheless held to be bound by the resale price stipulation. But by a third Supreme Court ruling, in 1931, it was held that a retailer could sell below the prices fixed for certain rubber goods in that the manufacturers had been unable to practise their complex price and rebate system with the thoroughness and firmness deemed to be a necessary condition if all dealers were to be bound to observe the resale prices.

It appears, then, that on the whole the civil law aimed at protecting manufacturers who had established clear and firm systems of r.p.m. based upon reciprocal obligations, and that their protection extended against price-cutting resellers who acquired supplies without having bound themselves to observe the fixed resale prices.

The growth of industrialisation gave rise to a number of manufacturing firms that were quite large by Danish standards. Agreements in restraint of competition also occurred more frequently. It was no longer possible to assume, as before, that a firm pursuing its own interests would automatically also be acting in the public interest. In the inter-war years there was increasing concern as to whether the Government should intervene and restore competition where it had disappeared or was tending to disappear.

The first legislation on price agreements, in 1931, contained no provisions about r.p.m. It is true that the problem of r.p.m. was raised during the reading of the bill, in that a rule was discussed to the effect that suppliers should not be allowed to agree on the resale prices to be observed by subsequent resellers; but the suggested provision was dropped.

The economic background to the second law on price agreements included the import restrictions of the 1930s. In commodity fields subject to these restrictions competition was eliminated or seriously curtailed, and some commodities became so restricted in supply that there was a danger of 'unfair' prices. Therefore, in addition to provisions directed against the detrimental effects of collective price agreements, the Act of 1937 was made applicable also to the policies and business practices of individual firms, the main target being the r.p.m. arrangements practised by dominant firms.

The Act of 1937 did not include any special provision on the fixing of resale prices; the practice was merely made subject to the general rules of the statute. Like all other prices, fixed resale prices were subject to price control. In fact, in only one case – the radio trade – did the price control authorities order that a system of r.p.m. should be abolished. In 1948 it was found that competition in the granting of trade rebates by the manufacturers of radio sets had resulted in high trade margins which, because of r.p.m., were not passed on to consumers. After the abolition of the system, retail prices dropped by as much as 15 to 20 per cent.[3]

The wider question of the compatibility of r.p.m. with the public interest was taken up on a broader basis by a Trust Commission appointed in 1949, as well as by the price control authorities who, in the early 1950s, began to discuss realistically the advisability of abolishing systems of fixed resale prices instead of having to keep the resale prices themselves under constant control.[4]

The General Prohibition of Resale Price Maintenance, 1955, and the Exempted Trades

Since the end of the period of scarcity after the Second World War, the Danish economy has been characterised by increases in

[3] For further details see Gammelgaard, *op. cit.*, pp. 104–5.

[4] Some of the price inquiries made by the Price Control Board are referred to in Gammelgaard, *ibid.*, pp. 107–9.

production, in exports of industrial products, and in money and real incomes. Immediately after the war, foreign trade was largely controlled in terms of bi-lateral trade and payments agreements, as in the 1930s. From 1948, however, Danish co-operation with the OEEC brought about a liberalisation of imports resulting in more abundant supply and keener competition. To meet this foreign competition Danish industry launched comprehensive and successful efficiency drives that improved its competitiveness in world markets. This development continued when the plans for a European market gained substance from the middle of the 1950s onwards.

Especially towards the end of this period there have been marked changes in the structure of the Danish retail trade: the dividing-lines between the various branches of trade have become blurred, and there has been a tendency towards larger firms in retailing.

In this economic situation the problem of r.p.m. was drawn repeatedly into economic-political debates. An expert group, the Trust Commission, was appointed by the Government to analyse the competitive situation of Danish trade and industry and to submit draft legislation on monopolies and restrictive business practices. In a report of 1953[5] the Commission suggested, *inter alia*, that the operation of r.p.m. arrangements should be made conditional upon advance approval by the cartel authorities. However, this proposal of the Commission encountered stiff head-winds from trade organisations and some politicians. Rules on the fixing of resale prices were, nevertheless, finally enacted, although in a different form, as is described below.

The arguments in support of the view that the practice of r.p.m. is, *per se*, detrimental to the national economy are more or less the same everywhere. In Denmark the Trust Commission emphasised, among other things, that the practice of r.p.m. must presumably have some detrimental effects because a system of fixed prices means an end to price competition in the retail trade. In consequence, retailers turn their attention towards methods of competition which involve additional costs, such as increased advertising, more extravagant shop decor, and free delivery of goods – a development in

[5] *Konkurrencebegrænsning og monopol*, Trustkommissionens betænkning nr. 3 (Copenhagen, 1953). R.p.m. is discussed on pp. 75–81. It was the intention of the Trust Commission first to describe the prevailing competitive situation within Danish trade and industry. But this work had not progressed very far before Parliament urgently asked for the completion of the draft legislation.

which by no means all consumers are interested. Moreover, the supplier, in his desire to have his goods carried by as many retailers as possible, is inclined to grant higher trade discounts. The Commission also underlined the fact that under a system of fixed resale prices shops operating with low costs are bound to charge the same prices as all the other retailers in the trade, a matter of great significance where unorthodox types of retail outlets such as voluntary chains and self-service shops are trying to gain a foothold in the market.

In the bill eventuating in the present Monopolies Control Act of 1955, the proposal of the Trust Commission that the fixing of resale prices should be made subject to the advance approval of the cartel authorities was altered to a direct prohibition of r.p.m., provision being made for exemptions. According to the bill, sales made subject to a condition that minimum resale prices or minimum margins be observed were prohibited, offenders being liable to punishment. This proposed new rule was eagerly discussed by those concerned, and trade and industry opposed it almost *en bloc*. Only the grocery trade showed a very slight conciliatory attitude by stating that it was all in favour of free prices although strongly opposed to any legislation in this field. The specialised trades, including booksellers, dealers in wine and spirits, dealers in perfumes and toilet requisites, and the like, maintained a solid opposition to the proposed ban. Eventually, however, the prohibition was enacted in a somewhat modified form as part of the political compromise reached on the whole new anti-trust legislation. A factor which contributed to this outcome was, no doubt, the newly enacted prohibition of r.p.m. in the Swedish legislation of 1953 on restraint of competition.

The prohibition is laid down in Section 10 of the Monopolies and Restrictive Business Practices Act of 1955 (as amended), which is still in force: 'Agreements, decisions, and business practices fixing minimum prices or margins to be observed by subsequent resellers must not be enforced unless the Monopolies Control Authority has approved the agreement, etc., in question. Such approval may be given if warranted by circumstances of special importance'. Both individual and collective r.p.m. are governed by the Act. The ban on enforcement concerns only minimum prices and margins. Offenders are not directly liable to penalties, the punishable offence under the law being disregard of any order issued by the Authority under the Act.

In its interpretation of the words 'must not be enforced' the Parliamentary Commission on the bill ruled that all agreements, etc., as to minimum resale prices and margins were to be regarded as no more than recommendations to resellers, unless they had been approved by the Monopolies Control Authority. Viewed in this light, all sanctions applied by suppliers, such as refusal of supplies and boycotts, must be understood to come within the scope of the word 'enforce'.

In order to give trade and industry as well as the authorities time to adapt themselves to the new legal situation, the rules applying to vertical price-fixing did not take effect until one year after the passing of the Act, that is, in 1956.

In the course of the year between the passing of the Act and the implementation of the ban, the Monopolies Control Authority received about sixty applications for permission to maintain fixed resale prices. The great majority of the applications were refused. When dealing with the applications, the crucial question was how the words of the Act, 'circumstances of special importance', were to be interpreted. The Act itself does not give any clue as to the desired interpretation. In the original bill it was said that exemptions might be granted 'when justified by considerations as to cost economies and price reductions', while the Parliamentary Commission relied on the following guiding statement: 'By the expression "circumstances of special importance" the Parliamentary Commission has had in mind instances, *inter alia*, where the commodity in question is sold in competition with goods supplied by foreign firms which maintain minimum resale prices and margins and against whom the Monopolies Control Authority cannot intervene, and instances where an article subject to r.p.m. has been used, nevertheless, as a loss leader by resellers. Further, the Commission has had in mind instances where considerations of economic efficiency require that the distribution of the commodity in question takes place continuously throughout the whole year. The Commission has also taken into consideration cases where it is practical and desirable that an article can be exchanged in any retail shop within the trade in question. Finally, the Commission has had in mind instances where obligations as to service of a very special character are connected with the sale of the commodity'.

In the event, then, it has been left to the Monopolies Control

Authority to decide which kinds of important circumstances should carry enough weight to warrant exemption from the general rule that prescribed minimum resale prices shall be deemed to be merely resale prices recommended by suppliers to resellers. When considering applications for exemption, the Authority has judged each case on its merits, and no general line of administrative practice has developed.

From the beginning, in 1956, the Authority showed great reluctance in granting exemptions; and during recent years, as will appear, the number of exemptions has been even further reduced, which means an appreciable decrease in the extent to which binding r.p.m. is currently practised in Denmark as compared with previous decades.

The exemptions granted include the categories of goods discussed below. Among them are some of the very first commodities to have been made subject to r.p.m. in Denmark. The categories of goods are grouped here according to the reasons for their exemption.

(1) As regards books, newspapers, weeklies and other periodicals, cultural considerations motivated the exemptions granted in 1956. In Sweden, the book trade had recently obtained a similar exemption. In Denmark, importance was attached to the general view that the prevailing system of fixed resale prices seemed to have acted as an incentive for booksellers to carry a wide range of books from all the publishing houses instead of concentrating on those books that were easiest to sell. In consequence, it was argued, under a system of r.p.m. publishers were encouraged to venture into the publishing of commercially more risky books and books likely to be sold only in modest numbers, in which category the most valuable contributions to literature were frequently to be found. This consideration was of particular significance in Denmark, where many books by necessity can be published only in quite limited numbers because of the limited area in which the Danish language is used.

Although these arguments carry some weight, it is open to dispute, on the other hand, whether the present price system is the best one. The r.p.m. arrangements for books seem to have affected the structure of the book trade in that the total volume of business has been distributed over a rather large number of bookshops, many of which are quite small. This feature may involve unnecessarily high costs of distribution, and many of the bookshops cannot hope to achieve a turnover large enough to enable them to carry the comprehensive assortment of books without which they cannot make the literary and cultural contribution which is advanced as an argument in support of the system of r.p.m.

Although the exemption continues at present, the system of r.p.m. for books, which originated in 1837, will soon be given renewed consideration, partly in view of the experience gained in other countries.

In respect of newspapers, which are sold at fixed resale prices in most countries, it was pointed out that in all fairness the diffusion of political opinions should not be influenced by competition among the various distributors of newspapers.

(2) In 1956 fertilisers were granted exemption in accordance with the Parliamentary Commission's statement that a system of fixed prices might be necessary to ensure efficient distribution throughout the year of a commodity which is used during a short season. In order to provide sufficient quantities of fertilisers, production and imports have to be spread over the whole year, involving considerable building up of stocks. The trade established the system of r.p.m. in order to maintain a price structure according to which consumer prices rise gradually through the year, reaching a peak in the season when the fertiliser is used. This price structure encourages farmers to buy their requirements early and thus take over part of the stock-holding function. In support of its case the trade argued that trade margins on fertilisers were so low that any gain to farmers from price competition among dealers would be negligible when compared with the loss to farmers if the abolition of r.p.m. should disturb the availability of supplies at the time of the year when they were most needed. The Authority also took account of the fact that, according to information received, trade margins on fertilisers were lower in Denmark than in most other countries.

(3) Practical fiscal considerations explain the exemptions granted in 1956 for perfumes and toilet requisites, certain brands of wine and spirits, and tobacco. When the applications were being considered, the Ministry of Finance on fiscal grounds supported the maintenance of the fixed resale price systems in operation for these goods. The excise duties levied on tobacco, perfumes and toilet requisites are calculated as a percentage of the retail price, which is printed on the revenue label affixed to the goods as proof that the duty has been paid. As the duty is payable either by the importer or by the manufacturer, it is necessary for them to know the retail price

with certainty. One of the advantages of this system of collecting excise duty is that it does not require a complicated machinery of control. For this reason the Ministry of Finance found that it was necessary to allow the suppliers to maintain fixed resale prices for these goods. The excise duty levied on wine and spirits, on the other hand, is calculated as a percentage of the wholesale price; the Ministry was nevertheless of the opinion that for practical reasons it was desirable to permit r.p.m. for these commodities also. Only such well-known brands of wine and spirits as were included in the wine merchants' price lists were exempted. No conditions were attached to the exemptions granted for wine and spirits and perfumes and toilet requisites. The permission granted for tobacco, however, was made conditional upon the continuance of the practice of allowing retailers to offer rebates (of up to 4 per cent.) to customers buying sizeable quantities and to give rebates off the fixed retail prices in the form of rebate coupons. As fiscal considerations were not included in the report of the Parliamentary Commission as a ground on which exemptions could be granted, the exempted trades were told that in due course the exemptions granted would have to be reconsidered.

Early in 1964 the Monopolies Control Authority informed the trades concerned that it had concluded that the grounds on which the exemptions had been granted were not thought weighty enough to justify the continued practice of r.p.m. This development was accelerated by a decision of the Monopolies Appeal Tribunal in April 1964 concerning a complaint from a reseller who wanted to be free to price perfumes and toilet requisites without external constraint. In its ruling the Tribunal said that the levy of excise duties (the fiscal ground) was not a circumstance which warranted permission to continue the fixing of resale prices. Accordingly, the exemption granted for perfume and toilet requisites was revoked immediately. The exemption for wine and spirits was revoked on 1 July 1964. After several investigations and inquiries, the exemption granted for tobacco was revoked in the beginning of 1965 to take effect on 1 January 1966. However, in July 1965 the Appeal Tribunal over-ruled this decision of the Authority so that r.p.m. is still being practised in respect of tobacco products.

(4) Exemption from the prohibition of r.p.m. was granted in respect of the leading brands of rubber footwear and bicycle tubes and tyres manufactured by the two dominant firms in this field in

the Danish market, on the grounds that the trade margins were relatively low and that free prices would mean higher retail prices. The retail trade, however, was interested in having the fixed price system abolished, and the manufacturing firms desisted from maintaining resale prices. While no sufficiently exact information has been obtained about the subsequent development of the margins and prices of rubber footwear, test inquiries have shown that since the termination of r.p.m. the prices of bicycle tubes and tyres have risen by approximately 10 to 15 per cent., with trade margins taking the lion's share of this increase.

(5) Special export and import considerations and the need to render special services explain the exemptions granted in respect of certain porcelain and faience articles made by a small number of firms, and of a special metal-grinding belt manufactured abroad.

One of the arguments in support of the proposal to intervene against the fixing of resale prices was that the practice was said to be widespread. Actually, however, at that time very little was known about its extent, and the first systematic data were not published until 1960.

As has been mentioned in the introduction, in Denmark by r.p.m. is meant the practice of suppliers to prescribe binding as well as recommended resale prices. After the imposition of the general prohibition of r.p.m., the distinction between binding and recommended resale prices is of decisive importance; but such a clear distinction had not been made before 1955, and the sporadic information on the extent of the practice included both categories of prescribed resale prices. In view of the fact that binding resale prices were relatively uncommon after 1955, later statistics of the extent of r.p.m. refer primarily to recommended resale prices.

There are various ways of measuring the extent of r.p.m. One method is to estimate the proportion of consumer expenditure directed towards goods subject to r.p.m. Another method is to estimate the share of total retail turnover covered by r.p.m. Both these methods are costly if they are to yield accurate information. A Swedish inquiry into the extent of r.p.m. in the retail trade in 1950 showed that 28 to 40 per cent. of the goods sold in food shops were sold at fixed resale prices.[6] It may be assumed that a similar inquiry in Denmark would have shown a similar result.

[6] This inquiry is discussed above, pp. 103–4. (Ed.)

The following table showing the extent of r.p.m., including both binding as well as recommended resale prices, in Danish industry in 1958 has been prepared on the basis of information in the public register of the Monopolies Control Authority.[7]

PERCENTAGE SHARE OF DOMESTIC INDUSTRIAL PRODUCTION AFFECTED BY R.P.M., 1 SEPTEMBER 1958

	%
Food, beverages and tobacco	20
Textiles and clothing	—
Leather, leather goods and footwear	17
Wood, wooden goods and furniture	3
Paper, cardboard and related goods	—
Chemicals	19
Stoneware, earthenware and glassware	15
Metal and metal products, and metal fittings and goods for the building industry	2
Machinery, other than electrical	12
Electrical machinery and other electrical equipment ...	38
Automobiles and other vehicles	20
Other goods	44

In interpreting these figures, it should be noted that the Danish register includes only restrictive practices, including r.p.m., that exert a substantial influence on the competitive situation. It may be mentioned, for instance, that in 1958 r.p.m. was practised in respect of various articles of clothing (such as shirts and ladies' stockings), so that it may be presumed that other entries in the table also are under-estimated.

In 1958 r.p.m. was the most common restrictive practice in commerce.[8] In most cases the resale prices were prescribed by manufacturing firms acting in varying degrees of collaboration with trading firms; in some instances, however, importers or wholesalers fixed the resale prices. There were registrations concerning the recommendation of resale prices for one or more resale stages in

[7] *Konkurrencebegrænsninger i Dansk Erhvervsliv*, Trustkommissionens betænkning nr. 8 (Copenhagen, 1960), pp. 55–6.

[8] *Ibid.*, pp. 91–2.

respect of many categories of goods such as bread, coffee substitutes, Danish paper, paper bags, automobile tubes and tyres, washing preparations, petrol, kerosene and fuel oils, service and household glasses, stoves and kitchen ranges, nails and wire products, farm and garden implements, radio sets, incandescent lamps, agricultural machinery, automobiles and photographic equipment.

The extent to which recommended resale prices were observed by resellers is discussed in the next section.

The Scope and Application of the Law

The prohibition of r.p.m. is the only deviation from the leading principle of Danish cartel legislation that restrictive business practices are not unlawful as such but that any detrimental effects of such practices are to be remedied through public control. The philosophy underlying the legislation is that in normal economic conditions the public interest in ensuring reasonable prices and the greatest efficiency in the economy is best served by the operation of free competition in the market. For the purpose of preventing abuse by cartels and dominant firms, any practices which are found to be obstructing the full play of free competition should be subjected to control. It should be borne in mind, however, that certain forms of co-operation and large-scale operation may foster efficiency to the benefit of the economy. In contradistinction to English anti-trust legislation, under which the onus is on the cartel to prove that it is operating in the public interest, in Danish anti-trust law the burden is placed on the cartel control authorities to prove the existence of detrimental effects of restrictive practices. The rules of procedure are quite different in the two countries.

Danish anti-trust law is administered by the Monopolies Control Authority consisting of a Council and a Directorate under the Ministry of Commerce. Final decisions are made by the Council, on which the main organisations of trade and industry are represented; the majority of the Council members, however, are independent of business interests. Decisions made by the Council cannot be over-ruled by the Minister of Commerce but can be brought before the Monopolies Appeal Tribunal, which functions as a special court of law. Appeals against the rulings of the Monopolies Appeal Tribunal lie with the ordinary law courts, final appeals being to the Supreme Court.

The Monopolies Control Act of 1955 as amended[9] applies solely to restrictive business practices that exert or may be able to exert a substantial influence on the competitive situation (Section 2 of the Act). Only where this condition is fulfilled is the Monopolies Control Authority in a position to negotiate with the enterprises concerned for the purpose of having the detrimental effects eliminated. If such negotiations fail, the Authority can intervene by issuing orders to the effect, for instance, that the firms in question shall cancel agreements, change business terms and conditions, or resume delivery to stated buyers (Sections 11 and 12). Offending firms are not liable to punishment under the law until it is evident that they have violated the provisions of the law, which means, generally speaking, that liability to punishment does not arise until an order issued by the Authority has been flouted.

The Monopolies Control Authority has assumed that the ban on r.p.m. applies to all cases of the fixing of binding resale prices, notwithstanding the fact that the Act is applicable only to situations where competition is restricted to a substantial degree. But even if this interpretation by the Authority is valid, orders to suppliers to resume delivery to price-cutting dealers can be issued only in pursuance of the control provisions of the Act; and this means that the legal enforcement of the prohibition is still subject to the requirement of the law that its application is conditional on there being a restrictive practice which exerts a substantial influence on prices and distribution. In administrative practice, however, the severity of this requirement has gradually been relaxed. The mere fact that a dealer can establish a substantial interest in handling a commodity frequently implies that the supplier of the commodity holds such a strong market position that his business practices necessarily come within the scope of the legislation in pursuance of Section 2.

In so far as the condition requiring the presence of a restrictive practice of substantial significance cannot be fulfilled in practice, the prohibition of r.p.m. must be described as a *lex imperfecta*; for although it is true that the Authority can investigate the matter and declare that the practice violates the ban, it has no legal power to take direct action in such cases by ordering suppliers to resume delivery to price-cutters.

Such cases have occurred several times within the practice of the

[9] A more detailed account of the procedure followed under the Danish antitrust legislation is found in *Guide to Legislation . . . , op. cit.*

Monopolies Control Authority, and by way of illustration one case may be mentioned. A retailer complained that he could no longer obtain deliveries of a certain brand of ladies' stockings. The reason for the cessation of supply was that the retailer had granted a rebate off the recommended resale prices of the stockings, and some of the retailer-customers of the supplier had objected. Finding that the particular brand represented a small part of the total sale of ladies' stockings, the condition for the issue of an order to resume delivery was not fulfilled, and the Authority could do no more than direct the supplier to observe the ban on r.p.m.[10]

Under Sections 11 and 12 of the Act, the Authority may be able to order suppliers to supply 'unorthodox' retail outlets or to continue supplying price-cutting retailers (subject to the situation falling within the scope of Section 2). The following example illustrates the position, and shows the power of the Authority even where the prohibition of r.p.m. does not apply directly.[11]

The Co-operative Society of Copenhagen operates a large number of speciality shops and supermarkets. As an integral part of a systematic attempt in recent years to extend its sales of durable consumer goods, the Society adopted a new price policy. Previously, dealers in kitchen ranges, refrigerators, washing machines, radio and television sets, and the like, frequently negotiated individual reductions to customers off the resale prices recommended by the manufacturing firms. Under its new price policy, the Society advertises 'open' prices which are below the recommended prices, and, in addition, the Society continues its usual practice of giving an annual patronage bonus or dividend to its members according to their total purchases. When, in 1962, the Society advertised its new prices which, for example, for electrical and gas kitchen ranges, were first 10 per cent. and later 17 to 18 per cent. lower than the recommended resale prices, the suppliers of these goods and of radio and television sets discontinued supplies. In due course the case was brought before the Monopolies Appeal Tribunal, which found that the ban on r.p.m. in Section 10 of the Act did not apply directly. In its ruling the Tribunal held that Section 10 did not apply to every action a supplier might take against resellers who were charging lower prices than those recommended, but that it applied only to cases which involved such price or profit arrangements as are covered by the agreements,

[10] *Meddelelser fra Monopoltilsynet*, 1963, pp. 64–5.

[11] The case is discussed in detail in *Guide to Legislation . . .*, *op. cit.*

decisions and practices specified in Section 10. According to the Tribunal, however, the withholding of supplies could be brought to an end by the Authority if it acted under Sections 11 and 12, because the suppliers in question held dominant market positions and their actions therefore were subject to the provisions of the law. The Tribunal concluded that the withholding of supplies had such detrimental effects as to warrant the issue of orders to require the suppliers to resume deliveries to the Society.

The two cases discussed above provide illustrations of the not uncommon tendency for suppliers to tolerate modest reductions off their recommended prices, but to take action against particularly severe price-cutting. Such interference in retail pricing can have similar effects to those of r.p.m. itself in frustrating efforts aimed at making distribution cheaper and more efficient. This is particularly the case where such actions are directed against enterprises taking the initiative in introducing new business methods and achieving economies which they wish to have reflected in reduced retail prices. Even though in practice it is possible for the Authority to enforce the prohibition of r.p.m. in many cases, it would have been more straightforward as well as more in harmony with the ideas underlying the prohibition had it been made to apply to all cases of interference with selling below recommended resale prices.

As will appear from the preceding examples, it is often quite difficult in practice to apply the theoretically clear distinction between binding and recommended resale prices. Even if the prices are said to be recommended only, ostensibly leaving the retailer free to charge whatever prices he chooses, the supplier nevertheless sometimes attempts to have his prices observed by taking measures against under-selling. It is a moot point, therefore, whether the fact that the recommendation of resale prices is lawful does not to some extent curb the price competition which the prohibition of the enforcement of resale prices in retailing was intended to promote.

In order to gain some impression of the effectiveness of the prohibition of r.p.m., it is of great interest to ascertain the degree to which *recommended* resale prices are being observed. Unfortunately, only two investigations have been made, for groceries and ladies' stockings, respectively.

An inquiry published in 1960 showed that in most instances the recommended prices for goods in the grocery trade were being observed.[12] The assortment of goods examined included various brands of detergents, soap flakes, dish-washing preparations, toilet soap, toothpaste, razor blades, polish, floor wax, tea, powdered coffee, chocolate, biscuits, crispbread, vinegar, incandescent lamps and deep-frozen foods. The percentage of compliance varied distinctly from one article to another. As regards washing and cleaning preparations, the recommended prices were observed in about 77 per cent. of the observations made; for one brand, however, the percentage was only 51 per cent., while it amounted to 98 per cent. in respect of another. It was found that the goods were frequently sold at prices well below the recommended ones; in 19 per cent. of the observations the prices actually charged were at least 5 per cent. lower than those recommended. The percentage of observance of the resale prices recommended for powdered coffee was rather low, namely, a little less than 50 per cent. (In a little more than a third of the observations the prices actually charged were more than 5 per cent. lower than the recommended prices.) The percentages of compliance for the remaining articles, except crispbread, showed little variation. The highest percentages were found for razor blades and frozen foods, the recommended resale prices for these articles being observed in all the shops visited.

Similar inquiries have been made in Norway and Sweden (published in 1959 and 1955, respectively), and the following table shows in percentages the extent to which the recommended resale prices for goods in the grocery trade were observed in the three Scandinavian countries:

	Denmark	*Norway*	*Sweden*
Dish-washing preparations, solid ...	94	—	90
Dish-washing preparations, liquid ...	94	—	99
Soap and washing preparations ...	77	94	75
Toothpaste	92	98	81
Razor blades	100	99	99
Crispbread	56	93	—
Vinegar	93	98	—
Floor wax	92	96	—

[12] See *Meddelelser fra Monopoltilsynet*, 1960, pp. 153 ff.

The main finding of the Danish inquiry was that the recommended resale prices were observed in 85 per cent. of the cases investigated, and that the prices actually charged were lower than the recommended prices in 13 per cent., and higher in 2 per cent. of the cases. In Norway the overall percentage of compliance was about 95 per cent.; and in Sweden it was 90 per cent. in respect of 60 per cent. of the items included in the inquiry.

Comparison of the results of the investigations in the three countries involves many uncertain factors, as for instance the differences in the assortment of goods traditionally carried in the shops of the three countries and the different periods of time covered by the investigations. The table, therefore, can serve only as an indication of the extent to which recommended prices were observed in the three countries.

An interesting finding of the Danish inquiry was that large shops were more inclined to deviate from the recommended resale prices than the small shops. It was found, further, that observance of recommended prices was less frequent in Copenhagen and the large towns, the frequency varying inversely with the size of the community in which the shops were located. It appears, then, that the prevailing competitive situation is a decisive factor.

The results of an inquiry into the prices of ladies' stockings were published early in 1965.[13] The following findings are based upon observations made in a relatively small number of shops. The inquiry showed that a third of the stockings made in Denmark were sold under brand names, and that resale prices were suggested for most of them. Two-thirds of imported stockings were sold under brand names, but prices recommended for only half of the brands. The probable explanation of this difference is that the Danish brands relate to first-quality stockings in the higher-price group, while imported brands include a great many sold at relatively low prices.

Observance of recommended prices was far more frequent for ladies' stockings than for groceries, the recommended prices being observed in virtually all the cases examined. The inquiry revealed the remarkable fact that, while the gross profit obtained for the majority of ladies' stockings in the retail trade varied from somewhat less than 30 per cent. to about 50 per cent., the gross margins included in the resale prices of those brands with recommended prices varied from about 50 to over 70 per cent. Part of the explanation

[13] See *Meddelelser fra Monopoltilsynet*, 1965, pp. 18 ff.

may be that the branded articles predominate in the higher quality ranges. In explanation of the fact that the recommended prices for ladies' stockings were being observed everywhere, the report on the inquiry states that the general attitude of the retailers was that any attempt at under-selling would lead to interference by the suppliers in the form of strong suggestions to observe the prices combined with threats of discontinuance of supplies. Further reasons for the unanimous observance of prices were considerations of loyalty to other retailers and concern with the reactions of competitors. A competitor, for instance, who felt his business threatened by under-selling might ask the supplier to put an end to the offending practice; and ordinarily the shopkeepers would comply with requests by suppliers because they would be interested in stocking the customary range of brands.

The disturbing fact that the effect of the ban on r.p.m. is undermined by widespread compliance with manufacturers' price recommendations has aroused surprisingly little discussion. On two occasions, however, the Minister of Commerce has been asked in Parliament whether he thought it necessary to strengthen the ban; and in his answers the Minister said that it might be worth considering whether advertisers should be obliged to state that the advertised retail prices were only recommended prices. The Minister did not think he was justified in imposing a prohibition on the recommendation of resale prices without further investigation. It was argued that in certain instances the use of recommended prices might simplify invoicing and reduce selling costs. It appears, then, that at present there seems to be no reason to expect any strengthening of the prohibition of r.p.m.

To complete the picture and present it in perspective, it should be noted that since the prohibition of r.p.m. lively price competition has developed in certain trades, accompanied by substantial price reductions; these developments are discussed below.

Effects of the Prohibition

The practice of fixing resale prices affects competition in distribution with possibly unfortunate effects in raising resellers' prices and profits. First, trade margins included in fixed resale prices are generally rather high compared with the general level of margins prevailing within a trade. Second, fixed resale prices are almost always calculated on the basis of the traditional structure of the distributive trades and, therefore, tend to preserve the prevailing system of distribution and number of resale stages, and so to frustrate the development of more efficient methods of distribution.

Recent developments in Denmark offer many examples of changes in distribution. Chain stores and voluntary chains are being established increasingly, and the old demarcation lines between trades are tending to disintegrate. Such developments dislocate the basis of existing resale prices and make it difficult to continue the system of graduated trade discounts underlying them. A large retailer, for example, may often buy larger quantities than a small wholesaler, and he would of course prefer to buy directly from the manufacturer at wholesale prices and terms. In such a case the large retailer would be able to sell at low prices and still obtain a 'normal' profit. Thus developments within distribution themselves contain elements counteracting the use of r.p.m.; but, on the other hand, these developments affect traders operating on traditional lines, and in particular those in the specialty trades, who become even more interested supporters of r.p.m. systems than before.

In assessing the effects of the ban on r.p.m., one may start by investigating the direct effects either on the price level as a whole or on the prices of the goods previously subject to r.p.m. In the long run the effects depend upon the extent to which the ban has contributed to the adaptation of the competitive structure of trade and industry to technical and economic developments and opportunities. However, because the prohibition of r.p.m. is but one among many factors affecting this process, any exact evaluation of its particular effects on the economy is virtually impossible. Great difficulties also arise in connection with an analysis of the effects of the ban on the price level in general, and such an analysis has not been attempted in Denmark. In respect of certain goods and commodity groups, however, there is some more precise statistical information as to the effects of the abolition of binding resale prices.

Already before the revocation of the permission to practise r.p.m. for wines and spirits in the summer of 1964, price competition had sprung up in certain brands not included in wine merchants' lists and therefore not subject to r.p.m. After the revocation, this price competition spread to the formerly price-maintained brands. Thus competition in rebates at the wholesale stage has appeared in the sale of 'Akvavit', for which the Danish manufacturer recommends resale prices. In many cases wholesalers have increased their usual cash discount to retailers from 1 to 3 per cent., and to some extent the manufacturer's quantity discounts to wholesalers have been passed on to the retailers. The recommended consumer price for 'Akvavit' was under-sold in 26 per cent. of the observations made in Copenhagen in August 1964, and in 42 per cent. of the observations made in November of the same year. Resale prices were up to 10 per cent. lower than the recommended prices. Outside the metropolitan area, however, such under-selling was found to be limited.

In respect of various brands of cognac (brandy), gin, vermouth and whisky, an inquiry throughout the country showed that the actual resale prices were from 11 to 17 per cent. lower than the recommended prices. The inquiry seemed to show that under-selling was practised more in grocery shops and supermarkets than in specialty wine and spirits shops.

As the legislation pertaining to the taxation of perfume and toilet requisites has not been changed, retail prices are still stamped on the articles. No inquiry has been made into the effects of the recent revocation of the earlier exemption of these goods; but it is the general impression that resale prices are being observed for the exclusive brands and that under-selling is practised only to a limited extent and then mainly in non-specialty shops.

As previously mentioned, the decision of the Monopolies Control Authority to revoke the permission to practise r.p.m. on tobacco was over-ruled by the Appeal Tribunal. While the case was being dealt with by the Authority, the effects of revocation both on the competitive structure of the trade and also on prices were much discussed. In support of their request to continue r.p.m., the trade organisations argued that for years the Authority had controlled tobacco prices and kept profit margins at a very modest level. It was the opinion of these organisations that the abolition of fixed resale prices would lead to loss-leader selling of some brands by shops not formerly in the tobacco trade, and that the specialty shops would be unable to cope with this competition. A structural change of the tobacco retail trade involving the disappearance of the specialty shops would have unfortunate social consequences and make it difficult for the manufacturers to serve the customers with the great variety of brands at present carried by the specialty shops.

While the arguments about the unfortunate social effects of structural changes in the trade did not carry much weight in the discussion the Authority attached more importance to the effect on prices should r.p.m. be eliminated. Information from Sweden revealed that since the abolition of r.p.m. for tobacco there had been some increase in trade margins, which had always been higher than in Denmark. It was to be expected, on the other hand, that the revocation of permission to practise r.p.m. would have a stimulating effect on competition in Denmark. A contributory factor was the prospect of the abolition of the agreement between organisations in the Danish tobacco trade determining the types of shops entitled to stock tobacco products. In the opinion of the Authority, moreover, Danish legislation, unlike the Swedish, would have made it possible for the cartel authorities to keep a supervising eye on any recommended prices, for the purpose of counteracting any tendency for prices and margins to rise.

During the hearing of the case before the Appeal Tribunal, decisive importance was attached to the probable effect on prices if the permission to practise r.p.m. was to be revoked. The present average retail profit margin on all tobacco products in Denmark is only 7·5 per cent. – and for cigarettes alone 5·2 per cent. – of the consumer price; these margins have been declining since permission to continue r.p.m. was granted in 1956. In Sweden, on the other hand, the corresponding profit margins rose from 8 to 15 per cent. for all tobacco goods, and from 7·5 to 14·7 per cent. for cigarettes alone, since the abolition of r.p.m. In its ruling the Appeal Tribunal emphasised that, as it had been practised, the Danish system of r.p.m. for tobacco had not involved the customary and crucial features of such a pricing system, namely, higher costs, gross profits and prices. On the contrary, it had been demonstrated that the retail margins on tobacco were considerably lower than on wine and spirits, perfume and toilet accessories. Further, the Tribunal attached importance to the recent developments in Sweden, where the abolition of r.p.m. for tobacco – but not for various other goods – had resulted in quite appreciable increases in gross profit margins.[14] The Tribunal found, therefore, that a revocation of the exemption for tobacco would in all probability involve higher gross profit margins and correspondingly higher consumer prices, notwithstanding the (limited) opportunities which the Monopolies Control Authority might have of supervising tobacco prices. On these

[14] For further discussion of these Swedish developments, see pp. 142–3, above. (Ed.)

grounds the Tribunal ruled that the tobacco trade should be allowed to continue to practise r.p.m. under the system in operation since 1912, which seemed to have worked satisfactorily. For the time being, therefore, the permission to practise r.p.m. should be allowed to remain in force.

In recent years, very active competition has manifested itself within the photographic equipment trade in step with the appearance of non-traditional forms of retail outlets and the abolition of the so-called 'photo-arrangement' which regulated competition in the trade. Under this arrangement, the importers' and manufacturers' association collaborated with the other trade organisations for the purpose of regulating the sale of photographic equipment by means of a joint discount system. Recommended resale prices were fixed, and the arrangement included rules to determine which dealers could be accepted as dealers entitled to trade discount. Although the resale prices have been merely recommended prices since 1956, the whole arrangement and the sense of loyalty prevailing among the members of the trade had the effect that the suggested prices were generally observed. An inquiry by the Monopolies Control Authority early in the 1960s into the effects of the 'photo-arrangement' on prices and margins disclosed high trade margins and showed that the rebate system allied with the rigorous control of entry to the trade curbed any tendency towards price competition in retailing.

While the cartel authorities were negotiating with the trade to have the 'photo-arrangement' terminated, strong price competition was introduced by a few shops in Copenhagen. These were non-traditional enterprises which used new selling methods such as self-service and mail-order sales which enabled them to cut prices drastically and advertise the fact in all important newspapers. This rather unexpected price competition was a strong contributory factor in the final abolition of the 'photo-arrangement' in 1963. Competition in prices has continued, especially in Copenhagen and certain provincial towns. In Copenhagen and the metropolitan area prices seem to have dropped by about 20 per cent. The trade did not give in to this new price competition without resistance, and tried to re-establish 'normal' price conditions by taking such measures as refusal to supply rebelling dealers. The cartel authorities have regarded these actions as attempts to revive some of the restrictive practices of the former 'photo-arrangement', and in some instances have issued orders to suppliers to make deliveries to retailers charging low prices in their shops.

Finally, a brief account of the competitive situation in the radio and television trade follows. As has previously been mentioned, binding resale prices were made unlawful as early as 1948, which measure resulted in price reductions of about 15 to 20 per cent. After the abolition of binding resale prices, suppliers began to recommend resale prices which became the customary prices charged by resellers, with the important proviso that a customer who paid cash could quite easily obtain 'confidential' reductions ranging from 10 to 20 per cent.

In 1940, chain-store firms with at least four retail outlets were estimated to have been handling about 10 per cent. of the total sales volume of the trade; today their market share amounts to more than 25 per cent. At the same time, the formerly sharp distinction between radio and television shops and other retail shops has become blurred, and today the former also sell other durable consumer goods, while radio and television sets are sold in co-operative shops and by retailers in other trades. This development has made it increasingly difficult for the radio and television trade to have its recommended resale prices observed. Large retail chains, for example, at certain times have openly reduced their prices by up to 15 per cent. below those recommended by the manufacturers. These reductions were motivated, it was claimed, by a wish to put pricing on a sound basis by openly charging competitive prices and obviating the practice of giving confidential or secret rebates. As a countermeasure manufacturers discontinued deliveries to the shops concerned on the ground that the announced price reductions were tantamount to a price war or loss-leader selling; after intervention by the Monopolies Control Authority, deliveries were resumed.[15] The size of the price reductions granted are extremely difficult to ascertain precisely, because the trade-in prices paid for used radio and television sets remain an important feature of competition.

Policy towards Loss-Leader Selling

In Denmark, as in other countries, the dangers of loss-leader selling have been advanced by business firms as an argument against the imposition of a ban on r.p.m. In spite of this advocacy, rules on

[15] See above, p. 163.

loss-leader practices were not included in the Monopolies Control Act of 1955. In the explanatory memorandum to the Act, however, it was stated that evidence of loss-leader selling might influence the grant of permission for firms to maintain their resale prices. It was said, further, that an order to a supplier to supply a price-cutting dealer would not necessarily be made where the dealer was using the item as a loss leader. But unfortunately no guidance was given as to what was to be understood by the term loss leader.

Since the passing of the Act of 1955, only a very few cases concerning loss-leader selling have been dealt with by the Monopolies Control Authority. In none of these cases did the Authority find sufficient reason to grant permission to suppliers to maintain their resale prices or to allow suppliers to discontinue supplies on the grounds of loss-leader selling.

In 1964 the problem of loss-leader selling received renewed attention,[16] after the scope of the earlier exemptions from the prohibition of binding r.p.m. had been greatly reduced. The organised grocery trade, supported by other trade organisations, submitted applications to the Authority asking for a new approach to loss-leader selling. The Authority should introduce a clear definition of the practice, and suppliers should be allowed, without the intervention of the Authority, to discontinue supplying dealers who sold their goods at prices which obviously were loss-leader prices according to the definition. The grocery trade organisation emphasised that the grocers did not object to the ordinary practice of selling at low prices, and that their scheme was directed solely against flagrant cases of loss-leader selling of nationally advertised branded articles boosted by special sales efforts. It was claimed that such loss-leader selling created considerable 'disturbance', spreading far beyond the clientele of the offending dealer. The grocers also voiced the opinion that loss-leader selling was an unsound business practice devised for pulling the wool over the eyes of customers, which at the same time forced dealers in a large area to charge the same unrealistic prices in self-defence.

During the negotiations with the Authority, the grocers' organisation conceded that the concept of loss-leader selling should be delimited so as to include nothing except cases where a commodity is sold at or below the price paid by the dealer in question. Some

[16] See 'Lokkevaresalg som Begrundelse for Leveringsnægtelse', *Meddelelser fra Monopoltilsynet*, 1965, pp. 33 ff.

organisations, however, went further and asked for a wider definition. Thus the organised perfume and toilet requisites trade, then but recently deprived of its former exemption from the ban on r.p.m., applied for permission to be given to suppliers to discontinue or refuse supplies to dealers in cases where their resale prices did not cover their purchase prices and normal overheads. It may be added that some of the other organisations which supported the grocers, whose application was confined to non-durable consumer goods, pointed out that arguments similar to those advanced by the grocers' organisation could be put forward in respect of durables also.

It is difficult to draw a clear distinction between, on the one hand, the price competition in retailing which the ban on r.p.m. sought to encourage, and, on the other, loss-leader selling which may be considered as a special form of price competition. No generally accepted or statutory definition of loss-leader selling has been developed in Denmark. The Trust Commission had stated that goods are used as loss leaders when a shopkeeper sells them at a loss or at prices including very low profit margins in order to lure customers into his shop in the hope that they will also buy other goods at prices including normal or even higher profit margins, so that any losses sustained on the sale of the loss leaders are compensated for by profits earned on other goods.[17]

It is extremely difficult to demonstrate that loss-leader selling is detrimental to the interests of the manufacturer or the consumer. Consequently, it is equally hard to show that competition in the form of loss-leader selling has any adverse effects from the point of view of the public interest, while it is nevertheless clear that this special form of competition may greatly inconvenience many retailers.

It would be at variance with the general practice of the Danish cartel authorities of judging each case on its merits if, in loss-leader cases, the authorities adopted the administrative policy of refraining from ordering suppliers to resume supplies to loss-leading retailers, as suggested by the grocers' organisation. Moreover, such an inflexible procedure would make it impossible to take into account the variety of circumstances in evidence in each individual case. Again, in times of intensive price competition in fields where non-traditional business methods and sales policies are being introduced, it is

[17] *Konkurrencebegrænsning og Monopol*, Trustkommissionens betænkning, nr. 3 (Copenhagen, 1953), p. 77.

important that the 'natural' forces of price formation are given free rein. For these reasons, the authorities have hesitated to lay down fixed lines to be followed in deciding the circumstances in which loss-leader selling should justify the discontinuance or refusal of supplies.

Thus the final outcome of the discussions on loss-leader selling was that the Monopolies Control Authority decided that under the present law it could not introduce any general administrative ruling or give any general administrative directive. Consequently, the Authority has maintained a free hand to decide on the evidence of each individual case whether or not loss-leader selling is being practised and whether or not an established case of loss-leader selling may justify refusal or discontinuance of supplies. In judging whether such a measure is justifiable or not, great importance would no doubt be attached to the size of the price reduction, and whether the commodity in question was sold at a loss or not. This latter factor would not, however, be the only factor bearing on the decision; in practice, apparently similar circumstances would carry different weight from one case to another, especially when viewed in the light of the prevailing competitive situation.

Concluding Observations

It is not possible to arrive at an exact evaluation of the effects of the ban against r.p.m. Its encouragement of competition has operated simultaneously with other developments influencing the competitive situation and pricing, and it is not feasible to isolate the effects contributed specifically by the prohibition of r.p.m.

When judging the effects of the prohibition, general economic developments since 1955 should be taken into consideration. While the comprehensive liberalisation of foreign trade has brought about keener competition, the high rate of employment and the increase in money incomes have kept consumer spending at high and rising levels. In such circumstances, incentives to increase sales by means of price reductions are not as strong as in periods when over-all demand is less buoyant.

Competition cannot be created by legislative means alone if the enterprises are not interested in competing with one another. It is a fallacy, therefore, to believe that the abolition of horizontal price agreements, the breaking-up of mergers, or the prohibition of r.p.m.

will automatically result in an appreciable degree of competition. Whether such a situation will develop depends, *inter alia,* on the number of enterprises choosing to take advantage of the new situation, the nature of the goods, and differences in the size and efficiency of the enterprises in the trade. As has been shown in respect of the photographic equipment and radio and television trades, the establishment of new firms organised on non-traditional lines and operating new sales methods can be a decisive factor in converting a trade to more competitive conditions. The prohibition of r.p.m. contributes to the rise and growth of such new enterprises.

A widespread use of r.p.m. is said to preserve too many small retail shops operating at a low rate of efficiency. In fact, already before 1955, when the ban on r.p.m. was imposed, there had been a development towards voluntary chains, supermarkets and other forms of large-scale operation in the retail trade, and the establishment of non-traditional retail outlets such as self-service shops and mail-order shops selling at low prices. In some trades, the ban on r.p.m. has helped to make it easier for non-traditional and new shops to obtain supplies of goods, and owing to their efficiency, goods are being sold in them at correspondingly lower prices. In this way the ban has influenced the pricing policies and practices of dealers, and has facilitated the adaptation of the structure of retail trades to changing technical and commercial opportunities. It must be admitted, however, that there still are a fair number of commodity fields where pricing is rather rigid on account of the widespread observance of *recommended* resale prices. In these cases, the ban on r.p.m. can be said to have had hardly any effect so far.

Fairly frequently r.p.m. has been found to form only part of a comprehensive system of regulations restraining competition. To activate competition it will often be necessary, therefore, to combine the elimination of r.p.m. with such measures as intervention against restrictions on the number of dealers accepted in the trade (as illustrated in respect of the tobacco and photographic equipment trades). If r.p.m. has been practised in conjunction with agreements on exclusive dealing, boycotts, restrictions limiting entry to a trade, or refusal or discontinuance of supplies to price-cutters, abolition of r.p.m. alone will not be sufficient to create the freely competitive situation which is the objective. It is logical, therefore, that the provisions on r.p.m. in the Danish anti-trust legislation are closely linked with provisions concerning other forms of restrictive practice.

The beneficial effects of the prohibition of r.p.m. would have been appreciably greater had the emphasis in its statutory formulation been rather different. It would have been better, both to achieve greater clarity and also to promote more competition, had the legislation been phrased (as had been suggested in the original bill) so as to make it a punishable offence to sell goods subject to an expressed or implied condition that the buyer would observe stipulated minimum resale prices or margins. It would then have been beyond all doubt that the prohibition applied to all resale price stipulations, including those which took the ostensible form of price recommendations, and also that it applied regardless of whether the supplier exerted a substantial influence on competition. Difficulties experienced with the present legislation would have been avoided; and the impediment to the greater effectiveness of the prohibition of r.p.m. caused by the widespread observance of recommended prices would have been far less important.

6

THE EUROPEAN ECONOMIC COMMUNITY

F. D. Boggis

The restraints which have been placed on the practice of resale price maintenance in Europe have arisen from a variety of motivations. The decision to curb r.p.m. is inevitably political, but has to be interpreted in the context of economic policy. In Holland, for example, the decision to ban collective and later individual r.p.m. was taken in a situation where inflationary pressures were evident in the economy and the prospect of reducing prices through the effects of competition was seen as a means of curbing price increases.

Restraints on the practice of maintaining prices have been seen by governments in a number of European countries as an integral part of a comprehensive policy for regulating incomes and prices. There are few countries in Europe which have not adopted some form of price control during periods of national emergency. Given the existence of such 'emergency' controls, it was an easy transition to intervention in business affairs in more 'normal' conditions, by government regulation of the formation of prices and the size of trading margins.

The climate of economic opinion in Europe has changed since the war from one of hostility to competition to one of a general, if grudging, acceptance of the inevitability and desirability of competition. The public authorities now firmly believe that business should be conducted in a competitive manner. Changes in the structure of industry and distribution have taken place within this changed climate. The formation of the Common Market has given added impetus to these changes.

The form of the institutions and the relative severity of the legislation on r.p.m. in the different European countries reflect the differing strengths of the forces involved. In Germany, for example, the adoption of the free-enterprise market philosophy played an important part in the formulation of the ban on r.p.m., although the persistence of pre-war attitudes towards cartels seems to have played some part, at least, in the lengthy debates which resulted in a number of excepting clauses to the ban. In Holland, where the pre-war empirical approach to the cartel question may have been regarded as pre-disposing the authorities towards the persistence of r.p.m., a partial ban has now been adopted. The determination of the administration to encourage the newer forms of competition and to remove obstacles to innovation has strengthened the force of decisions taken under the previous law favouring freedom in pricing.

There is considerable diversity in the countries of the European Economic Community in their approach to the regulation of the practice of r.p.m. In the case of France the tradition of administrative centralisation has led to what is, in the main, a purely administrative solution. Elsewhere the legislative bodies have played a greater part in the formulation of the law. In every country where the law is used as a serious instrument of policy, however, the courts are presented with the difficult task of deciding how policy should be put into practice.

Finally, it must be mentioned that nowhere has a simple restraint of r.p.m. sufficed. Competition has been further encouraged by ancillary laws; for example, it has been backed by regulation of dealers' access to supplies.

The adoption of the Treaty of Rome places the laws of the Six dealing with the restraint of r.p.m. within a common framework, the implications of which are only now becoming apparent. The first important decision concerning r.p.m. at the Common Market level suggests that there may be a difficult problem of reconciling national laws permitting r.p.m. with the right of importers to price imported goods freely. Yet this will be necessary since the Common Market Commission's interpretation of the relevant article of the Treaty encourages the development of freely priced imports.[1]

France

When the initial attack on the practice of r.p.m. developed in France in the early 1950s, it took place in a climate of opinion hostile to 'Malthusianism' in the French economy. The term 'Malthusianism' was used by critics of French industry and trade to describe the prevailing attitude towards competition. At that time French in-

[1] I wish to make a general acknowledgment to *Guide to Legislation on Restrictive Business Practices.* This publication of the OECD contains details of legislation, legal decisions and other related information, on which I have drawn.

dustry was characterised by its retreat into a protected home market, a refusal to compete through innovation, and the avoidance of price competition by means of vertical and horizontal agreements fixing prices.

The campaign against Malthusianism was initiated in part by the 'administrative technocrats' who during the Occupation had formulated their plans for the re-shaping of the French economy, and in part by the younger generation of French industrialists who were impatient with the customary restrictions. As industry and government were re-staffed by these new men, so the campaign against Malthusianism gathered strength.[2]

The adoption of the initial legislation concerning restrictive business practices was not a simple matter. Premier Pinay's attempt to introduce a bill outlawing price-fixing cartels, within the context of a stabilisation plan, was strongly opposed by the organised interests. The employers' organisation, the Confédération Nationale du Patronat Français (C.N.P.F.), lobbied vigorously against the introduction of legislation on price-fixing. Even before the bill was submitted to Parliament, the C.N.P.F. successfully pressed the administration to exclude from the regulation all established prices for household and similar branded goods. The parliamentary situation was such that the Government by-passed the two chambers by issuing a decree dealing with price-fixing.

During the discussion of the abortive bill before Parliament the arguments of the C.N.P.F. spokesman were viewed with suspicion. The dire consequences of the freeing of prices predicted by him were so over-stated as to be unconvincing. The pleas of the C.N.P.F. were not assisted by mounting suspicions of the work on interest groups within Parliament. Leading politicians denounced pressure groups as subjecting Parliament to 'pressures as impudent as they are scandalous', and spoke of the 'economic congregations' which 'paralyse the State within these walls'.[3] Outside Parliament the work of the pressure groups had for long been held in opprobrium. The representations of the 'respectable' pressure groups such as the C.N.P.F. were, so far as the general public was concerned, confused with the pressures exerted by ' . . . a "mafia" of disreputable hotel

[2] See C.P.Kindleberger, 'The Postwar Resurgence of the French Economy', in S.Hoffmann (ed.), *France: Change and Tradition* (1963).

[3] See P.M.Williams, *Crisis and Compromise: Politics in the Fourth Republic* (1964).

keepers, alcohol merchants, supporters of colonial expansion, swindlers or "merchants of death" '.[4]

Apart from changes in the political climate which prepared the way for reform, there also were changes in the social climate which made inevitable the freeing of prices. During the post-war recovery there had occurred amongst French consumers what has been described as 'the revaluation of mass consumption'. With the greater acceptance of mass-consumption goods went a more ready acceptance of the idea of mass distribution. Although in the early 1950s the inroads of mass distribution into conventional French retailing were still relatively modest, they were sufficiently important to give impetus to the political protest of the Poujadist movement.[5]

The Regulation of Prices

The French approach to freedom in pricing has to be viewed against a long-standing and elaborate system of official price controls, which have in turn been eroded and then made good on a number of occasions during the post-war period. The general effect of the changes has been to reduce the area over which the government has control.

The basic law on which the regulation of prices and margins is based was introduced by the immediate post-war de Gaulle Government. The law of 30 June 1945 was a stabilisation measure, and pegged prices at their 1939 level or at a level subsequently fixed by the authorities. It was basically a law against the black market. It sought to turn trade back into conventional channels and to bring prices into line with the various maxima and minima fixed by the authorities. The penalties provided for under the law were severe – imprisonment, confiscation of assets and heavy fines. Although the law on prices may be regarded as 'un texte d'exception qui avait trouvé son origine dans les circonstances du temps de guerre et de l'occupation ennemie, puis dans le disette qui durant quelques années les prolongea', it is also, as will become evident in reviewing the German and Dutch laws, far from exceptional in that it permits state intervention in the process of price formation. However, it is true, as Franck observes, that the French administration by basing

[4] See G.E.Lavau, 'Political Pressures by Interest Groups in France', in H.W. Ehrmann (ed.), *Interest Groups in Four Continents* (Pittsburgh, 1958).

[5] S.Hoffmann, *Le Mouvement Poujade* (Paris, 1956).

later regulations dealing with competition on the Price Ordinance have given the regulations 'un caractère quelque peu ambigu'.[6]

The most recent example of direct government intervention in the area of prices began with the Stabilisation Plan of September 1963, when producer prices for industrial products were frozen at their level on 31 August 1963, and ceiling prices for services were fixed. In addition, the Government launched an operation with the code-name '100.000 points de vente'. The retailers concerned, all in the food trades, agreed to sell certain products at reduced margins and at stable prices. Press and radio publicity was given to the products coming within the scope of the scheme. Producers, wholesalers and retailers of other goods, in particular textiles, footwear and household cleaning articles, also agreed to collaborate in the campaign. The Plan further sought to achieve a number of reforms in the distributive trades. A first approach was to reduce the number of shops, especially the smaller shops, and to concentrate trade on larger, more efficient outlets operating on lower margins. This proposal was accompanied by another for the 'despecialisation' of certain outlets, to enable them to sell a wider variety of products.

The system of official price controls developed in France is very flexible. The techniques used range from the severe price freeze (le blocage) through freedom in pricing subject to official approval (la liberté contrôlée) to the least stringent form of control where there is freedom to fix prices subject only to prior notification to the authorities (la liberté surveillée).

The attitude of the authorities towards these price controls is somewhat ambiguous. As recently as 1961 an influential Frenchman, Pierre Masse, writing shortly after a 'big bonfire of price controls' stated: 'Setting up price controls and price ceilings were perhaps necessary evils to prevent still greater disorders. But they were a cure that attacked the consequences and not the causes of monetary depreciation. They were able to slow down the latter but were not able to vanquish it. Moreover, their persistent use had grave repercussions on the lives of millions of French people.'[7] Within the space of two years of this statement, a new stabilisation plan and further price controls were introduced. Despite set-backs such as these, it probably remains true that direct official intervention in the realm of prices is now regarded as a matter of expediency aimed solely at

[6] L.Franck, *La Libre Concurrence* (Paris, 1963), p. 92.

[7] Quoted in J. and A.Hackett, *Economic Planning in France* (1963).

correcting or reducing temporary market disturbances. It has been appreciated that the indiscriminate use of price controls introduces distortions in the economy which it is most difficult to correct except in the very long term.

It will be evident from the foregoing that, whatever the regulations concerning r.p.m. might be, there are a number of controls through which the authorities may influence prices and margins. These controls are concerned with price ceilings rather than with the freedom of a distributor to arrive at his own price lower than that recommended or prescribed by a supplier.

The Law on Resale Price Maintenance

The Decree of 9 August 1953, which made it illegal 'to stipulate, maintain, or impose minimum limits on prices of goods or services, or on profit margins, whether by means of price list or schedules, or under private business agreements of any description', drew its authority from general powers granted to the Government by Parliament 'to take measures to maintain or re-establish free competition in industry and trade'. The prohibition of r.p.m. was not an isolated measure, but was part of the Pinay stabilisation plan for the French economy, designed not only to bring down prices but to hold down costs.

The ban introduced in the 1953 law and confirmed in the Decree of 24 June 1958 applies to both individual and collective r.p.m., and no distinction is drawn between branded and non-branded goods, as is done in the German law. There is provision for exemption from the ban for limited periods on grounds of (1) the novelty of the good or service; (2) exclusive rights stemming from a patent, licence or registered design; (3) the requirements of conditions of sale involving a guarantee of quality or specifications concerning packaging; and (4) the advertising cost of launching a new product.

Before an exemption to the ban is made, the Minister of Economic Affairs, the Minister of Trade, and the Minister of the appropriate department for the product in question must give their consent. Exemptions have not been granted easily, and in the main have been restricted to durable consumer goods and perfumes. It seems to be the leading firms producing such products which have benefited from the exemption. Exemption does not seem to have been gained by these firms, however, without concession on their part to the authorities. Prices are fixed subject to a 'marge à double détente': manufacturers are given the right to stipulate a fixed resale price provided that traders are allowed to cut the price within a certain fixed limit. The limit is relatively narrow; in the case of Moulinex domestic electric appliances the authorised discount is 5 per cent., while for Kodak-Pathé 'Instamatic' cameras the discount cannot exceed 7 per cent. In the main the fixed price seems to prevail in the resale of the various exempted goods.

It is not sufficient simply to forbid manufacturers to fix prices for their goods if they are able by selecting their outlets to channel their output only to those traders who will observe the recommended prices. In France the ban on r.p.m. is buttressed by regulations dealing with refusal to supply and discriminatory terms of supply. In March 1960 an Official Circular (known as the Fontanet Circular) made a considerable stir by restating the Government attitude to discrimination and refusal to supply. The Circular does not have the force of law but it does seem to have influenced subsequent legal decisions since they appear to be fully in line with the doctrine set forth in it.

In the Circular it is stated that the revisions in June 1958 of the Price Ordinance 'are clear proof of determination to prevent discrimination between purchasers even more effectively than in the past and to punish any interference with the regulating mechanisms of free competition'. In a situation where the structure of distribution is changing and the Government is committed to restoring competition in distribution, emphasis must be placed on freedom in pricing. When the imposition of minimum prices is prohibited, price competition becomes possible. 'But,' continues the Circular, 'it cannot be effective unless, whatever the form of commerce and methods of sale employed, all purchasers have the same possibilities of obtaining supplies without fear of encountering refusal to sell or discriminatory terms of sale, most often applied at the instigation of certain competitors.'

The very broad prohibition against refusal to sell is qualified by certain exceptions listed in the Circular. Supplies may be refused (1) where requests for supplies come from purchasers showing bad faith (for example, indulging in systematic denigration of the supplier's product by means of adverse comparisons or through selling at a loss); (2) where requests for supplies have 'un caractère anormal' (for example, the order size is larger than normal; special delivery is requested; the request comes from a trader whose usual line of business, qualifications or installations make it inappropriate); or

(3) where the supplier does not have sufficient goods to meet all orders. Some aspects of these exceptions are of particular interest. Selling at a loss is defined as a sale made at less than the price paid for the goods, plus carriage and turnover tax. Where a sale is refused on the grounds that the trader is insufficiently qualified, all other such traders demanding supply must be treated similarly.

So far as discriminatory terms of supply are concerned, sales must be made on customary trade terms, and the same terms must be offered to traders purchasing equivalent amounts at regular intervals. These principles do not rule out the granting of advantageous terms for the purchase of large quantities if it can be shown that this involves lower costs to the supplier. Similarly, the supply of a customer on more favourable terms is permitted where he is developing a difficult sales area (for example, a sparsely populated area), or where he holds a complete range of the manufacturer's goods when other dealers do not. It would not conflict with the restrictions for a wholesaler to supply a group of retailers who bulk their orders but take separate delivery and make individual payments on terms different from those applied to a large order of similar size received from and delivered to a single purchaser. Broadly, it has to be shown that the difference in the price at which the goods are supplied to different purchasers is warranted by an equivalent difference in the costs of supplying them.

A way round the ban on the enforcement of resale prices was seen by many manufacturers in the development of exclusive dealing contracts. The Fontanet Circular recognised that this was a legitimate form of commercial arrangement; however, the Circular states explicitly that '. . . no clause may have the object or effect, even indirectly, of restricting the dealer's freedom to determine at will – subject, as regards the maximum price, to the provisions of the price regulations – the selling price of the product unless, of course, exemption has been granted from the prohibition of minimum prices. This rule must be applied the more strictly because distribution through exclusive dealers is by its very nature an obstacle to free competition and, what is more, gives the supplier an effective instrument for coercing the trader whose concession can usually be withdrawn at very short notice.'

Exclusive dealing contracts do not contravene the law if in practice they are advantageous to consumers, do not bring about price increases, do not result in prices being held at an unreasonably high level, and do not reduce the supply in such a way that market demand cannot be met.

A recent development in the position regarding price competition has been the prohibition of loss-leader selling (2 July 1963). Resale of goods at less than their real purchase price (purchase price less discounts or rebates plus turnover tax) is forbidden. A blanket prohibition of selling at a loss is not possible and hence the law lists those cases in which a trader can sell at a loss. These relate to sales of perishable goods likely to deteriorate rapidly, of seasonal goods at the end of the season or when they are out of season, of obsolete or out-of-fashion goods, and of goods for which replacement stocks have been obtained at a lower price. A trader may also sell below cost to meet the lawful lower price of a competitor for the same goods, as well as in voluntary or forced sales occasioned by changes in business activity.

From the foregoing brief description of the law regarding r.p.m. and related practices, it will be seen that in France the practice of r.p.m. has been attacked relentlessly by the administration, but that no simple solution has been found. Since 1952, ordinances and decrees have been introduced almost every year bearing on the practice. During this period perhaps the most remarkable development has been the issue of the Fontanet Circular. As Franck explains, '. . . la circulaire a créé un cadre juridique administratif, ou si l'on veut *institutionnel*, à l'intérieur duquel les diverses formes commerciales, des plus traditionnelles aux plus modernes, peuvent s'affronter dans les conditions équitables et déployer librement l'éventail de leurs possibilités; elle devrait donc être l'instrument d'un souhaitable assainissement des structures'.[8]

It is an impossible task to disentangle the effects of the prohibition of r.p.m. on the price level and the changing channels of distribution in France. Innovation in retailing and a law which encourages change and facilitates competition interact with the changing incomes and habits of the French consumer and the drive of new entrepreneurs.

It is clear from the establishment of discount houses and the widespread use of discounts for clubs and groups that the idea that durable consumer goods have to be purchased at a fixed price is no longer accepted by many French consumers. The French are now

[8] L.Franck, *op. cit.*, p. 108.

far more interested in mass-produced consumer goods than they were before the war. The contrast in attitudes is perhaps more marked in France than in any other country in Europe. Rather than emulate the aristocrat by acquiring a pale imitation of a piece of craftsmanship at a high price, the Frenchman is content with the mass-produced, cheap but usable alternative. Kindleberger argues that the change is '. . . intimately linked to a change in the reproductive pattern. Instead of living for the future of the dynasty, French people today seek enjoyment, including enjoyment in children'.[9] The change in attitudes extends to savings and to credit (which is now more readily available), and hence has facilitated the revaluation of mass consumption in French society.

The department stores, which had anticipated the change in the law by introducing their own brands and their own prices for manufacturers' brands, played an important part in the change in climate regarding fixed prices. In food distribution, which has been a particular thorn in the side of the French Government, at the retail level the Leclerc Distribution Centres and Saveco have taken full advantage of their opportunity to cut prices. Discounting in foodstuffs has now become more general. Once again clubs and groups to whom discounts are given have grown in importance as purchasers.

Enforcement

In cases involving enforcement of resale price, refusal to sell, or discriminatory terms involving individual traders and their suppliers, the normal procedure would be to place the facts before the Economic Enquiry Branch (le Service des Enquêtes Economiques) of the Direction Générale des Prix et des Enquêtes Economiques. An offence can be prosecuted as an ordinary criminal matter by filing a complaint with the Cours Tribunaux, but in practice control rests with the administration. It is the administrative service, the Economic Enquiry Branch, 'which applies the indispensable economic criteria in appreciating the facts which are referred to it'. Every attempt is made to settle cases without recourse to the courts either by arranging a settlement or by the imposition of a fine. Proceedings are only taken if the offender refuses to discontinue the practice. The Economic Enquiry Branch has been described as attempting 'to secure the observance of the law without legal proceedings by substituting education and conciliation for repressive action'.

[9] C.P.Kindleberger, *op. cit.*

Cases concerning resale prices, terms of sale and refusal to supply involving groups of manufacturers or wholesalers and a trader can be dealt with under the articles of the Ordinance concerning 'ententes' (combines). Once again it is possible for the matter to be dealt with through the courts; but since January 1954, when the Technical Commission on Combines (la Commission Technique des Ententes) was set up, it is most likely to be settled through this machinery. The Commission was established to investigate and evaluate the judicial, economic and social problems concerning combines. The Commission is composed of a judge from the Conseil d'Etat, la Cour de Cassation or la Cour des Comptes as chairman, five other judges as members, six members chosen for special technical competence (of which two are trade-unionists), and two members with expert economic knowledge.

Matters are referred to the Commission solely by the Minister of Economic Affairs, and hence there is a preliminary administrative investigation of any complaint by the Economic Enquiry Branch. The report of the preliminary investigation goes to the Minister, and, if he decides to submit the matter to the Commission, to the Commission also. With the report go the observations of the parties and the comments of the appropriate ministries. A rapporteur is appointed by the Minister for Economic Affairs and the Minister for Commerce, and, after investigation, he reports to the Commission and the Minister. Observations on the rapporteur's report are again made by the parties, members of the Commission and appropriate ministers. The next stage is an investigation (including oral hearings) by the Commission, and in due course consideration of their conclusions. The Commission states if there is an infringement of the Ordinance, and may make recommendations for dealing with the matter and restoring competition, for example, by removing the offending clauses in an agreement or terminating the offending practice. If the Minister agrees with the Commission's recommendations, the matter may be settled (given the agreement of the parties) at this stage; otherwise the matter will go to court, always provided the Commission states that there has been an infringement of the law.

Thus the lengthy procedure is essentially administrative in character and the Economic Enquiry Branch plays an important part in it. The activity of the Commission during its early days was shrouded in mystery; but, since a decree of 1959, recommendations of the

Commission and decisions of Ministers have been published and hence cases settled out of court have been given greater publicity.

Refusal to sell has been the issue in almost all the important litigation concerning r.p.m. In *Colin et Société Radio-Matériel*, the manager of a department store complained that the manufacturer of an electric gramophone had refused him supplies. The manufacturer defended his action on the ground that the department store lacked the requisite technical competence. The court of first instance (Tribunal Correctionnel, Lyons, May 1960) held that since electric gramophones were articles of common use there was no requirement for technical skill on the part of the reseller. The Court of Appeal upheld the lower court's ruling that the Decree (of 24 June 1958) under which the action was brought was valid, but disagreed with the judgment on grounds of substance and discharged the case. The public prosecutor appealed to the Cour de Cassation which, while expressing no opinion on the issue of the requirement of skill by a reseller, quashed the judgment of the Court of Appeal on the ground that insufficient reasons had been given for over-ruling the lower court (July 1961).

A further case involving refusal to sell turned on the packaging of the product. In *Barjolle et Biscuits Olibet*, a retailer alleged refusal to supply, on the ground that the biscuit manufacturer would only supply his products to him in a package which differed from that in which they were usually sold. The court of first instance (Tribunal Correctionnel, Bordeaux, June 1960) dismissed the case on the grounds that the Decree of June 1958 under which the action was brought was illegal. This judgment was reversed by the Court of Appeal which accepted the legality of the Decree of 1958 but dismissed the case on other grounds. Refusal to sell had not been proved since the manufacturer had undertaken to supply a substitute – the same product, bearing the manufacturer's name but differently packed. The request was abnormal, since the retailer was likely to resell the product in question at cost; and the retailer's conduct was contrary to trade usage. On appeal, the Cour de Cassation (July 1961) reaffirmed the legality of the Decree of 1958 but quashed the judgment of the Court of Appeal: 'A brand has a mercantile value and the buyer who acquires a branded product acquires a brand as well as the product. Hence refusal to sell the product in its normal packing amounts to refusal to sell. There can be price competition in respect of a branded product only if all the competitors are in a position to sell a product which is identical not only in its substantial properties but also in its presentation.' The court held that the prohibition of r.p.m. by the Price Ordinance had altered trade usage regarding sales at cost, and that trade usage referred only to the purchase and not to the resale of the goods.

The sale of photographic goods has been an area of fierce competition in France in recent years. Two interesting cases concern these goods. The first is *Nicolas et Société Brandt* which arose from the refusal of a wholesaler with the exclusive distributorship for cine-cameras of a particular brand to supply a retailer who systematically was cutting prices. The wholesaler had placed a chain of 'exclusive' retailers under contract with him. The Tribunal Correctionnel de Seine (July 1960) held that this was simply a device for circumventing the requirement not to enforce resale prices and a means of cutting off supplies to retailers who did not wish to observe the recommended prices. The contracts themselves were of doubtful standing since they did not define the exclusive area of the dealers nor did they forbid them to deal in the branded products of competitors. The Paris Cour d'Appel (February 1961) also held that sole agency contracts could not be regarded as justification for refusal to sell.

In the Cour de Cassation hearing it was held that a sole agency contract by which contracting parties limit their freedom to trade can be beneficial if it is designed to improve consumer service, provided it does not directly or indirectly restrict the agent's freedom to fix his own selling price. Since the contract may have the effect of making merchandise inaccessible to other retailers, the practice has to be examined in relation to the degree of skill required in the trade or the quality of the merchandise involved. The Amiens Court, re-examining the case in May 1963 in the light of this ruling, found that it was impossible to justify the refusal to sell on the grounds of the existence of the sole agency contracts.

The second case, which has yet to reach finality, involves a Paris firm, the importer and exclusive distributor of certain Japanese cameras. The firm had made contracts with retailers whom it described as 'independent agents'. Under the terms of the contracts the retailers were to observe the resale prices laid down by the firm. The firm refused to supply a low-margin shop in Paris. While the Tribunal Correctionnel de Seine (May 1964) found that there was insufficient evidence to support the charge of refusal to sell, it stated that the agreements with the 'independent agents' had as their principal aim and intention the evasion of the law banning the enforcement of resale prices. Such practices, because of their scale and purpose, tended to control the market for photographic goods and were an attempt to restrict competition. The Court imposed a severe fine on the importer (Frs 20,000) and a less severe fine on the retailers (Frs 1,500) and confiscated the cameras held in stock.

This last case is especially interesting since this is the first conviction for the infringement of the ban on r.p.m. Other cases, amongst them those described above, have been concerned firstly with refusal to sell and only secondarily with r.p.m.

The Netherlands

The Netherlands is engaged in one of the long-standing European experiments in the area of comprehensive policies for wages, prices and profits. From this country has emerged also some impressive work on the forecasting of short- and medium-term developments in the national economy. It is doubly interesting therefore that its Minister for Economics should have recently initiated a fundamental change in Dutch policy concerning r.p.m.

Prices Policy

Prices policy in Holland is regarded as a normal part of general economic policy; it is linked closely to wages policy (so as to prevent the development of a wage-price spiral) and to profits policy (in order that profits do not, independently, generate an inflationary situation). While the Government has extensive powers in the area of prices, its policy is developed in close co-operation with industry and trade, which is accomplished without difficulty in the relatively small Dutch economy. Prices policy is primarily the responsibility of the Ministry of Economic Affairs assisted by the Economic Control Office. Through regular discussions with industry general rules are established for dealing with prices. There are, for example, general rules which have been adopted in an endeavour to achieve reasonable price stability although in certain circumstances departures from these rules are authorised. It is possible to operate within the general rules concerning price changes not only because of the extensive system of consultation but also because there is a requirement of prior notification of price increases for all goods and services to the Ministry of Economic Affairs. With the notification there must be a justification for the price increase. The Ministry of Economic Affairs consults with industry about possible price reduction in sectors where productivity is rising fast.

If the Ministry regards a price increase as not being justified, the Minister asks the industry or the enterprise to rescind the change. In most cases it is possible to obtain the industry's voluntary co-operation; but where this is not forthcoming the Minister can use his powers under the Price Act to impose a maximum price. The range of prices for which maxima have been fixed is relatively small, although during the inflationary period at the end of 1964 additional controls were introduced.

Prices policy has been given particular stress during periods of strong demand when inflation threatened. The distinct threat of an inflationary situation developing in the course of 1964 not only brought the active prices policy into force but also resulted in the Minister applying the once-for-all check of the abolition of r.p.m. This represented somewhat of a reversal of traditional Dutch policy.

Cartel Policy

The Netherlands adopted its first cartel legislation in 1935 when the country was still suffering from the effects of the depression. The Entrepreneurs' Agreements Act not only enabled the Government to attack restraint of competition by declaring agreements illegal but also permitted the authorities to set up compulsory cartels in situations where cut-throat competition had developed. A Cartel Decree enacted in 1941 followed similar lines and made provision for a closed cartel register. The most recent legislation, the Economic Competition Act of 1956 (amended in 1958), follows the same tradition. Restraint of competition is examined against the state of the industry or trade in question; it is basically an empirical approach. The Act requires the notification of all agreements in restraint of competition. While the register is not public, the authorities may publish agreements which they regard as detrimental to the public interest. Where the regulation of competition is judged to be contrary to the public interest, the agreement may be declared to be non-binding.

There were under the 1956 Act (and its precursors) a number of decisions bearing on r.p.m. and related aspects (such as refusal to supply) which even before the most recent change in policy represented a considerable restraint on the practice.

Various exclusive trading agreements, for example, effectively excluded certain types of enterprise (co-operative societies, department stores and buying combines) from participation in a particular trade. The agreement on stoves, to which virtually all dealers and suppliers adhered, obliged the parties to refrain from supplying co-operative societies. While the Minister conceded that enterprises in the private sector had a right to defend or enlarge their market, he held also that certain limits had to be placed on the means used. It was held contrary to the public interest that these enterprises should prevent the co-operatives from trading in stoves. Similarly it was deemed inadmissible for an exclusive dealing cartel involving manufacturers, dealers and retailers to stipulate that only owners of specialised businesses (or specified 'horizontal combines') might be admitted as retailers. The gramophone record cartel which had such a requirement was held to constitute too great an obstacle to economic development and was hence invalidated in that form. Again, the exclusion of a voluntary chain (a highly developed form of retail organisation in the Netherlands) from the financial benefits of collaboration with wholesalers was held to be inadmissible.

In some cases agreements required that the participants should observe market rules. An exclusive trading agreement involving leading dealers in surgical instruments and commercial agents in medical and related articles included the compulsory observance of market rules. Since surgical instruments were imported from abroad through agents, it was difficult for dealers who were not parties to the agreement to obtain supplies, and hence they were virtually forced into membership and into compliance with the requirement to observe minimum prices.

Some horizontal trade agreements also came under attack. A decision in 1951 ruled that an agreement amongst dealers in solid fuel in Friesland, which adopted the Government's maximum price as a fixed price, was contrary to the public interest, since those concerned had failed to show that it was necessary to prevent disastrous competition. The Government took the view that those who could supply solid fuel more cheaply, while still operating on a sound business basis, were being forced to charge higher prices than they needed. The Government has ruled that in minimum price agreements the minimum prices should not exceed the average cost (including 'wages' of management but not profits) of the most efficient enterprises. Neither the level at which the price is fixed nor the method of arriving at the price must be such as to hamper 'economically justified' price competition. An agreement of a trade association of beer dealers and mineral water manufacturers which laid down minimum prices for supplies to the retail trade was held to be admissible only if it complied with these rules for arriving at minimum prices.

Individual r.p.m. backed by a system of collective detection, prosecution and adjudication had also been declared inadmissible in particular trades. The most interesting decision in this connection concerned the radio cartel, an exclusive trading agreement involving manufacturers and importers and their customers, the wholesale dealers and retailers. Under the terms of the agreement manufacturers and importers were to fix prices at all levels, including the prices to be charged to the final consumer, and were to police the system. The Government's opinion was that 'a generally applied system of individual price maintenance leads to rigidity in principle, because it excludes price competition between the dealers in the articles concerned. This rigidity is enhanced by collective price maintenance, because the relationship in the form of a contract between a dealer-buyer and his supplier is thereby replaced by a relationship between a dealer-buyer and a body set up by the collective suppliers and/or dealers-buyers, which does not allow the normal personal element in the commercial relationship between a buyer-dealer and his supplier'. In the case of the radio cartel the Government held that '. . . the collective enforcement of prices led to a widespread and rigorous regulation of competition, and supported trade-margin warfare between manufacturers which resulted in excessive dealer margins and increased consumer prices'.

An aspect of the gramophone and vacuum cleaner cartels which attracted adverse attention was the requirement that a price set by any member of the cartel (manufacturer, dealer or retailer) had to be maintained by all members of the cartel.

From the foregoing short account it will be seen that even before the decision to end r.p.m. was taken, there already had been a considerable body of rulings which made the practice difficult to enforce except in a relatively sophisticated manner.

The Banning of Resale Price Maintenance, 1964

The decision of the Minister of Economic Affairs, Dr Andriessen, to ban collective r.p.m. in June 1964 took Parliament somewhat by surprise. The Economic Competition Act provides for the appointment of a Consultative Committee of experts, which can be asked for its opinion on measures to be taken under the Act. In 1960 the Minister of Economic Affairs consulted the Committee on the question of whether or not both individual and collective r.p.m. should be prohibited. The Committee deliberated for three years, consulting sixtytwo industrial and trading organisations and the two Dutch consumer organisations, Consumenten Contact Orgaan and the Netherlands Household Council. The latter organisations alone advocated total abolition of r.p.m. The Committee's report showed that a unanimous conclusion on the question of a general prohibition could not be reached. The majority of the Committee (it is not known how large this was) stood out against the general prohibition of individual r.p.m. The prohibition of collective r.p.m. was rejected too, but by the smallest possible majority. There was, however, a large majority for government regulation of the practices concerning the enforcement of r.p.m. (the private systems of investigation and adjudication). The Committee found it impossible to weigh objectively the arguments for and against general prohibition and to find a decisive argument on either side.

If the first element in the situation which suggested the preservation of the *status quo* was the report of the Committee, the second was the delicate political balance existing at that time and the fact that two of the parties in the Government coalition drew support from the small shopkeepers who could be expected to oppose the abolition of r.p.m. Both the Catholic and Liberal parties are dependent on the shopkeepers' vote. In Holland, where the voluntary chain came into existence earlier than in any other European country, small shopkeepers remain a numerous, if only marginally viable, group of traders. Small traders, and small firms generally, are actively encouraged by the Government, which carefully follows the fortunes of this 'middenstand'. However, the Minister of Economic Affairs resolved to make a change in the face of this apparently adverse situation.

In the autumn of 1963 agreement was reached for a national wage increase of about 10 per cent., which when translated into actual terms would amount to about 15 per cent. The potentially inflationary effect of such an increase played an important part in the decision to move against r.p.m. The new initiative came in two stages. In April 1964 the Government made an order under Section

10 of the Economic Competition Act; this order, which was revised and re-drafted in August 1964, dealt with collective forms of r.p.m. The second stage was reached in August 1964 when an order was made to the effect that individual r.p.m. for certain specified durable consumer goods would not be binding.

The order relating to collective forms of r.p.m. in effect prohibits the practice when it is collectively imposed, administered or enforced. The order excludes from its scope the individual form of r.p.m., except that the collective enforcement of individually imposed resale price restrictions is not exempted and hence is prohibited. The order does, however, provide for the granting of exemptions from its general prohibition of collective r.p.m. Temporary exemption is granted until requests for permanent exemption have been decided. The views of the Consultative Committee have to be sought before an exemption is made.

The explanatory memorandum accompanying the first order deals with the effect of r.p.m. on price formation, margins and efficiency. It is argued that uniform prices prevent efficient distributors from passing on to the consumer in their selling prices any savings stemming from lower operating costs. The consumer's choice between lower prices with less service and higher prices with more service is removed. Because the manufacturer has to engender an interest in his goods amongst high-cost distributors, he has to fix his resale price at a level which generates a sufficient margin for these distributors. Even if the costs of high-cost distributors are not used as the reference point and average costs of distribution are used instead, prices will be higher than they need otherwise be. It is argued in the memorandum that this leads to prices at the consumer level remaining permanently higher than is necessary for the efficient and economically profitable operation of the distributive system. Where manufacturers seek competitively to influence retailers by raising their margins, this effect is likely to be more marked. Emphasis on trade margins is more likely where the distributor's role in making sales is relatively more important and the consumer's judgment of the comparative merit of the goods is relatively difficult. The argument that competition in the form of service to the consumer is an acceptable alternative to price competition is rejected in the memorandum. The memorandum puts much stress on the consumer price level, and the possible effect of an increase in prices in remote locations is discounted on the grounds that the bulk of purchases are made from distributors who are in competition with one another.

In dealing with r.p.m. in its collective form the memorandum asserts that the practice restricts the reseller's choice of supplier, particularly where the number of suppliers outside the agreement is small. Collective r.p.m. circumscribes suppliers in their ability to adapt sales policy to current market conditions. Because the individual buyer is remote from the price-enforcing body, the possibility of local sales flexibility is thereby reduced.

The order affecting individual r.p.m. stems from the earlier order on collective r.p.m.; it takes the form of an exclusion from the general exception concerning strictly individual r.p.m. Certain sectors in which individual r.p.m. is not to be binding on resellers are defined by reference to characteristic articles. These sectors are as follows: (*a*) radio and television sets, record-players and tape-recorders; (*b*) electrical refrigerators, toasters, mixers, vacuum-cleaners, washing machines, spin-driers, flat irons, shavers and hair-driers; (*c*) cars and station wagons; (*d*) cameras, flash-light apparatus, cine-cameras and photo-slide and film projectors; and (*e*) records.[10]

In a background paper presented to Parliament in preparation for a debate on the r.p.m. issue, the case for and against the practice was outlined and the conclusions reached in the Ministry of Economic Affairs stated. On the issue of the effect of r.p.m. on the level of prices, the paper concedes that is does not necessarily result in higher prices and margins in all sectors. However, it was argued, price competition is most effective when it takes place at both the productive and the distributive stages. The problem of localised retail monopolies is dismissed as of slight importance. In a situation of retail competition there is a possibility that differences in buying power (of retailers) may be translated into differences in price to the consumer. The contribution that r.p.m. may make to production planning is regarded as being exaggerated. Even with r.p.m. there can be fluctuations in the level of trade margins, and its removal

[10] The prohibition of individual r.p.m. in respect of records, vacuum-cleaners and photographic articles has subsequently been suspended pending a decision on the request by their suppliers for exemption from the earlier prohibition of collective r.p.m. *Cf. Sales Promotion in Europe* (INTAM Ltd, London, 1964), p. 32.

facilitates more rapid adaptation to changes in market conditions. 'On the whole, restricted price flexibility cannot be considered a socio-economic advantage. Moreover, in present economic circumstances, with so-called "administered" prices, of which r.p.m. is an example, the danger cannot be ignored that prices will be adjusted in an upward, rather than in a downward direction, and this can lead to inflation.' Turning to the issue of the possible effect on the structure of distribution of r.p.m. and its place in mass marketing, the background paper concludes that r.p.m. can have a detrimental effect on the dynamics of retailing. In those trades where r.p.m. predominates, cost differences in distribution are inadequately reflected in prices, with a consequent dampening effect on the development of new sales methods amongst small and medium-size firms, which would stimulate competition. It is argued in the paper that increased concentration in the distributive sector is not to be expected from the abolition of r.p.m.; the forces responsible for this development are altogether different. Dealing with the matter of branding, quality, and knowledge of prices amongst consumers, the case is put that there is no reason to believe that the prices of branded goods will fall unreasonably in the absence of r.p.m. It is also assumed that quality standards will be maintained. If national brands are cut in price, there will be less incentive for retailers to develop their own private brands. The paper accepted that in those sectors where r.p.m. currently predominated the effect of abolition might be to reduce the number of existing brands. Finally, in dealing with the issue of the connection between fixed prices, margins and service, the paper comes down on the side of giving the consumer the choice between lower prices or more service on the ground that this would reduce the economic waste of undesired services which was present in the case of certain consumer durables.

The provision for exemptions from the ban on collective r.p.m. immediately attracted a number of applications, and the extent of the exemptions which will be granted is not yet clear. The abolition of individual r.p.m. for the various groups of goods listed above came into force on 1 December 1964, and hence its impact is also not yet clear. Philips, a company which manufactures several of these articles, has already adopted a policy of advertising 'advisory' prices. This position has been taken on the grounds that consumers should know what the company regards as a reasonable retail price.

So far as Philips goods are concerned, retailers are under no obligation to observe the 'advisory' prices, but they are required to observe various obligations regarding servicing, advertising and demonstration of Philips' products and they may not sell below the purchase price paid. Failure to observe these requirements would result in a reduced rate of discount or removal of recognition as a Philips dealer.

Industry and trade have claimed for the goods on which there will no longer be individual r.p.m. that margins and prices are such that there is no need for corrective action and that competition is already keen. The Government's view is that since there had been some price competition even under the system of r.p.m., the removal of restrictions would encourage further developments. Most retailers are opposed to abolition, although some of the vigorous grocery chains using self-service methods have welcomed the change. It was three of the larger food multiples which pioneered a system of coupon sales which enabled them to sell certain household electrical goods at considerably lower prices than were ruling amongst conventional electrical goods dealers.

Changes in the law regarding r.p.m. in Holland have been introduced in part to deal with a short-term threat of inflationary price increases; but the major reason is to be found in the desire to open up the way for new sales channels and more efficient methods of distribution. It must be added, too, that the system of private justice which backed the collective enforcement of r.p.m. in Holland had attracted much criticism.

It might be added by way of footnote to this account that the Dutch Government is assisting the consumer to become a more discriminating buyer by subsidising comparative testing of consumer goods and price investigations as well as by fostering the establishment of an institute for informative labelling. A Consumers Interests' section has been set up in the Ministry of Economic Affairs. This represents an important development in the balance of market forces in that it assists the consumer to become a more knowledgeable buyer.

Germany

Before the Second World War the German Government's position with regard to cartels was typified by the Cartel Ordinance (Kartell-

Verordnung) of November 1923 which aimed at the prevention of abuses of this form of restriction of competition. The law did not condemn cartels; rather, it recognised their existence and potential usefulness while it attempted to control the abuse of economic power. Price-fixing agreements attracted government intervention during the period before the National-Socialist regime came to power, while under Hitler the cartels became an integral part of the planning machinery of the State.

After the defeat of the Nazis the Occupation Powers in the Western Zone introduced a comprehensive programme of deconcentration and decartellisation. The influence of the American Government in the adoption of this programme was initially strong, although in the course of time United States resolve weakened.

When the Federal Parliament adopted the Act Against Restraints of Competition in July 1957, the law reflected not only the seven years of debate which preceded its passage – the first Government draft was submitted to Parliament in June 1952 and the debate had begun before that date – but also the experience which industry and trade as well as the administration had had of two basically different approaches to restriction of competition: American abhorrence of restraints on competition, and the pre-war German approach via the prevention of abuse.

The Law Relating to Resale Price Maintenance

The Act Against Restraints of Competition, commonly called the Kartellgesetz, is a formidable document with 109 sections. The statute begins boldly by declaring that vertical and horizontal agreements restraining competition are invalid, but then it goes on to describe the numerous exceptions. Section 2 states that agreements dealing with uniform application of terms of trade, deliveries or payments, including cash discounts, are excepted, provided these do not relate to prices or components of prices. Export cartels, crisis cartels, and standards agreements similarly fall outside the scope of the prohibition.

Section 15 deals with r.p.m.: 'Agreements between enterprises with respect to goods or commercial services relating to markets located within the area of applicability of this law are null and void in so far as they restrict any party to them in its freedom to establish prices or terms in contracts which are concluded with third parties in regard to the goods supplied, other goods, or commercial services'.

Again this is a bold start, but the sting goes out of the clause when Section 16 is read, because this exempts '. . . agreements made between an enterprise and the purchasers of its branded goods which are competing in price with similar goods of other producers or dealers, as far as such agreements bind the purchaser contractually or economically to maintain certain resale prices or to impose the same obligation upon their own purchasers down to the resale to the ultimate consumer'. Books also fall outside the prohibition of Section 15. Branded goods are defined as products whose delivery in equal or improved quality is guaranteed by the price-fixing enterprise, provided that the goods or their 'wrappings or adornments' or the container from which they are sold carry a distinctive mark indicating origin.

Before an enterprise can take advantage of the exemption from the ban on r.p.m. for its branded goods, it must register the agreements with the Federal Cartel Office (Bundeskartellamt), which is described below. In addition to information on sales prices charged to the initial dealer and subsequent distributors, the producer must supply information on trade margins and the services the dealer is expected to render customers. The Cartel Office may either upon its own initiative or upon the application of a purchaser invalidate a resale price agreement. The grounds for invalidation are (1) that the conditions regarding brand competition and brand identification no longer apply; (2) that r.p.m. is being abused; and (3) that r.p.m. 'as such or in connection with other restraints of competition is apt, in a manner not justified by general economic conditions, to raise the price of the goods affected, to avoid the lowering of such prices, or to restrict production or sale of such goods'.

Sections 25 and 26 of the Act forbid boycotts, refusals to sell and discriminatory pricing in connection with enforcement of resale prices. Section 38 (2) forbids recommendations 'which, by causing a uniform conduct, have resulted in an evasion of the prohibitions set forth in the law'. This clause hinders the use of price recommendations in place of formal r.p.m.

From this outline of the provisions of the Kartellgesetz dealing with r.p.m. it will be clear that the impact of the law on the competitive climate turns on the level of activity of the Federal Cartel Office (Bundeskartellamt), since it has the important role of supervising the notification of agreements and keeping itself informed of the state of competition. This Office, which is described in the law as an independent Higher Federal Authority, comes within the jurisdiction of the Federal Ministry of Economics. Should the Federal Minister of Economics issue an instruction concerning a decree issued by the Office, this must be published in the Official Gazette (Bundesanzeiger); hence the degree of political intervention in decisions can be seen. The Cartel Office issues an annual report which goes before the Bundestag. The Office is staffed by economists and legal experts and its President, Dr Günther, has become a well-known figure both through the reports and decisions of the Office and because of his active interest in anti-trust matters internationally.

The extent of the Cartel Office's task may be judged from statistics of notification of r.p.m. agreements presented to the Bundestag in 1962. At the end of 1961 there were 198,059 agreements notified by 1,109 firms (87,196 agreements concerned motor-car spare parts and accessories). Two years earlier the number of notifications had been as high as 203,109. More recently the statistics show a falling off in the number of notifications, with 161,739 in 1962. Because every individual article has to be notified, a particular branded good may appear as a number of entries because of different package sizes. Since 1963 the Office has increased its supervision of r.p.m., and there are now a number of decisions on the practice from which the legal position can be seen.

A case which turned on the issue of notification concerned two manufacturers of eau-de-Cologne. Manufacturer 'A' marked his product with a price but did not register it with the Cartel Office, while manufacturer 'B' both marked and registered his product. The Court held that 'A' had violated the Act Against Restraints of Competition (as well as the Act Against Unfair Competition) since the non-obligatory character of the price recommendation on his product was not apparent.

Ladies' stockings featured in a case involving differential pricing. A manufacturer sold the same quality of stocking in two different packs; one was trade-marked and price-maintained, the other was free of price-fixing. The decision reached in this case was that the lower price ruling in the free market was the market price, and that the price fixed for the price-maintained goods should be reduced or r.p.m. should be abandoned.

The supply of price-maintained photographic film to a mail-order firm, which also operated department stores and other sales outlets, came under examination by the authorities. The manufacturers of two branded films defended their refusal to supply this firm on the ground that they limited their sales to specialised photographic shops. By supplying film to the mail-order house, the producers feared they would lose their specialist retail outlets. It was shown, however, that the film in question was in fact sold, with the permission of the manufacturers, by some shops which were not specialised photographic shops. Since the mail-order firm operated photographic departments in its department stores in order to meet the requirements of their customers for a complete range of services, there appeared to be no reason for the withholding of supplies. The Cartel Office called on the manufacturers to supply the film, which, after hesitation, they finally agreed to do.

Despite the elaborate procedure for notification of r.p.m. agreements, the competitive conditions existing in distribution in Germany today are such that r.p.m. is rapidly being eroded. The expansion of supplies of durable consumer goods partly through over-production and the saturation of the home market and partly through the impact of foreign competition led to the breakdown of r.p.m. for radios, television sets, washing machines and refrigerators. In the trade in these goods the department stores, mail-order houses and discount traders made an early impact. For other goods where for some time the line held (for example, chocolate and spirits), the development of the 'grey market' (direct sales by wholesalers to consumers) undermined price-fixing and made inevitable a general breakdown. Some chocolate manufacturers have tried to repair the breach in the r.p.m. dyke by setting their resale prices at a lower level and making fresh notifications to the Cartel Office. The adoption of this expedient by manufacturers of cameras led the Cartel Office to press for still lower prices since cameras were on sale below even the new list prices.

The problem which manufacturers face in a price-cutting situation is that once prices are reduced by a sufficient number of traders, it is difficult to justify the enforcement of the fixed price and virtually impossible to prosecute all the offending traders. (One detergent manufacturer has more than 1,000 cases pending.) Once prices are cut it can no longer be argued that the enforcement of r.p.m. is 'gapless', and hence this defence fails.

Further Reforms

In the face of the widespread disregard of r.p.m. amongst producers and wholesalers, it is little wonder that politicians are discussing the possibility of changes in the law. In August 1962 the Government submitted a 'Report on Amending the Act Against Restraints of Competition' to the Federal Parliament in which the total abolition of r.p.m., even for books, was advocated. Political caution and the nearness of elections led to a modification of this view, although the Economics Minister, Herr Schmucker, has declared his opposition to r.p.m. The Free Democrats, as supporters of economic liberalism, argue for the continuance of the manufacturers' right to fix resale prices for their goods. The Christian Democrats support the continuance of r.p.m. since they find substantial support amongst the smaller traders and shopkeepers who regard r.p.m. as a defence against competition from other retailers and direct-selling manufacturers. The Socialist Opposition favours the outright abolition of r.p.m.

Two draft Bills have been introduced. The Government Bill seeks to amend the law on r.p.m. in several respects. (1) In filing particulars with the cartel authorities, price-fixing enterprises will be required to identify those groups of trade purchasers they do not intend to supply. (2) Notifications of r.p.m. agreements will be placed on a public register. (3) A r.p.m. arrangement will be presumed invalid where it can be shown that substantial quantities of the price-maintained goods are sold below the prescribed resale price, or that the supplier, besides selling price-maintained branded goods, also sells the same goods unbranded at a substantially lower price.

The Social Democrat Bill would abolish r.p.m. outright, except for books.

Of the government proposals it may be said that they represent some advance. The open register for price-maintenance agreements would certainly lend itself to close examination and comment particularly by consumer-oriented groups. Potential trade purchasers would be able to establish the range of terms available from a manufacturer. Similarly the proposal that the existence of a series of actions to enforce a resale price would lead to the presumption that the agreement was invalid (because it would be evidence of extensive price-cutting) would inhibit prosecution of price-cutters and liberate pricing still further.

These progressive changes in the law would certainly bring Germany closer to complete abolition of r.p.m., and the Social

Democrats' proposals are probably a truer representation of the shape of the law to come.

Belgium

There is no specific ban on r.p.m. in Belgium. The Act on Protection Against the Abuse of Economic Power, 1960, does contain a prohibition of any abuse by one or more persons which 'shall prejudice the public interest by practices which distort or restrict the normal play of competition or which interfere with the economic freedom of producers, distributors or consumers or with the development of production or trade'. But as a Belgian observer comments, 'the Belgian anti-trust law is a most indulgent legislation and, until now, its enforcement has been rather soft'. Of the rulings which have been given it would be true to say that they accept the *status quo*, accepting, for example, the use of loss leaders as a common commercial practice at the opening of a new retail outlet, and on the other hand approving the imposition of r.p.m. as 'a commercial practice not illegal in itself' where it does not 'safeguard an unreasonable profit margin'.[11]

Associations of retailers in Belgium have recently been pressing the authorities to lay down regulations regarding minimum margins in particular trades. Through the machinery of the Prices Commission trade groups have persuaded the Minister of Economic Affairs to regulate the minimum margin for domestic electrical appliances. At the same time there is pressure from retailers for the advertising by manufacturers of fixed resale prices for appliances.

The apparently retrograde step taken in Belgium of moving back towards r.p.m. can be traced to the very large number of small shopkeepers who are seeking protection against the new supermarket traders who are establishing themselves in good town-centre sites. Small retailers, who until the beginning of the 1960s had been protected by the law which restricted the growth of multiple organisations (the 'loi de cadenas'), are now seeking protection through the associations they were permitted to form when that law was repealed. It is hard to believe that this reversion to guild organisation will persist for long as the economic integration of the Common Market proceeds.

[11] L.P.Suetens, 'Belgian Antitrust Law "In Action"', *Common Market Law Review*, December 1964.

Italy

Resale price maintenance is not permitted in Italy, save in respect of pharmaceutical products. The practice has not in recent years been the subject of policy proposals or discussions.

The European Economic Community

The principles underlying the Treaty of Rome were succinctly stated in the Spaak Report which was adopted by the Foreign Ministers of the Six in May 1956: 'The object of a European Common Market should be to create a vast area with a common political economy which will form a powerful productive unit and permit a steady expansion, an increase in stability, a more rapid rise in the standard of living, and the development of harmonious relations between the Member States'.

From the widening of the market in Europe the pioneers of the EEC expected that the consumers' standard of living would improve and that it would be possible for consumers to buy more easily and at lower prices. Such benefits to the consumer were expected to arise as industry began to operate on a European scale and the fruits of mass production and specialisation began to show themselves. But, as the report of the Heads of Delegations stated, there were barriers to progress to be anticipated in this process. 'In the economic conditions of the modern world, the widening of markets and of competition is not enough to ensure the most rational distribution of activity and the most favourable rate of expansion. The first fact which must be borne in mind is the size of firms or the existence of understandings between firms and consequent monopoly practices and facilities for market sharing. Rules of competition imposed on firms are, therefore, necessary to ensure that dual prices do not have the same effect as Customs duties, that dumping does not endanger sound economic production and that market sharing is not made a substitute for closed markets.'

The effect of the Common Market has been, as anticipated in the Spaak Report, to encourage the process of merger and concentration. This can be regarded as inevitable if firms are to be of a size and efficiency to survive in the new market area. Along with these changes have gone the conclusion of numerous trading and specialisation agreements and the setting up of joint subsidiaries. Such agreements may also be seen as enabling firms to fit themselves for survival in the new trading climate.

Apart from these changes in structure and relationships between firms, which might be broadly described as adaptive and aimed at rationalisation to achieve a more efficient scale of production, there have been agreements designed to frustrate the purpose of the Common Market. The removal of trade barriers has exposed well-entrenched national firms to the competition of outsiders whose efficiency and scale of operations threatened their home markets. In such situations there is the temptation to conclude agreements which effectively protect home markets or limit competition to third markets, and in such situations the promised benefits of economic integration for the consumer are lost.

The Treaty of Rome includes two Articles, 85 and 86, intended to ensure free competition within the Community. Article 85 bans agreements or concerted practices which prevent, restrict or distort competition; Article 86 deals with the action of firms which abuse their position of dominance in the market.

Arriving at a workable administrative scheme for the regulation of competition within the Community was a difficult task, because there were major differences in the national legislation of member-states. Thus, for example, while in Germany there was a requirement for the registration and notification of agreements, in France the burden of discovery and proof rested on the administration. Discussions concerning the implementation of Articles 85 and 86 dragged on for so long that it seemed that the Council of Ministers would have to depart from its unanimity rule and instead pass to qualified majority voting. However, when Regulation 17 dealing with the Rules of Competition was adopted, the process of conciliation had worked itself through and the final administrative scheme bears the signs of compromise, containing, as it does, distinct elements from both the French and the German systems. It may also be mentioned that even before the Regulation reached the Council of Ministersthere had been considerable re-drafting of the EEC Commission's proposals in the light of discussion in the Common Assembly of the Community.

The basic scheme of the Regulations concerning competition was for the registration with the Commission of agreements which were liable to infringe Article 85. Broadly speaking, agreements which were not registered were to be invalidated, and agreements which the Commission did not regard as infringing the Article were to be given a 'negative clearance', that is to say, they might remain in force, although the final question of legality was not determined thereby. The question of clearance is decided by the Commission with the approval of the Consultative Committee on Restrictive Trade Agreements and Domination of Markets.

Before examining in greater detail the relevance of Article 85 to the practice of r.p.m. in the Common Market, it is important to place the rules of competition within the context of wider economic policies. As has been emphasised when examining the position in the individual countries of the Community, it is possible for policy towards r.p.m. to be part of a more general active prices policy. Since the Community has only taken the first faltering steps towards the co-ordination of economic policies, there is as yet no common prices policy into which the policy towards r.p.m. could fit. Spokesmen of the Commission have been at pains to deny that the Commission is dirigist, inflationist and an advocate of planned economy. A statement made by a member of the Commission some years ago places the Regulations on Competition in a correct perspective: 'In a so strongly federal structure as our EEC, it is impossible to co-ordinate economic activity by intervention on the part of the central administration. A centrally administered economy is possible only where there is undisputed and very powerful authority able to decide on prices, wages, investments and the production plans of enterprises. The European institutions do not have authority of this type and it would be a hopeless business to try and work out general investment plans and price and wage regulations amongst six member states with often varying and at times even conflicting interests. It therefore remains *to leave economic co-ordination to the workings of the market economy* and to intervene only to the extent necessary to ensure that the machinery can in fact function'.

So far as the practice of r.p.m. is concerned, the vital article in the Treaty is Article 85. According to Article 85 (1) '. . . all agreements between firms, all decisions by associations of firms and all concerted practices likely to affect trade between Member States and which have the object or effect of preventing, restraining or distorting competition within the Common Market . . . shall be deemed to be inconsistent with the Common Market and shall be prohibited'. Certain prohibited agreements, decisions or practices are instanced in connection with the prohibition; amongst them is the indirect fixing of buying or selling prices. Thus the practice of r.p.m. would seem to be outlawed in intra-Community trade. There is, however, another clause, 85 (3), which exempts agreements, decisions, or practices which contribute towards improving the production or distribution of goods or promote technical or economic progress, 'while reserving to users a fair share in the profit which results'. This exemption is conditional upon there being no restriction other than that which is essential for the attainment of the object and that the firms are not given power thereby to eliminate competition in respect of a substantial portion of the products in question.

For an agreement to be granted a negative clearance by the Commission it is necessary that a notification of its existence be made to the Commission. The implementing regulation for Articles 85 and 86 (Regulation 17, Article 5) requires notification for all agreements, decisions and concerted practices with certain exceptions. These exceptions include agreements, etc., involving enterprises of only one member-state and not concerning imports or exports, and agreements between two enterprises the sole effect of which is 'to restrict the freedom of one party to the contract to fix prices or conditions of trading in the resale of goods which have been acquired from the other party to the contract'.

The insertion of the latter exemption from notification of resale price agreements between two enterprises was originally undertaken not because there was any doubt that such agreements would come within the scope of Article 85 but because they were thought to be so numerous that it would impose too great an administrative burden on the Commission. This would seem to have been a wise decision; the scrutiny of the agreements already notified to the Commission has proved a long task and the first block negative clearances are only now in prospect. The effect of the exemption from notification, however, was to add uncertainty to an already uncertain position. However, there can be few agreements regarding the fixing of resale prices which do not in fact also involve other restrictions, and hence many of the exclusive dealership agreements notified to the Commission will deal with r.p.m. too.

Some clarification of the position with regard to r.p.m. and associated matters is beginning to emerge. A crucial decision is that of the Commission in the Grundig–Consten case. Grundig manufacture radios, tape-recorders, dictating machines, and television sets in Germany. In 1957 Grundig entered into an agency contract with Consten, a French firm. Consten undertook to distribute only Grundig products and not to represent any other German firm. The French firm also undertook to maintain a repair service and a stock of spare parts for Grundig products and to advertise these goods. For their part Grundig undertook not to supply, directly or indirectly, their products in Consten's sales area except through Consten. Exports or re-exports by Grundig agents were similarly forbidden. Grundig registered a trade mark GINT (Grundig International) which was to be used only by Consten in France. Another French firm, UNEF, imported Grundig products into France and Consten took action against it for infringing the GINT trade mark. UNEF claimed that the sole-distributor contract infringed Article 85 and in due course the matter reached the Commission for decision.

UNEF imported its Grundig products directly from German traders and re-sold them on favourable terms to French dealers. UNEF claimed that it was able to act as a parallel importer to Consten because of the large differences in price ruling between Germany and France for these products. At the end of 1962 the catalogue price for a Grundig recorder was 44 per cent. higher in France than in Germany, after deduction of customs duties and taxes. The difference in actual prices (catalogue prices less discount) was at least 23 per cent. Although some narrowing in the price difference took place at the beginning of 1964, French prices were still 20 per cent. higher than prices in Germany. The difference was attributable to a higher wholesale margin in France.

The Commission concluded that the agreement was intended to restrict and distort competition within the Common Market for two reasons. First, by making Consten their sole agents and undertaking not to supply other dealers, directly or indirectly, Grundig were prevented from supplying any other French purchaser, and other dealers outside France were excluded from supplying the French market. Second, the use of the trade mark GINT was intended to protect the sole concessionaire against parallel imports. The Commission rejected the defence that the agreement was necessary to cover the costs of publicity and after-sales service on the ground that these constituted only a relatively small part of the total turnover, 1·9 per cent. and 1·18 per cent., respectively. The Commission placed particular stress on the need for competition at the distributive stage, especially between wholesalers selling the same brand. Consumers are offered a real choice when they can buy the same quality product at different prices. The Commission stated that experience in other countries of the Community led to the conclusion that ' . . . the possibility of parallel imports may be regarded as a useful corrective to the difference in price between the various countries which does not however to any extent impede a sales organisation in its activities'.

The Commission's decision has been contested and will go to the European Court of Justice.

The most interesting aspect of the case is that the Commission clearly intends to subject to severe scrutiny agreements being defended on the grounds of the indispensability of the territorial restrictions. In this case there were no arguments produced by the parties which the Commission found convincing. As a commentator has written recently: 'The Grundig–Consten decision is a warning signal to businessmen and anti-trust lawyers alike that the indispensable character of the restraint will be extremely difficult to prove to the satisfaction of the Commission'.[12] Apart from the question of the interpretation of 'indispensability', the case highlights the factual economic approach of the Commission. The figures concerning prices and margins and the differences between the French and German markets which are quoted more than once in the decision show the decisive importance attached to these considerations.[13]

The decision of the Grundig–Consten case exposes some of the problems facing the EEC. Within the countries of the Community there are very different basic approaches to the question of r.p.m., however much the reality of day-to-day application may be the same. Hence France bans the practice and Germany allows it for branded merchandise. Some manufacturers practising r.p.m. in a country where it is permitted will attempt to prevent, by inserting restrictions in their exclusive agency agreements with foreign distributors, the re-import of their goods and their sale below the fixed resale price in the country of origin.

[12] L.J. de Keyser, 'Territorial Restrictions and Export Prohibitions under the United States and Common Market Antitrust Laws', *Common Market Law Review*, December 1964.

[13] S.P.Ladas, 'Exclusive Distribution Agreements and the Common Market Antitrust Law', *Antitrust Bulletin*, 9 (1964).

The Commission has given negative clearance to exclusive distribution agreements where there is no prohibition on the distributor to export and no requirement that the manufacturer bar imports by other dealers within the exclusive distributor's territory.

Two other cases which have originated in France, one involving parallel imports of whisky, the other calculating machines, are awaiting decision by the Commission.

The Commission, like so many authorities dealing with restrictive practices, seeks to have agreements infringing the regulations on competition revised to bring them into conformity with the law. Many restrictive agreements will therefore be purged of their offending clauses without publicity being given to the cases.

Concluding Comment

In the countries of the Common Market one can see the compromise being reached between, on the one hand, the demand for the lowest possible distribution costs and, on the other hand, security for retailers. In Belgium the political importance of the small shopkeeper is such as to have swung the decision towards security and away from abolition of r.p.m. In Holland the desire, at the political level, for innovation in distribution (and hence the reduction of distribution costs) has resulted in a decision for abolition in the face of considerable opposition. It is difficult, however, to contain all the European experience within this simplified explanatory framework. The German case seems to show that in that country the stream of competition cannot be kept within the constraints sanctioned by law and that it breaks its banks from time to time. The phenomenon of the 'grey' market which undermined the formal system of r.p.m. has played its part in forcing the current re-thinking of the German law. In France there have been important social changes as well as political initiatives which help to account for the current state of the law.

In addition to the considerations noted above, it must not be lost sight of that the abolition of r.p.m. is now generally held to contribute to price stability. It is regarded as a desirable reform within the context of a general wages, incomes and prices policy.

Wherever one looks in the EEC, it is clear that r.p.m. is breaking down. The development of the Common Market is contributing to this breakdown by opening up new sources of supply to traders who might otherwise have been denied supplies which they could price for resale as they wished. To take the laws at their face value and to contrast the ways in which the different countries approach the practice would be to neglect the fact that the everyday interpretation of the law by business men, administrators and the courts is rapidly reducing the importance and effectiveness of the practice of r.p.m.: it is becoming little more than a trifling annoyance in the business of supplying the needs of a mass market. Before very long r.p.m. will no longer have any real importance in marketing within the Common Market.[14]

[14] Since this chapter was written, the following official assessment of the effect on prices of the elimination of r.p.m. in several trades in Germany has been published. 'In those fields in which price competition in trade had been able to develop fully since the abrogation of r.p.m., it was possible to determine in 1964 – after sufficiently long periods of time – that the index of retail prices had fallen by as much as 20 per cent. and more [. . . dass der Index der Einzelhandelpreise bis zu mehr als 20 v.H. sank.] By the reductions in prices in these fields substantial purchasing power would have been released for other purposes.' *Bericht des Bundeskartellamtes über seine Tätigkeit im Jahre 1964 sowie über Lage und Entwicklung auf seinem Aufgangengebiet* (Bonn, 1965), p. 12.

7

IRELAND

Catherine Brock

Introduction

Resale price maintenance and its control are both fairly recent developments in Ireland. In order to understand the evolution of r.p.m. a brief sketch must be given of Irish economic growth.[1]

Before the establishment of the Irish Free State in 1922, Ireland was part of the British market. Practically all manufactured goods were imported and the economy was at this time under-developed and mainly agricultural. For the first few years of independence Ireland remained, economically, part of the British market and it was only in the 1930s that specifically Irish economic development commenced. The impetus to this development was given by the imposition – for political as well as economic reasons – of high tariff barriers against a wide range of manufactured goods. As a result of the virtual exclusion of many British goods from the Irish market, new firms and industries came into existence in Ireland to supply the needs of the home market. The expansion of the industrial sector was extremely rapid in these years and by 1939 it was well established. During the years 1940 to 1945 the Irish economy suffered from considerable shortages, and in Ireland, as in England, this situation led to a great increase in government control of the economy. This control was often exerted through trade associations which gained both in power and in respectability. Thus, while there had been isolated instances of trade association activity, including some r.p.m., in the 1930s, such practices only became widespread in the post-war period.

As the emergency controls were relaxed, the extent of private

[1] This chapter is concerned with the 26 counties only, not with Northern Ireland.

In preparing this study I have been assisted by consultation of two unpublished theses. My thanks are due to the authors, K.A.Kennedy and C.Lysaght, for permission to refer to their theses presented for travelling studentship awards at University College, Dublin.

restrictions to trading in the economy became more obvious. There were in many trades severe restrictions to new entry, and trade associations controlled supply and distribution of goods in many ways including the encouragement and enforcement of r.p.m. Insufficient information is available to give any precise estimate of the extent of r.p.m. in Ireland during the late 1940s and early 1950s, but the practice was certainly widespread.

In addition to the organisation of r.p.m. internally by Irish suppliers, the continued dependence of Ireland on various imported manufactured goods, mainly from Britain, has led to some externally enforced r.p.m. A good example here is the book trade where the terms of the British Net Book Agreement have been and still are fairly strictly observed, although isolated instances of discounts to special buyers and sales not authorised by the Agreement do occur. In gramophone records also, control is exerted by British manufacturers who at present enforce individual r.p.m.

Growing public concern about the extent of all restrictive business practices led in 1952 to the introduction into the Dáil of the Restrictive Trade Practices Bill which became law in 1953. This was the first statutory control of restrictive trade practices to be introduced in Ireland and it is still the basis for control.[2] Before 1953, collective r.p.m. and its enforcement came nominally under the sway of the common law but, as in Britain, the common law was completely ineffective in controlling such practices. An unsuccessful case was fought under common law a few months before the introduction of the bill.[3] This concerned a cut-price trader whose supplies had been stopped, and it revealed clearly the weaknesses of the common law in protecting the interests of such traders.

Legislation Affecting Resale Price Maintenance

The full title of the 1953 Act is 'An Act concerning restrictive trade practices in regard to the supply and distribution of goods'. The Act is thus not concerned with monopoly nor with all restrictive practices of manufacturers and traders, but only with those affecting supply and distribution. Resale price maintenance does, however, fall clearly within the scope of the Act.

[2] In the 1930s there was some legislation for the regulation of prices in those trades protected by tariffs, but control was not of restrictive practices specifically.

[3] *Connolly v. R.G.D.A.T.A.*, 87 I.L.T.R.

The general aim of the Act is to promote fair competition in the supply and distribution of goods. There is no general prohibition of all or of any classes of restrictive practices; instead, a flexible system for the scrutiny of each individual case is set up. The body responsible for this scrutiny is the Fair Trade Commission, which consists of a chairman and not less than two and not more than four other permanent members. The members, who are all appointed by the Minister for Industry and Commerce, may not be members of either House of the Oireachtas, nor may they investigate any industry with which they have connections. So far the Commission has had three members including generally a senior civil servant, a senior counsel and an accountant or economist. In seeking to encourage and sustain fair competition, the Fair Trade Commission have two different methods of procedure and they may choose whichever seems more suitable.[4] First, the Commission may make 'fair trading rules' governing the supply and distribution of any goods. Such rules may be made at the request of the relevant trade association or on the initiative of the Commission. The Commission must publish their intention to make fair trading rules and must consider any representations made to them about the form of the proposed rules. It is the statutory duty of the Commission to keep all fair trading rules under review and to report to the Minister for Industry and Commerce if the rules are not being observed. Although the rules do not have the force of law, the provision for report to the Minister, who would then, if necessary, make an order giving legal force to the rule, ensures that the fair trading rules are not disregarded lightly.

The second procedure open to the Commission is to make an 'enquiry' into the conditions of supply and distribution of any goods. Such an enquiry may be instigated by the Minister or may be undertaken on the initiative of the Commission – often as a result of complaints received. While there is provision for secret hearings, as much as possible of the investigation is held in public. Notice of intention to hold such an enquiry is published to enable all interested parties to make submissions. A report of the enquiry is made to the Minister and is laid before the Oireachtas and published. Included in the statutory regulations for these reports is the provision that the Commission shall report on the existence and extent of r.p.m. If the Commission conclude that, in the trade under investigation,

[4] Following the convention of the Act, 'Commission' is treated here as a plural noun.

restrictive practices exist which are against the public interest, they are required to recommend to the Minister accordingly and to indicate the form of the order by which the Minister may give effect to their recommendation. If the Minister decides not to make an order on the recommendation of the Commission, he is bound to lay before each House of the Oireachtas a statement giving the reasons for his decision. An order, when approved by both Houses of the Oireachtas, is law and anyone contravening the provisions of an order is guilty of an offence. The penalties laid down in the Act are a fine not exceeding £500 and/or imprisonment not exceeding 12 months on summary conviction, or a fine not exceeding £5,000 and penal servitude not exceeding 10 years on conviction on indictment.

The Commission also are required to keep all restrictive practices under general review and to report on any significant developments. They are bound by statute to produce an annual report on their activities and, as well as detailing fair trading rules, enquiries and orders, the annual report gives details of this more general review work of the Commission.[5]

In order to carry out their work, the Commission have the power to summon witnesses and question them on oath, and they may also demand the production of any documents relevant to an enquiry. Failure to attend or produce documents is met with the same penalties as if the Commission were a High Court.

For the guidance of the Commission there is set out in the Act a list of unfair trade practices.[6] This list is not exhaustive and is not intended to limit the Commission in the exercise of their functions. The list covers actions by individuals as well as by parties to agreements 'express or implied' which keep prices unnecessarily high, which restrict freedom of entry, which unjustly eliminate trade competitors and lead to substantial control over the supply of a product, and which impose 'unjust or unreasonable conditions in regard to the supply or distribution of goods'. The wording of this part of the Act is very general and no practices are defined by it as unfair *per se*. In each clause there is a qualifying word or phrase such as 'unjustly', 'unreasonably', 'without good reason'; so the Schedule is not of great practical use in limiting the decision-making of the Commission. For example, elimination of trade competitors may apparently be acceptable at times; it is only 'unjust' elimination of

[5] The Commission have a staff of about 16 civil servants.

[6] Restrictive Trade Practices Act, Second Schedule.

a competitor which is unfair, and it is the Commission's task to decide when the practice is unfair.

The 1953 Act has continued in force until the present, but in 1959 it was amended in certain minor respects as a result of experience gained during the first six years of the Commission's life. The amendments allow for an enquiry to be held into 'one or more aspects of the supply and distribution'[7] of a good whereas previously enquiries had to cover all aspects of supply and distribution. Also, there is now a special procedure for the review of the operation of existing orders which facilitates their amendment where necessary. Both these measures have increased the flexibility of action of the Commission. The Amending Act introduces a further provision which could conceivably widen the scope of the legislation although it has not yet done so. This allows for an enquiry – but only at the request of the Minister – into the refusal of employers or employees to use particular materials or particular methods for manufacturing or construction purposes. Apart from this provision, the Irish legislation on restrictive practices does not cover the actions of employees.

In addition to the Restrictive Practices Acts there is one further piece of legislation which may affect the prices charged for goods sold and which is thus relevant to any consideration of r.p.m.; this is the Prices Act of 1958. This Act replaced emergency legislation on price control which had existed during the period of the Second World War and it allows the government to retain some limited powers for the control of prices should this prove necessary. Section 13 of the Act refers to the 1953 Restrictive Trade Practices Act and allows the Minister for Industry and Commerce to set maximum prices for a good where a report of the Fair Trade Commission has shown the existence of restrictive practices by means of which excessive prices are or could be charged. This provision has not so far been used.

The preceding summary of the legislation relating to r.p.m. and other restrictive practices in Ireland makes it clear that no very strong official disapproval of such practices exists. There is no dogmatic prohibition of all restrictions on competition or of any particular types of restriction. Instead, the attitude is one of flexibility; each case is to be looked at on its own merits and to be judged in terms of 'the public interest' and 'the principles of social justice'[8]

[7] Restrictive Trade Practices (Amendment) Act 1959, s. 2(1) (*a*).
[8] Restrictive Trade Practices Act, Second Schedule (*k*).

without much *a priori* definition of how the public interest is best served except for the very general presumption that there should usually be some degree of competition. In this respect the 1953 Act is strikingly different from the British restrictive practices legislation which was to follow in 1956. It is closer, perhaps, to the British legislation of 1948, but, as will be seen below, it has proved more effective in the actual control of business behaviour than did that statute.

The restriction of the major legislation to supply and distribution excluding restrictive activities in manufacturing alone is understandable in the context of the Irish economy. With a market of under three million, industry will always be on a fairly small scale and there is likely to be greater need for co-operative activity (which could be called 'restrictive') in order to achieve productive efficiency than in a larger economy. Given this small size, also, Ireland will continue to be dependent on imports of manufactured goods. Both these features would suggest that the concentration of formal control should be on supply and distribution where restrictive practices of both traders and importing agents can be regulated. It should be noted, too, that this concentration does not limit unduly the work of the Fair Trade Commission, because any manufacturers' practices which affect, however marginally, supply and distribution may be investigated by the Commission. This is particularly true in relation to r.p.m., which has been fully investigated and regulated by the Commission.

The Work of the Fair Trade Commission since 1953[9]

With the type of case-by-case legislation outlined above, the full meaning and impact of control can only be assessed by a detailed study of the work of the controlling body. No excuse is offered, then, for a fairly full account of the work of the Fair Trade Commission since 1953. This account is particularly significant in the Irish context since much of the available information about r.p.m. in Ireland has come to light only as a result of the Commission's investigations, and since, moreover, the major part of the work of the Commission has been concerned with various aspects of r.p.m.

Between 1953 and December 1963, the latest date for which figures

[9] I am indebted to J.J.Walsh, member of the Fair Trade Commission from 1953 to 1960, for a useful discussion of the work of the Commission.

are available, the Fair Trade Commission made fair trading rules affecting the supply and distribution of twentytwo commodities. In three cases the fair trading rules were later revoked since their functions were taken over by orders made consequent on reports of enquiry by the Commission, and in one case the rules were revised. In all other cases the periodic statutory review of the operation of the rules satisfied the Commission that no further action was necessary. Of these rules, seven are concerned with limited aspects of supply, particularly entry into the wholesale and retail trades, while all the rest cover most aspects of supply and distribution including r.p.m.

In pursuance of the second formal method of regulation open to the Commission, nine enquiries had been conducted and reports published by the end of 1963. Seven of these were full enquiries and two were concerned with only some aspects of supply and distribution (as permitted by the 1959 amending legislation). Eight of the nine enquiries referred to r.p.m., and for some of them it formed the chief topic for investigation. Resale price maintenance was also mentioned in the ninth report, on carpets, although it was not significant in this trade. Following recommendations made in these reports, nine orders affecting most conditions of supply and distribution in eight different trades were made. All these, except the order on carpets, concerned r.p.m. among other restrictive practices. The Commission have also published reports on the operation of the first three orders and have kept under review, although without separately published reports, the operation of the other orders.

The more general review work of the Commission is less easy to specify in terms of exact numbers, but, from some of their annual reports, the scope of this work by the Commission can be appreciated. Thus we find that in 1954 investigation of complaints and other general reviews, excluding those concerned with fair trading rules and enquiries, covered thirtyfour different commodities. In 1959 the figure was twentynine commodities; in 1962, twentyseven; and in 1963, eighteen. While some of these investigations were concerned with activities restricting freedom of entry into wholesaling and retailing, many of them dealt with r.p.m. itself or with activities ancillary to r.p.m.

Detailed discussion of the Commission's work on r.p.m. falls into three parts. First, the making of fair trading rules is discussed; secondly, the reports of enquiries and resulting orders are considered;

and finally, the general work of the Commission and their reviews of the operation of rules and orders are examined.

Fair Trading Rules

A full list of the fair trading rules published to date is given at the end of this chapter (pp. 247–8, below). Commodities for which fair trading rules which affect r.p.m. have been made are as follows:

ropes, cordage and twines
nails and screws
tableware (earthenware and china)
cutlery, spoons and forks
electric light bulbs
sole leather
files and hacksaw blades
dry batteries
carpets, carpeting and floor rugs
household textiles (non-woollen)
coal
aluminium hollow-ware
perambulators, folding-cars and sun-cars
pedal bicycles, spare parts and accessories
razor blades
cigarettes

Many of these rules were made in the first few years of the Commission's life – for the first twelve commodities listed above rules had been made by the end of 1955 and the remainder by the end of 1958. There have been a few rules relating solely to entry to a trade since then, but this part of the Commission's work has slowed down considerably in recent years. The timing of the rules reflects the intention of the Commission to avoid the inequity which can arise from an industry-by-industry approach to control. The issuing of fair trading rules provides a method of control which can be used to cover a number of different cases within a short period; generally, appropriate rules can be formulated quite quickly for each individual case. Since there had been no previous regulation of business practices, this speedy method of resolving a number of outstanding problems was used widely. The provision in the Act for review of the operation of Rules ensures that any weaknesses in the rules can be amended without delay, though in practice this has proved necessary for only one of the commodities considered here (carpets). As a guiding principle for the early rules, the Commission considered first commodities 'in the production of which there are conditions of monopoly or quasi-monopoly'.[10] In their investigations the

[10] *First Annual Report*, p. 3.

Commission drew on the experience and knowledge of the Department of Industry and Commerce and also advertised in the press and on radio in order to ensure that they received any complaints from the public. The material thus accumulated enabled preliminary judgments to be made about the suitability of fair trading rules or an enquiry for any particular commodity. At this stage many complaints and problems could be solved satisfactorily without recourse to either of the formal methods. When it had been decided that fair trading rules should be made, the Commission once again publicised their intentions and received much co-operation and assistance from manufacturers and traders who gave factual information to the Commission and also commented on the draft rules. As the procedure became established, some trade associations took the initiative in proposing to the Commission that fair trading rules should be made for their trade and in suggesting the form of the proposed rules.

The actual form of the rules has proved fairly standard over the years. In some cases the wording is varied slightly to take account of circumstances peculiar to the trade in question and in a few cases some of the usual provisions are omitted. Of the commodities considered here, the only ones for which the rules show significant divergence from the standard pattern are those for carpets, household textiles, coal, perambulators, bicycles, razor blades and cigarettes. Before considering these exceptions, the standard rules will be explained.

A clear summary of the import of the fair trading rules was given by the Commission in their *First Annual Report*: 'These Rules provide for freedom of entry to trade, freedom to compete fairly, assurance of supplies on equal terms and conditions, and liberty to traders fairly to determine their own resale prices; and they specifically prohibit price maintenance arrangements by manufacturers, price fixing, regulation of margins, conditional or exclusive dealing, territorial division of markets, the maintenance or publication of white or black lists and agreements by or between manufacturers, importers or traders for the limitation of competition by various devices'.[11] The prohibition of r.p.m., both collective and individual, is made quite clear by the actual wording of the rules. These specify, among other things, that, in quoting terms to the trade, retail prices with discount shall not be used; they prohibit any threats or intimidation leading to the restriction of price competition among traders

[11] *Ibid.*, p. 3.

and prohibit all agreements and understandings (expressed and implied) which fix resale prices or suppress price competition in any way. Manufacturers are generally required as well to file with the Commission statements of their terms and conditions of sale and to inform the Commission of any variations in the terms. This provision has enabled the Commission to ensure that individual contracts do not contravene any of the rules.

In the majority of fair trading rules, then, the Commission have decided that fair trading conditions imply freedom to compete in as many ways as possible, including price, and a minimum of restriction by firms. But, as already stated, some of the rules concerned with r.p.m. do not follow this standard pattern and the exceptions may now be considered. The rules for the supply and distribution of coal can be disposed of briefly. The main tenor of these rules is, like that of the standard pattern, to encourage freedom of competition, and to this end r.p.m. is prohibited. But, in the special context of the Irish industry, where practically all supplies are imported, the Irish suppliers are permitted to act collectively through their trade association in order to negotiate favourable prices from any foreign state organisation supplying coal. This rule is of no general significance and relates only to the particular conditions of supply of this commodity.

The other exceptions are, however, of wider significance and most of them – relating to carpets, household textiles, perambulators, bicycles and razor blades – can be considered together. It should be made clear, first, that the rules for carpets referred to here are a revised set of rules made in 1958, following various complaints, to replace the earlier rules of the standard pattern for this commodity. The revised rules had been in operation only from 1 April to 16 July 1958 when the Commission decided that conditions in the trade warranted a full enquiry. The main problem always related to conditions of supply rather than to pricing and r.p.m.; but, since the pattern of the carpet rules was followed in some respects in the other rules to be considered here, they are included in the discussion.

For all these five commodities r.p.m., both collective and individual, is prohibited, and concern is generally to promote free competition. The supplier of these goods may, however, on occasions use the sanction of withholding supplies in order to prevent excessive price competition characterised by the resale of the goods at a price at or below the supply price. In household textiles, supply may also be withheld if price competition takes the form of misleading the public as to quality, where, for example, goods labelled 'all linen' are sold cheaply when in fact they are of a linen and rayon mixture. In razor blades, supply may be withheld not only if resale prices are at or below cost but also if the price so little exceeds the purchase price 'as materially to injure the supplier's legitimate business interests'. (This clause may be intended to cover cases of loss to suppliers through the disruption of retail outlets which might follow severe price competition. There has, however, been no reference to it by the Commission in later years, so that an accurate interpretation of its meaning is difficult.)

For four of these five commodities (household textiles being the exception) the rules allow suppliers to quote a recommended or suggested retail price. While this must not be a minimum price, it may be a maximum price, and supplies may be withheld if sales are made at prices above the maximum. Finally, the sanction of withholding supplies may again be used for carpets, perambulators and bicycles if the buyer persists in 'dual pricing', that is, in advertising or displaying the supplier's suggested resale price in close conjunction with his own lower selling price.

The object of all these provisions is to temper the winds of competition in the particular circumstances of these trades where apparently excessive price competition was considered likely to develop. General comment on the rules is deferred until the enquiries and orders have been considered since similar provisions occur in some of them. Also, the Commission's reasons for this type of regulation are made clearer in the reports of enquiries than in the fair trading rules, for the latter are published without explanation by the Commission, except, on occasions, for a brief comment in their annual reports.

Before moving on to the reports, one set of fair trading rules remains to be considered: those relating to the supply and distribution of cigarettes. Unlike all the other fair trading rules, in this case the rules specifically permit individual r.p.m. by the manufacturer and the sanction of withholding supplies. Collective r.p.m. is, however, prohibited. This set of rules which is so very different from the rest is prefaced with a short note by the Commission giving their reasons for permitting individual r.p.m.; but the note is too brief to give much enlightenment. According to the Commission, r.p.m. is permitted only because of the special circumstances in this trade.

These circumstances apparently include the high proportion of the retail price which is represented by excise duty, the manufacturers' purchase of raw materials considerably in advance of production, and the very large number of retail outlets. The existence of price-cutting by retailers in the Dublin area is mentioned as well. We are, however, given no chain of reasoning to explain why these facts should lead to the support of individual r.p.m., and, considered in the context of the other fair trading rules, the Commission's decision in the case of cigarettes is hard to understand. Again, more general comment is deferred until all the work of the Commission has been considered.

It should be emphasised in relation to the six fair trading rules considered above that the sanction of withholding supplies is not to be used freely at the supplier's discretion. Whenever supplies are withheld, the Commission are to be informed, and they will permit the withholding of supplies only if they are satisfied that the conditions laid down in the relevant rules do prevail.

Reports of Enquiries and Statutory Orders

A list of the nine reports of enquiries so far published can be found in the List of Official Papers (pp. 247–8, below). As has already been stated, eight of these were concerned with r.p.m. among other things, and led to a total of nine orders regulating the trades in question.

The reports give a thorough survey of the trade in question generally including historical information and devoting considerable space to the submissions of the trade association as well as to those of other interested parties. Sometimes these submissions are printed in full and a complete list of witnesses is always given. The reports often reveal more information about the working of restrictive agreements than do similar reports and legal decisions under British legislation. In several of the reports, for example, private letters from trade associations threatening collective boycotts of price-cutters are printed in full. The Fair Trade Commission have been concerned to give as accurate a picture as they can of trade association activity, whether good or bad.

As pointed out in the analysis of the statute, the Commission are required to make recommendations in each report and to give the suggested form for an order if they consider that an order is necessary. This provision is analogous to that found in the British

Monopolies and Restrictive Practices Act of 1948, and has the advantage of forcing the analysis of each trade to a positive and precise conclusion. It also gives the Commission opportunity to present the arguments for the measure of control chosen, and for this reason the reports give more material for discussion than do the fair trading rules. Since the total number of reports is small, some account can usefully be given of each of them in turn, both as to the background and extent of r.p.m. in each trade and also as to the control measures proposed. This account will make clearer the pattern of r.p.m. and its regulation in Ireland than would merely a general review.

The first report to appear was on radio sets and accessories, including television sets. The structure of this industry derives exclusively from special features of the Irish economy and is thus worth specifying in detail. At the time of the report, 1954, production of television sets was very small and the main emphasis was therefore on radio sets. Production of these began in Ireland in 1946 when a tariff of 75 per cent. full and 50 per cent. preferential was imposed on imported fully assembled sets. The industry in 1954 consisted of seven firms and a number of distributors who imported sets or had them assembled in Ireland. Imports of assembled sets amounted to only 3 to 4 per cent. of total supply. Distribution was generally straight from manufacturer to retailer. The rather small and protected industry facilitated the development of strong restrictive controls on distribution. Manufacturers did not fix their resale prices collectively, but r.p.m. was strictly enforced collectively. This was done chiefly by means of an approved list of retailers and manufacturers controlled by the trade association which represented manufacturers, wholesalers and retailers. Firms which sold below the retail prices were struck off the approved list and could not thereafter obtain supplies. Similarly, a manufacturer who offered sets at a lower discount than the accepted one of 33⅓ per cent. would be struck off the list, and the 90 per cent. of all retailers who were on the list would no longer accept sets of that make nor would they repair them. The trade association employed agents to secure evidence of price-cutting and used fines as well as exclusion from the list in order to make traders obey the rules. The approved list had also been used to restrict the numbers of retailers in Ireland. Thus between 1941 and 1954 the numbers of retailers had increased only from 800 to 971 although trade in radio sets had increased ten-fold during the same period. The ostensible purpose of the list was to ensure good and efficient service in retailing radio sets; thus, stringent conditions about premises, repair equipment and repair staff were imposed. The requirement that a full-time, fully trained service mechanic had to be employed bore particularly severely on retailers in the country areas of Ireland where the population is small and scattered and where there would rarely be the volume of sales or service to justify such employment. As was pointed out by several of those excluded from the list, these conditions were only applied to new entrants and not to those already on the list.

In their conclusions and recommendations, the Commission stressed the protected nature of the Irish market and commented on the reduction in internal competition caused by the restrictions on entry and the maintenance of resale prices with a high discount. The form of order recommended and made law is similar to the form of some of the later fair trading rules already discussed. Compilation of an approved list and its use to discriminate among retailers or suppliers are prohibited and both individual and collective r.p.m. are banned. Suppliers are, however, permitted to suggest a retail price and they may recommend a maximum price. Supplies may be withheld from retailers who sell above the maximum price, those who sell at a price equal to or below their own purchase price, and those who sell at a price so little above the purchase price as 'materially to injure the supplier's legitimate business interests'. Any withholding of supplies must immediately be notified to the Commission, which must also be informed of the ordinary terms and conditions of sale of each supplier.

Fairly full detail has been given about the radio trade since this trade demonstrates many features common to distribution in Ireland. It was also one of the more fully controlled and restricted sectors of distribution. With this background, the other reports can be considered more briefly.

The next report, completed during the same year as was the first, was on building materials and components. In this sector there was a long history of control of distribution arrangements, including collective and individual r.p.m., dating back to the time when Ireland was part of the British market and when all such materials were imported. Now, however, most materials are manufactured at home; but control of distribution continued to be very extensive up to 1953 and included restriction of entry, use of approved lists and withholding of supplies if r.p.m. was not observed. Control was chiefly in the hands of sixteen trade associations, each concerned with one product only. There was considerable similarity in the rules of the various associations, whose membership interlocked – as one chairman put it to the Commission: 'We are all dovetailed into one another'.[12] In 1953 the passing of the Restrictive Trade Practices Act caused many of the associations to change their rules in anticipation of probable action by the Commission. These changes led to the development of some price competition in several building materials although many restrictions still existed.

The situation in the timber trade was particularly interesting and illustrates the close relation – which exists in other trades as well – between Irish and British markets. Most of the supplies of timber are still imported. There are three Irish associations of timber merchants and, although these associations had no formal links with external associations, practically all the Irish members were in fact members of the Timber Trade Federation of the United Kingdom and subscribers to the Softwood Sales Agreement. These agreements related to approved lists of dealers, and thus the British Federation in fact exerted control over distribution outlets in Ireland. The Irish associations then imposed r.p.m. as well, thus restricting competition in the distribution of timber almost completely. At the time of the Commission's enquiry the British Monopolies Commission had completed its investigation of the British timber trade and had found its arrangements to be against the public interest.[13] The Fair Trade Commission accepted the findings of their British counterpart, and the suggested order prohibits these practices.

This report as a whole contains rather more extended and general economic analysis of the arguments for and against r.p.m. than did the previous report. There is some discussion of figures provided by the Central Statistical Office showing wide variations in gross profit margins as a percentage of sales for builders' merchants. The Commission's general attitude is that restriction and rigidity in distribution are against the public interest and should be prohibited. Thus the order for this trade prohibits individual and collective r.p.m., discrimination, exclusive dealing, market-sharing arrangements, approved lists and so on. Again, a retail price may be suggested and also a maximum price for which the sanction of

[12] *Building Materials Report*, p. 24.
[13] Monopolies Commission, *Report on the Supply of Imported Timber* (1953).

withholding supply may be used. But in this case the sanction may not be used for sales below cost.

The report on motor vehicles and accessories which came next, in 1955, revealed a situation similar to that in the radio trade. Entry to the trade had been drastically restricted by the imposition of increasingly onerous conditions for acceptance as a member of the trade association through which practically all supplies of new cars and spare parts were channelled. These conditions applied only to new entrants, not to existing firms, and led to the situation where the number of garages remained unchanged between 1938 and 1953 despite an increase in the number of licensed vehicles from 59,000 to 142,000. Linked with this rigidity in distribution was a system of collective r.p.m. for new cars. Enforcement methods included fines ranging from two guineas to £50, apologies from erring traders printed in a trade journal, and attempts to stop supplies. Resale price maintenance was never very effective in this trade. About 90 per cent. of the sales of new cars involved the trade-in of a second-hand car and, despite some attempts by the association to fix allowances for second-hand cars, many traders used these allowances as a form of price-cutting. Such price-cutting was practically impossible to prove and to check, in contrast with the situation in radio sets where second-hand allowances were fixed and enforced fairly effectively.

The Commission considered fully the trade association's arguments for r.p.m. – its necessity in order to ensure good and efficient service and to protect the garage-owner's investment in equipment – but did not find these arguments altogether sound. The Commission obtained cost statistics from some members of the trade in order to test whether or not the official discounts, which were the same as those given in Britain at the time, were reasonable. The information, although rather incomplete, showed very wide variations in costs between different traders, and this substantiated the Commission's view that rigidity in distributive margins was against the public interest. The final conclusion of the Commission was that, given these conditions and especially in view of the fact that r.p.m. was even then only partially effective, both collective and individual r.p.m. should in future be prohibited. As well as giving effect to this recommendation, the order forbids any attempt to fix prices for services or for used cars. No approved lists or entry restrictions are permitted and supplies may only be withheld on three grounds: if a trader exceeds a maximum resale price fixed by the supplier, if a trader sells persistently at prices equal to or lower than his purchase price, and thirdly, if a trader *advertises* a new car for sale at a price less than the suggested list price. This last provision is already familiar from some of the fair trading rules, although it goes further than do the rules on 'dual pricing'. The Commission's arguments for these provisions are that, in an industry which experiences considerable fluctuations in trade and in which technical considerations set limits to the volume of trade which can be effectively handled by any trader at any one time, 'some safeguards should be provided against the emergence of extreme competition'.[14] The final provision about advertising, which appears to be inconsistent with the Commission's prohibition of r.p.m., is thought by the Commission to allow a framework within which individual bargaining between dealer and purchaser can take place and which at the same time prevents rapid shifts in sales which 'might readily result in a distortion of distribution and the inefficient use of technical service facilities'.[15] In practice this provision does not seem to be important.

The grocery trade was next considered by the Commission. This trade in Ireland is characterised by a large number of shops with low turnover and profits. The development of supermarket and self-service trading has lagged behind that of the British grocery trade. The trade falls into two very different sections: that serving the rural areas where the population is scattered and declining, and that serving the Dublin area. In the country areas the size of shops is very small – 65 per cent. of all country grocers, excluding general stores, have an annual turnover of less than £2,500. Population per shop in these areas is very low, for example 210 in Leitrim, 180 in Kerry. In Dublin, on the other hand, only 22·8 per cent. of grocers have a turnover of less than £2,500, and population per shop is 390.[16] Net profits as a percentage of sales of all grocers are moderate; in 1951 average net profits were not more than 3·48 per cent., and often less for various groups of grocers.[17]

There has always been considerable price competition in this trade particularly among wholesalers but also among retailers. At the time

[14] *Motor Vehicles Report*, p. 93.

[15] *Ibid*, p. 93.

[16] Figures from the 1951 Census of Distribution and Censuses of Population, *Grocery Report*, pp. 10–14.

[17] *Grocery Report*, p. 115.

of the Commission's enquiry, 1956, there was r.p.m. for some goods. The Retail Grocery, Dairy and Allied Trades' Association, the major trade association, estimated for the Commission that approximately 30 per cent. of grocers' goods were subject to official price control (butter, for example), 30 per cent. were proprietary goods with r.p.m., and the remaining 40 per cent. were 'free'. Margins on the 'free' goods were generally considerably lower than those on the price-maintained goods. For some goods only wholesale prices were maintained, not final retail prices. Resale price maintenance was encouraged by the major trade association in order to ensure reasonable profit margins for its members, but there was no restriction on entry. There had recently been some extension of price-cutting in the Dublin area, although price-cutting rarely occurred in rural areas. Enforcement measures including the withholding of supplies had not been very effective, and R.G.D.A.T.A. did not always obtain support from manufacturers in its attempts to get collective action in this field. The only products for which price-fixing had been thoroughly organised were salt and jam. The Commission found very little evidence of loss-leader selling: even the cut-price traders took at least a small margin on all items. Given the small profit margins earned generally, the Commission felt that the abolition of r.p.m. would not lead to any great extensions of price-cutting. They therefore recommended the abolition of collective and individual maintenance of wholesale and retail prices. To safeguard the position of the smaller grocer, however, the order stipulates that supplies may be withheld from any retailer who sells a branded product below the trade price charged to retailers. Where quantity discounts are applied, the trade price to be used is that for the minimum quantity supplied. This provision limits the extent to which economies of bulk buying can be passed on to the consumer and is clearly intended to protect the small grocer from extreme price competition. The first order passed for this trade was amended by a second order by the Minister; but the basic recommendations of the Commission were accepted and the amendments were relatively minor.

The report on chemists' goods which appeared in 1956 is noteworthy in that it is the only case so far where the order recommended by the Fair Trade Commission has not been accepted by the Minister, who took no action as a result of the report. In his statutory report to the Oireachtas giving his reasons for not implementing the suggested order, the Minister for Industry and Commerce stated that, in his judgment, the form of order proposed would not change conditions in the trade significantly.

In this trade there was almost complete acceptance of r.p.m., with fairly high margins to chemists. Collective enforcement did not occur, chiefly because there had been only a negligible amount of price-cutting. A considerable proportion of r.p.m. originated outside Ireland since many of the products were imported from Britain or produced locally under licence arrangements or by subsidiaries of British firms. As well as r.p.m. there was a policy to channel most trade through chemists by means of approved lists. It was, in fact, only in the few chemists' products retailed also through grocers that some price-cutting had appeared. The Commission gave some weight to the argument that the chemist's trade is of a 'unique character'[18] because of the professional skill necessary, the importance of the service provided, the wide variety of products stocked and the slow rate of turnover. Because of their acceptance, at least in part, of these arguments, the order proposed by the Commission was an attempt to compromise, to limit restrictions which were harmful while at the same time to permit the continuance of some practices which they felt were justified in the conditions of the trade. This compromise was inevitably less clear-cut and more complicated than a simple prohibition would have been and it is in this respect less satisfactory than a purely negative order. The provisions included prohibition of collective r.p.m., and prohibition of individual r.p.m. for infant foods and toilet preparations with the proviso that, at the Commission's discretion, individual r.p.m. might be permitted for some luxury toilet preparations. Individual r.p.m. was to be allowed for medical preparations. On the restriction of outlets, the Commission were prepared to let this continue as long as excessive enforcement measures were not used. As has already been stated, no action was taken as a result of this report. Nine years later, in 1963, a fair trading rule was made which prohibits collective action to restrict supply to chemist outlets; it was made after a survey by the Commission had shown 'an intensification of collective restrictions' in this trade.[19] But on r.p.m. no action has been taken.

The next report, on motor spirit and motor vehicle lubricating oil, was the last report to be completed before the 1959 amendment to the legislation came into force and is the last one so far to cover

[18] *Chemists' Goods Report*, p. 41.
[19] *Tenth Annual Report*, p. 14.

all conditions relating to supply and distribution. But, although all aspects of trading were covered, the main emphasis was on conditions relating to entry; price policy and r.p.m. were considered only briefly. In this trade a major part of pricing was decided externally and there was thus only a limited margin for internal variations in price policy. The Irish market was served by six firms of which three supplied over 80 per cent. of the market. There was no formal collective fixing of trade or retail prices either by these companies as a group, or by the companies in conjunction with any trade association. Of the three major companies, one acted as price leader, and informed the other firms in advance of any price changes, which always were followed quickly. While retail prices were recommended and generally followed, there was no enforcement of these prices. The Commission's recommendations relating to r.p.m. were that collective r.p.m. should be prohibited as a precautionary measure, but that no action be taken on individual r.p.m. The system of consultation by suppliers before price changes are made was considered by the Commission to be a restriction on competition and therefore has been prohibited.

The final two reports to be considered were concerned only with r.p.m. The trades covered were cookers and ranges and women's nylon stockings and hand knitting yarns. Both reports appeared in 1962.

The first of these reports can be disposed of quite briefly. It covered the supply of electric, bottled-gas and solid-fuel domestic cookers and ranges. For the first two types, recommended retail prices were observed by retailers though the suppliers used no enforcement measures. One of the two chief manufacturers of solid-fuel cookers had attempted to set up a distributive system allowing different discounts for different classes of wholesalers and retailers and strictly enforcing retail prices and discounts. This system had not received the co-operation of distributors and had never been really effective. It did, however, lead to some discrimination and inequity among different dealers. The Commission therefore banned individual r.p.m., and any enforcement measures for all three types of cookers.

The other report considers two commodities where, as in cookers, there had been some partial r.p.m. by individual firms but with no collective enforcement action. For nylon stockings the Commission proposed no action. Retail prices have only been maintained by one firm whose products are in competition with several other non-maintained brands, and it was felt that there was sufficient competition to prevent the firm from behaving in a way detrimental to the public interest.

The trade in hand knitting yarn was dominated by three firms, one of which had attempted to fix and to enforce resale prices. While enforcement had not been very successful it had, the Commission decided, 'the effect of unreasonably restricting competition'.[20] They therefore recommended an order banning individual r.p.m. in this trade.

This completes the description of the enquiries and reports of the Fair Trade Commission. In this section only the basic reports themselves have been considered; the measures for the review of both orders and fair trading rules raise some interesting general points and are therefore discussed together in the next section.

Other Activities of the Fair Trade Commission

One of the most valuable features of the Irish system for the regulation of restrictive practices is the provision for the review of industries already investigated and of those where previously no action has been deemed necessary. In part, this review is of a continuous nature. Any complaints about restrictive practices or about the operation of fair trading rules or orders are investigated by the Commission immediately, and even in the absence of complaints the Commission keep a general eye on trading sectors where restrictive practices are, or have been, significant. There is, additionally, a more formal periodic review of trades in which the Commission have introduced control. Thus in 1956 the Commission decided to review the operation of some of the early fair trading rules which had been in existence since 1953 or 1954. To this end advertisements were issued calling for submissions from interested parties for consideration by the Commission. This process has continued over the years for all fair trading rules and orders (for which the procedure was altered by the 1959 legislative amendment). In only a few cases (radios, motor cars and building materials) have separate reports of these reviews been published. Generally the conclusions of the reviews can be expressed quite briefly and are given in the annual reports of the Commission.

The review procedure, both general and formal, serves two useful

[20] *Women's Nylon Stockings and Hand Knitting Yarns Report*, p. 34.

functions: it enables the Commission to ensure that their regulations are observed, and it provides an opportunity for the Commission to test the practical effectiveness of their regulations and to check on the accuracy of their predictions about future developments in trading patterns.

The control measures imposed by the Commission do not appear to have been infringed to any great extent. The ready flow of complaints from all sections of business keeps the Commission aware of possible infringements to be investigated. There is some dissatisfaction among traders about the difficulty of proving to the Commission that an infringement of a rule or order has occurred, for, without a written contract of sale which is unusual for many retail goods, firm evidence of contravention is difficult to obtain. Thus there has been price-cutting in cigarettes in the Dublin area, but the Commission have not been convinced of the need for any action. While this difficulty of proof may permit limited contravention of rules or orders, any serious or persistent contravention would be controlled by the Commission. Where contraventions have occurred, they seem usually to have been in minor matters such as 'dual price' advertisements or as a result of ignorance, for example when a new manufacturer or importer starts in business. The intervention of the Commission in cases of infringements has generally been sufficient to ensure that the control measures are obeyed. In a few cases protracted negotiation has been required before a satisfactory solution has been reached, but it has not yet been necessary to bring a court action as a result of infringement of any of the Commission's regulations.

The reviews have generally confirmed the Commission's earlier decisions about regulation and in only a few cases have changes proved necessary. No changes have occurred in the regulations for the control of r.p.m. as a result of the review procedure despite a considerable volume of complaint from traders. The most interesting trades in this respect are the trades in radios, motor cars, building materials and groceries. In all of these, it will be remembered, r.p.m. was prohibited – by orders confirmed in 1956 for the first three and in 1958 for the last. As early as 1957, reports of reviews were published for radios and cars and some survey was made of building materials. The report of a thorough review of the building materials trade was published in 1959 and in the same year complaints in the grocery trade were investigated. In the three following years more grocery complaints were investigated, and the trades in radios, building materials and cars were further reviewed to determine whether or not any significant change had occurred since the previous review. This chronological summary reveals the thorough way in which the Commission have interpreted their review duties under the Act, and such frequent reviews reduce considerably the possibility of any persistent faults in the distributive system. The reviews have provided useful information about changes in the structure of trading resulting from control measures, and some account will therefore be given of developments in the four trades mentioned above.

The review of the operation of the radios order of 1955 was the first such review to be completed and published. The Commission's investigation was thorough, as were all such reviews: authorised officers of the Commission visited ninetyfive retailers, large and small, in town and country, in order to discuss the effect of the order. Submissions were also invited from all interested parties.

The effect of the prohibition of r.p.m. in this trade had varied considerably from area to area. Price competition had become quite intense in Dublin and some firms were explicitly cutting prices and providing no maintenance and repair services. In the Dublin county area, however, there was no evidence of price-cutting. For the rest of Ireland, price-cutting had occurred on a severe scale in some localities, often at the instigation of just a few traders, while in large areas the order had had no effect on price competition. One factor which had influenced the situation was the development of a considerable trade in television sets since the original enquiry. The Commission found that price competition was at its most severe in areas where the demand for television sets was highest. There were, according to the Commission, two explanations for this. First, because television sets were a novelty at this time and reception was very uncertain in many areas, dealers needed to use every inducement to encourage sales. Second, because television sets were new to Ireland, retailers rarely could provide adequate maintenance and repair services, and thus sold sets at cut prices leaving it to the manufacturers to provide the service. The Commission found that there already were signs of a lessening of the initial severity of price competition and that the structure of distribution had not changed significantly after prohibition of r.p.m. Services continued to be provided adequately by some traders (including new entrants), the only difficulty being in relation to television sets where, as explained above, there was a general scarcity of the necessary skills. The Commission commented on the fact that, despite the provision in the order for action where sales were made at cost or little above, little use had been made of this provision. This led the Commission to consider less seriously the complaints of suppliers about extreme price-cutting. The Commission's final conclusion was that no change was necessary in the order.

In the years following this report the Commission have continued to keep the trade under review. This review work included a survey in 1960 of prices in the Dublin area showing that extreme price-cutting was no longer occurring and that retailers' discounts had settled to a fairly steady 10 to 12½ per cent. off the manufacturers' list of recommended prices. The survey also disclosed that firms still demanding the full margin in order to cover service costs were able to continue trading on this basis. Later, in 1963, the Commission asked manufacturers to furnish a breakdown of sales figures for several years in order to discover the trend in sales to television rental firms. The figures revealed a striking increase in these sales which now account for about one-third of total home manufacture, and the Commission are keeping this form of trading under review.

The next trade for consideration is the motor car trade. Here a review of the operation of the order took place in 1958. It was contended by the trade association that the operation of the order had had a serious effect on employment, that prices of new cars were being cut to an alarming degree, and that new traders who were unable and unwilling to provide proper after-sales service had entered the trade. These traders were competing unfairly with traders who had invested in equipment and garage space and who employed qualified mechanics. The Commission admitted that competition had become more severe since the making of the order but pointed out that this was due as much to general economic conditions as to the order. At this time the Irish economy was in a rather depressed state with balance-of-payments problems. Imports were restricted severely, hire-purchase controls were tightened and consequently sales of new cars fell substantially. Moreover, the Suez crisis caused petrol to be rationed during 1956 and 1957 and this adversely affected the motor trade. In these circumstances the Commission felt that it had not been shown that the regulations about r.p.m. were harming the motor trade and they therefore remained in force. The Commission were, however, persuaded that there had been some unfair competition from traders with no service facilities and therefore very low overheads. In order to prevent this, they formulated a set of fair trading rules laying down minimum standards of entry to the motor trade in terms of equipment and employment of a fully qualified mechanic. These rules were promulgated in 1959; but in the course of their continued reviews the Commission found that some of the requirements were unrealistic and made the rules difficult to enforce. Accordingly, a revised set of rules was issued in 1962 and appeared, by 1963, to be working reasonably effectively. No changes have occurred in the r.p.m. control of the motor trade and, despite occasional complaints from year to year about excessive price-cutting, the prohibition of r.p.m. does not appear to have changed the structure of distribution to any great extent.

In building materials, as in motor cars, the order for the trade had come into operation at a time when the industry as a whole was moving out of a boom into slump conditions. This had exacerbated the development of severe price competition which occurred on the prohibition of r.p.m. Another factor affecting only the timber trade was the sharp fall in the price of imported softwood leading to considerable losses on stocks by several merchants. The prohibition of r.p.m. and of the earlier rigid control of distribution arrangements had led to considerable changes in the structure of trading. New traders who sold at very keen prices had entered the trade and there were now considerable sales made direct from manufacturers to the larger building contractors (including public authorities). Also, small country merchants and co-operative societies had formed groups for the purpose of bulk-buying from manufacturers. These changes had affected the cement trade particularly, but in all building materials there had been a considerable increase in the flexibility of trading arrangements. As a result, the old-established builders' providers had lost considerable trade and some had gone out of business.

The Commission examined census of distribution figures for this trade to check the assertions of low profits and excessive price-cutting. These figures showed no reduction in gross margins during the period of operation of the order. The wholesale price index number for building materials had also increased in line with the price index for total home production; and the increase was significantly in excess of the increase for materials in use in all industry including building. As a result of the investigations the Commission decided to take no action. They felt that the increase in price competition and in the flexibility of the distribution system had been beneficial and had led to increased economic efficiency. In the years following this report the building materials trade has been kept under review but, apart from informal investigation of individual complaints, no further action has been necessary.

In the groceries trade no report on the operation of the order has been published, though there have been several reviews by the Commission of conditions in this trade. Thus in 1959 the annual report stated that there had been complaints of serious disruption of trade and an abnormal number of business failures among small independent grocers following the abolition of r.p.m. The Commission carried out surveys of the trade in Dublin and found no evidence to support these contentions. They found, however, some changes in the structure of the trade, with certain traders extending the range of products offered and others offering lower prices instead of credit facilities. By 1960 price competition had become less severe and the trade appeared to have reached a position of stability following the initial effects of prohibition of r.p.m. Price competition in groceries continues to be keen, however, and the Commission have in more recent years investigated complaints of excessive price-cutting, but have not found it necessary to take any action.

As well as these reviews of trades in which control has already been imposed, the Fair Trade Commission continue to investigate and review trades so far uncontrolled. Here informal investigation of complaints has often caused changes in trade practices, thus obviating the need for the formal control by rules or orders. In the small Irish economy this informal control has proved very effective and co-operation from traders is generally good.

Comment

The development of r.p.m. and of policy measures for its control in Ireland have been moulded by the particular features of the Irish economy which were outlined at the beginning of this chapter. The detailed discussion of policy measures has made clear the effect which high tariffs, small numbers of manufacturers and continued high levels of imported manufactured goods have had on r.p.m. in the economy. The small size of markets and the diversity of patterns of supply and distribution preclude the operation of general, inflexible rules for the regulation of private enterprise, and the case-by-case approach introduced in 1953 seems to be the most effective way of regulating restrictive practices in this economy. The freedom of approach permitted to the Fair Trade Commission by the 1953 Act places a heavy onus on the body responsible for applying the control measures, and, with very few exceptions, the Commission have carried this burden successfully.

The Commission's decisions as regards r.p.m. have generally been to prohibit the excessive rigidity which may result from this practice. The Commission have, however, considered seriously the disruption to distribution and the hardship which may result from excessive price competition. This consideration has been expressed both in the detailed provisions of certain rules and orders and also in the general review work of the Commission. The task of trying to strike a balance between too little price competition and excessive price competition is a hard one involving many difficult judgments about future developments. It is not surprising, then, that some criticism of the Commission can be made. Three particular decisions call for comment.

The first is the report on chemists' goods which has already been considered in detail. The Commission's recommendations on r.p.m. in this trade were not accepted by the Minister and thus never became effective; but the rather complicated provisions for r.p.m. suggested would probably have proved difficult to enforce in practice. In this report the Commission seemed to apply too little critical analysis to the trade arguments for r.p.m. Thus the argument about the necessity of skilled service and advice for the sale of all chemists' goods was accepted almost without comment by the Commission – in striking contrast to the analysis which the same argument was to receive from the British Restrictive Practices Court a few years later.[21] Second, the fair trading rule allowing enforcement of individual r.p.m. in cigarettes is open to criticism not necessarily for the Commission's decision but for the way in which the decision was made. A rule so very different from most of those on r.p.m. warranted the publicity and full consideration of all arguments which result from an enquiry. The fair trading rule, while a very useful instrument of control, is best suited to non-controversial issues; the preface to the rules on cigarettes is quite inadequate as an explanation of the reasons for allowing r.p.m. in this case. Finally, some comment should be made on the provision which occurs in both fair trading rules and orders prohibiting 'dual pricing'. If price-cutting is to be allowed, it appears to be inconsistent to prohibit the

[21] *Re Chemists' Federation Agreement* (*No. 2*) (1958), L.R. 1 R.P. 75.

public announcement of such competition. If this provision is to work effectively, it can only do so by encouraging consumer ignorance, and such an aim is open to strong criticism. In fact, however, in a small economy such as the Irish there are enough channels through which information is efficiently disseminated to make the particular provision relatively ineffective.

Comment so far has been on action taken by the Commission. However, the detailed review of the Commission's work reveals a few surprising omissions from the list of commodities covered. Most noticeable are two important r.p.m. commodity groups – gramophone records and books. While these trades may have been considered by the Commission in its general review work, the commodities have not been mentioned in any annual reports nor in any other publications of the Commission. Both commodities provide good examples of external control of r.p.m. in Ireland since supplies are mainly imported. Resale price maintenance is quite strictly enforced with the threat of supplies being withheld if any price-cutting occurs. In other cases of external control the Commission have occasionally contacted external manufacturers directly and persuaded them to discontinue restrictions or, as was seen in the timber trade, have accepted the findings of a British control body. For books and records, however, despite the existence of a British Restrictive Practices Court decision on the Net Book Agreement,[22] neither course of action has been taken. The problem of extra-territorial jurisdiction is a familiar one from American experience and is not easy to solve. In the Irish context a degree of external control of home distribution arrangements is likely to continue permanently; it might therefore be useful if some contact between the Fair Trade Commission and the Registrar of Restrictive Trade Agreements in Britain were considered.

Particular criticisms of the Commission are few, and in general the Commission have interpreted the new legislation effectively. Their work in the control of r.p.m. echoes the general Irish attitude to industrial organisation and its regulation, not seeking to impose a uniform structure on all trades and industries nor one simple solution to all problems, but by means of continued review, investigation and discussion to organise each trade or industry in the way most conducive to the sound development of the private sector of the economy.

[22] *Re Net Book Agreement, 1957* (1962), L.R. 3 R.P. 246.

IRELAND

List of Official Papers

LEGISLATION

Restrictive Trade Practices Act, 1953
Restrictive Trade Practices (Radios) Order, 1955
Restrictive Trade Practices (Building Materials) Order, 1955
Restrictive Trade Practices (Motor Cars) Order, 1956
Restrictive Trade Practices (Groceries) Order, 1956
Restrictive Trade Practices (Groceries) Order, 1956 (Amendment) Order 1958
Restrictive Trade Practices (Amendment) Act, 1959
Restrictive Trade Practices (Carpets) Order, 1960
Restrictive Trade Practices (Motor Spirit and Motor Vehicle Lubricating Oil) Order, 1961
Restrictive Trade Practices (Motor Spirit and Motor Vehicle Lubricating Oil) Order, 1961 (Amendment) Order, 1962
Restrictive Trade Practices (Cookers and Ranges) Order, 1962
Restrictive Trade Practices (Hand Knitting Yarns) Order, 1962

FAIR TRADING RULES

Serial No.

1. Ropes, Cordage and Twines
2. Nails and Screws
3. Tableware (Earthenware and China)
4. Cutlery, Spoons and Forks
5. Entry into the Retail Trade in Petrol (Revoked as from 25 July 1962)
6. Electric Light Bulbs
7. Sole Leather
8. Files and Hacksaw Blades
9. Dry Batteries
10. Carpets, Carpeting and Floor Rugs (Revoked as from 1 April 1958)

10a. Carpets, Carpeting and Floor Rugs (Revoked as from 16 July 1958)

11. Household Textiles (Non-Woollen)
12. Coal
13. Aluminium Hollow-ware
14. Perambulators, Folding-cars and Sun-cars
15. Pedal Bicycles, Spare Parts and Accessories

16. Entry into and Trade in the Co-operative Wholesale Distribution of Grocery Goods and Provisions (Revoked as from 21 June 1960)
17. Supply of Alcoholic and Non-alcoholic Apple Drinks, Juices and Concentrates to Wholesalers
18. Razor Blades
19. Cigarettes (Maintenance of Resale Prices by a Manufacturer)
20. Entry into and Trade in the Sale and/or Repair of Motor Vehicles (Revoked as from 1 March, 1962)
20a. Entry into and Trade in the Sale and/or Repair of Motor Vehicles
21. Entry into the Wholesale Trade in Domestic Electrical Goods
22. Collective Restrictions affecting the Supply and Distribution for Resale of Proprietary Household Remedies, Infant and Invalid Foods, Non-alcoholic Health Drinks and Toilet Preparations

REPORTS

Reports of Enquiries into the supply and distribution of
- Radio Sets and Accessories
- Motor Vehicles, Tyres, Other Spare Parts and Accessories
- Building Materials and Components
- Grocery Goods and Provisions
- Proprietary and Patent Medicines and Infant Foods and Medical and Toilet Preparations
- Carpets, Carpeting and Floor Rugs
- Motor Spirit and Motor Vehicle Lubricating Oil

Report of Enquiry into the operation of Resale Price Maintenance in the supply and distribution of Cookers and Ranges

Report of Enquiry into the operation of Resale Price Maintenance in the supply and distribution of Women's Nylon Stockings and Hand Knitting Yarns

Report on the operation of the Restrictive Trade Practices (Radios) Order, 1955

Report on the operation of the Restrictive Trade Practices (Motor Cars) Order, 1956

Report on the operation of the Restrictive Trade Practices (Building Materials) Order, 1955

Fair Trade Commission Annual Reports, 1953–63.

8

UNITED KINGDOM

B. S. Yamey

Origins and Development of Resale Price Maintenance

During the second half of the nineteenth century two major changes were taking place in the distribution of consumer goods: goods were being packed, branded and advertised on a rapidly increasing scale; and large-scale retailing firms were becoming established and expanding greatly. The two changes were largely independent of each other; together they gave rise to extensive and unprecedented price competition in retailing. The department stores and multiple shop organisations almost invariably traded on the basis of low selling prices. The availability of packaged branded goods facilitated price competition by making consumers readily aware of price differences among shops.

In these circumstances many of the traditional retailers – typically owner-operators of small shops, each specialising in one of the traditional divisions of retail trade – experienced reductions in their profits and turnover, and most of them were fearful of the future. Articles appeared in the trade press foretelling the end of the small shopkeeper and the triumph of the new giant firms. The threatened ranks of retailers turned to organisation to protect their interests and to fend off hostile developments. The advocacy of resale price maintenance as a device to raise margins and to arrest the advance of price-cutting competitors became widespread and organised. Associations of traditional retailers pressed their claims on the manufacturers of branded goods and urged them to introduce r.p.m. or 'price protection' as it was often called. Manufacturers, both individually and in groups, were canvassed intensively. Organised attempts were made in several trades to influence manufacturers by diverting sales to brands which were price-maintained from brands which were not. The first successful price maintenance association was formed in 1896 (the Proprietary Articles Trade Association in the chemists' trade), and others followed, with varying degrees of success. The practice of r.p.m. sprouted and spread in several branches of the distribution of consumer goods.[1]

Resale price maintenance, historically, was not the indispensable complement to the successful introduction and marketing of branded goods by manufacturers: it was, rather, a consequence of conditions in retailing to which the success of branded goods had contributed. Had r.p.m. been prohibited in these early decades, the history of retailing in some trades would have been different; the practice of branding and advertising would have been unaffected.

The history of r.p.m. in the distribution of books was rather different from the standard pattern in that it started earlier and the development of large-scale retailing played only a small part in it. The standardisation of books grew in the first half of the nineteenth century, when, increasingly, publishers issued each of their new titles in uniform bindings at advertised prices. Retail price competition gave rise to r.p.m., which, however, was abandoned in 1852 in the face of an aroused public opinion. A half-century of retail price competition ensued, in the form of retailers offering discounts on all

[1] A detailed account and analysis of the origins of r.p.m. in chemists' goods, groceries and tobacco products is given in B.S.Yamey, 'The Origins of Resale Price Maintenance: A Study of Three Branches of Retail Trade', *Economic Journal*, 62 (1952), pp. 522–45. The broad outlines apply equally to other trades which I have studied.

An official committee of inquiry, which reported in 1920, presented a different explanation of the origins of r.p.m. According to this explanation, it would seem that the initiative in the introduction of r.p.m. was taken by manufacturers to preserve the retail outlets of their goods and to prevent selective price-cutting by large-scale retailers which was damaging to the interests of the manufacturers. A version of the second half of this explanation of the origins of r.p.m. was repeated by another committee in 1931, echoed once more in 1949, and quoted with apparent approval in 1955. [*Findings and Decisions of a Sub-Committee Appointed to Inquire into the Principle of Fixed Retail Prices*, Cmd 662 (1920), pp. 3–4; *Restraint of Trade: Report of Committee appointed by the Lord Chancellor and the President of the Board of Trade to consider certain retail practices* (1931), para. 16; *Report of the Committee on Resale Price Maintenance*, Cmd 7696 (1949), para. 147; Monopolies Commission, *Collective Discrimination . . .*, Cmd 9504 (1955), para. 171.] This alternative explanation, in terms of the manufacturers' reactions to the depredations caused by selective price-cutting (in one report said not to be 'legitimate competition') by unscrupulous retailers, finds no support in contemporary accounts and discussions in the formative decades of r.p.m. The report published in 1949 gives the correct explanation in para. 36: 'The early history of resale price maintenance in this country is one of distributors' attempts to organise themselves in such a way as to bring collective pressure on manufacturers of branded lines to fix and enforce retail prices for their goods'.

books off their published prices. The growing department stores joined in this price competition, though they did not initiate it. Eventually in the 1890s strong organised pressure among retailers for r.p.m. was built up, and by the turn of the century publishers collectively agreed to give favourable consideration to the practice in the form of the publication of books on 'net book' terms, although they themselves were 'content to let matters go on as they are'.[2] As in other trades, the introduction of maintained resale prices meant that consumers were required to pay higher retail prices for the items in question.[3]

By the early 1930s r.p.m. was well entrenched in the distribution of various classes of consumer goods. 'Among the trades in which it is most prevalent [in 1931] are books, newspapers and periodicals, stationery, drugs, photographic goods, gramophones and records, motors and cycles, tobacco and cigarettes, confectionery and groceries.'[4] According to an estimate ('rough calculation') made several years later, 'between 27 per cent. and 35 per cent. of all consumer

[2] Statement by the president of the Publishers' Association, *Publishers' Circular*, 25 March 1899, p. 320.

[3] An account of the development of r.p.m. in the book trade is given in B.S. Yamey, 'Price Maintenance of Books in Britain: The Historical Background', in *Studi in Onore di Marco Fanno* (1966).

As is well known, one of the very first books to be published subject to r.p.m. after the practice had generally been abandoned for books in 1852 was Marshall's *Principles of Economics* in 1890. 'For many years economists have wondered how it came about that Alfred Marshall, in general a strong opponent of restrictive practices, should have agreed to his [book] being used as a sort of spear-head in Messrs Macmillan's campaign in favour of a net price for books.' The recent publication by C.W.Guillebaud of some correspondence clears up the mystery: Marshall 'misunderstood the proposal' made to him by his publisher! The published letters make it clear that, after his book had been published, Marshall in fact disliked what he considered to be the effects of r.p.m. for books and had a poor opinion of the arguments advanced in favour of the practice in the 1890s. See C.W.Guillebaud, 'The Marshall-Macmillan Correspondence Over the Net Book System', *Economic Journal*, 75 (1965), pp. 518–38, *passim*. The new mystery is what Marshall thought the original proposal *was* about. Further problems are posed by Guillebaud's observation that 'Marshall reveals himself (for rather *special* reasons *of his own*) as decidedly critical of *certain* aspects of the net book system, especially when applied to works of scholarship' (p. 518, italics added). A reading of the published correspondence suggests that his criticisms were in the main those which have been 'standard' for many decades, and, moreover, does not reveal *any* aspect of the net book system of which Marshall declared himself to be in favour.

[4] *Restraint of Trade* . . . (1931), para. 12.

goods sold to the private domestic consumer in the United Kingdom in 1938 were sold at prices fixed or recommended by the producers'.[5] Not all recommended retail prices were enforced; indeed, not all supposedly fixed or minimum resale prices stipulated by manufacturers were effectively enforced, especially in the depressed years of the 1930s. Not all manufacturers were anxious to disturb price-cutting retailers who were selling their goods; and even those who were most determined to enforce their resale prices were not always able to block supplies to determined price-cutters. In some trades there was a running battle of wits, with the manufacturers contriving intricate methods of coding to trace the flows of supplies and with the price-cutters discovering the code-marks and mutilating or removing them.

The practice of r.p.m. was not limited to consumer goods. It flourished also in the distribution of such goods as office equipment, dental supplies and building materials, and in them was not restricted to branded lines alone.

The Inquiries of 1920 and 1931

Although the introduction and early expansion of r.p.m. attracted little hostile public attention, the practice did not escape official scrutiny, especially at times when there was much public concern about the level and movement of retail prices generally.

Shortly after the end of the First World War, a sub-committee of the Standing Committee on Trusts (established in terms of the Profiteering Act, 1919) was appointed 'to report the extent to which the principle of fixing a minimum retail price by manufacturers or associations prevails; what are its results, and whether the system is, in the interests of the public, desirable or otherwise'.[6] The Com-

[5] James B. Jefferys *et al.*, *The Distribution of Consumer Goods* (Cambridge, 1950), p. 112. See Table 7, pp. 46–8, for a detailed picture of the extent of r.p.m. and recommended resale prices.

For a detailed examination of the extent of r.p.m. in the grocery trade in the years immediately before the Second World War, see J.D.Kuipers, *Resale Price Maintenance in Great Britain* (Wageningen, 1950), *passim.* On p. 229 it is estimated that between 18·6 and 21·2 per cent. of aggregate grocery turnover was subject to r.p.m., but the author notes that 'a proportion of such transactions took place under conditions less rigid than those associated with resale price maintenance policy in other trades, such as to allow the distributor some latitude in the matter of his selling price for the lines in question'.

[6] *Findings and Decisions of a Committee . . .*, Cmd 662 (1920). The report consists of only five large pages, so that detailed page references are unnecessary.

mittee found in favour of the fixing of retail prices. 'We believe it to be the case that where, as at the present time, the demand [for proprietary articles] is in excess of the supply, the method of fixing retail prices has undoubtedly restrained or tended to restrain any undue inflation of prices, such as might easily have taken place if no such method had prevailed.' Where, on the other hand, 'the supply is in excess of the demand, the ordinary conditions of competition will usually necessitate the price of proprietary articles being adjusted so as to meet the conditions of the market'. 'In times of plenty it [r.p.m.] tends to ensure to all classes, including labour employed in manufacture and distribution, a fair rate of remuneration for the services respectively performed by them', and, moreover, prevents the speculating middleman from 'taking undue advantage of violent market fluctuations and allocating to himself what properly belongs either (*a*) to the consumer, or (*b*) to the trader or manufacturer'. The Committee could find no fault with so virtuous a practice. Its only qualms were about the level of trade prices (not retail prices) set by price-maintaining manufacturers who were monopolists or members of restrictive associations. It is not clear why this problem should have been thought relevant in the context of r.p.m., more particularly since the report does not explore the possible effect of r.p.m. on prices at the manufacturing stage.

One member of the Committee, John Hilton, was more critical of r.p.m. Unlike the Committee as a whole, he did not believe that competition among manufacturers would ensure that margins allowed the distributors would be no more than moderate. In his view, except where there was a complete monopoly, 'the policy of fixed prices will generally be accompanied by a practice of immoderate discounts [to distributors]'. Hilton also addressed himself to the practice in some trades of denying supplies to consumer co-operative societies, on the ground that their patronage dividends were a form of price-cutting. He said: 'This is a particular instance of one general result of the fixed retail price system, which is that retailers who by reason of their circumstances and methods are able to do with a trading margin lower than the average are precluded from doing so'. This central consideration was not mentioned in the main report.

The next general inquiry took place in 1930–1. A committee was set up jointly by the Lord Chancellor and the President of the Board of

Trade to consider r.p.m. as well as other trade practices involving the withholding of supplies of goods from particular retail traders. The first subject occupies the major part of the report published in 1931.[7] The inquiry took place against the background of declining prices and deepening economic difficulties. There was some concern over the alleged fact that retail prices were declining more slowly than wholesale prices; and the treatment of co-operative societies by some price-maintaining manufacturers and associations was also a source of some disquiet in government circles.[8]

The Committee concluded that 'no sufficient case has been made out for interfering with the right of the manufacturer to sell his goods upon conditions which permit him to name the terms on which such goods shall be re-sold'. Although the Committee referred to disadvantages of the r.p.m. system (for example, its inability to allow for differences in the costs of different distributors),[9] and although 'we must not be taken as finding that the prices charged to the public and the margins allowed to the retailer are in all cases reasonable', the Committee was 'quite unable to say that the interests of the public would be better served by an alteration in the law which would prevent the fixing of prices of branded goods'.[10] It also saw no reasons for interfering with r.p.m. as it affected supplies to co-operative societies.[11] In one respect, however, the report was prophetic of future policy developments: 'The trade practices into which we have enquired impinge upon a much wider problem – the problem of monopolistic combinations and trusts – which is outside the scope of our reference. If, at some future time, the question of public policy in relation to this wider problem should

[7] *Restraint of Trade* . . . (1931).

[8] See footnote 11, below, for the treatment of co-operative societies by price-maintaining suppliers.

[9] *Ibid.*, paras 29–31.

[10] *Ibid.*, para. 59.

[11] *Ibid.*, para. 73(*e*).

The Committee noted (para. 66) that manufacturers who took the view that the payment of co-operative patronage dividends was a form of price-cutting 'in some cases refuse altogether to supply their price-maintained products to co-operative societies, or, as is more often the case, supply them on condition either that sales of the price-maintained goods are not to rank for dividend or that the amount to be paid as dividend is added to the price charged across the counter in the first instance'. It may be added that in some trades co-operative societies were in fact allowed to pay patronage dividends without let or hindrance, whilst their private trade competitors were not allowed to follow similar practices.

be examined, the possibility of support being given by the price maintenance system and boycotts to monopolistic combinations and trusts ought, we think, not to be overlooked'.[12] Indeed, after the Second World War the first policy decisions affecting r.p.m. were made in situations of this type.

The Committee's approval of r.p.m. rested heavily on the idea that retail price competition (except when it was effected through the granting of patronage dividends or rebates) took the form of selective price-cutting of leading lines, and that this was harmful to all concerned: 'We have been impressed by the volume and force of the testimony as to the harmful effects of price cutting upon the manufacturers and distributors of advertised branded goods and ultimately, as was contended, upon the public'.[13] The report does not include any example of the evidence of the alleged deleterious effects of price-cutting on the interests of manufacturers and the consuming public. A contemporary critic of the report noted this lacuna, and pointed out that the Committee seemed to contradict its own major finding when it reported that 'manufacturers are not always anxious to enforce without exceptions the retail prices which they prescribe for their products'.[14] In the absence of more detailed documentation, the report's discussion of price-cutting and its effects is unsatisfactory. The Committee clearly disliked price-cutting, an attitude which was widespread in the 1930s. For example, a judge referred to a price-maintenance organisation as one 'formed with the object, among others, of stopping price-cutting by either wholesale dealers or retailers – an object not only unobjectionable in law but also desirable'.[15]

The New Post-War Attitude towards Monopoly and Restriction

Before the Second World War public opinion was largely tolerant of organised restraints on competition. The growth of restrictive agreements in industry and trade provoked no official action to deal with them. After the war, however, the mood changed. Already in its statement on employment policy the wartime Coalition Government indicated the lines along which monopoly policy was to move.

[12] *Ibid.*, para. 73(*f*).
[13] *Ibid.*, para. 48; also paras 14–16.
[14] Arnold Plant, review of the Report, *Economic Journal*, 42 (1932), pp. 142–6.
[15] Goddard, J., in *Imperial Tobacco Co. Ltd v. Parslay*, 52 T.L.R. 61 (K.B.).

As part of its general policy of maintaining full employment after the war, and of keeping prices and wages 'reasonably stable' in order to achieve this, the Government announced that it would 'seek power to inform themselves of the extent and effect of restrictive agreements, and of the activities of combines; and to take appropriate action to check practices which may bring advantages to sectional producing interests but work to the detriment of the country as a whole'. However, the approach was to be in the spirit of the statement that 'such agreements or combines do not necessarily operate against the public interest; but the power to do so is there'.[16] In due course the pursuit of this policy was to give rise to the establishment of the Monopolies Commission in 1948, and the setting up of the Restrictive Practices Court in 1956. Resale price maintenance was not only one of the restrictive practices which became subject to scrutiny in the course of major inquiries into particular industries; it was also singled out for special investigation and, eventually, in 1956 and 1964, for special legislation.

A few *ad hoc* official inquiries encountered r.p.m. shortly after the war. A committee which investigated milk distribution reported in 1948. It stressed that the 'first necessity' in the retail field was 'to ensure that the pre-war system by which the [statutory] Milk Marketing Boards enforced through their contracts a scale of minimum retail prices does not return. This substituted for competition in price, competition in services, so adding, in our view substantially, to the costs of distribution'. It recognised that 'to abolish minimum prices will of course remove the protection distributors obtained from the system. But we see no justification for protecting those whose costs are high against their more efficient competitors or for maintaining a system which permits an excessive number of retailers to persist'.[17] The pre-war system of r.p.m. has not been re-introduced by the statutory milk marketing monopoly. Maximum retail prices have been prescribed officially. There seems to have been little price-cutting below these maxima.

Resale price maintenance again came under fire in the report of a committee which investigated the distribution of building materials and reported in 1948. The Committee described and analysed a

[16] *Employment Policy*, Cmd 6527 (1944), para. 54.

[17] *Report of the Committee on Milk Distribution*, Cmd 7414 (1948), paras 163–5. For a critical discussion of pre-war r.p.m., see P.T.Bauer, 'The Fixing of Retail Milk Prices', *Manchester School*, 10 (1939), pp. 134–43.

number of inter-acting restrictive agreements which pervaded virtually the whole field. Associations of manufacturers and merchants supported one another against outsiders; and r.p.m. played an important part in the arrangements. The Committee concluded that these arrangements were against the national interest. 'In particular, they have tended to lead to a higher level of prices than would have obtained in their absence; to an inflation of gross and net distributive margins; to the consumer being deprived of improvements, actual or potential, in the efficiency of distribution; to an over-elaboration of services provided in the field of distribution and therefore to a waste of manpower and other resources; to there being too many merchants; . . .'[18] The Committee recommended as a long-term measure that the restrictive practices should as far as possible be eliminated, but left this to be dealt with in terms of the promised general legislation to deal with monopolies and restrictive practices. As a short-term and temporary solution, it recommended that the government should control distributors' margins on building materials and components.[19]

The Report of 1949 and the White Paper of 1951

In the meantime the President of the Board of Trade had set in motion, in 1947, a general inquiry into r.p.m. The Lloyd Jacob Committee reported in 1949; its report marks a major step in the development of policy, even though its recommendations were not in the event carried out immediately or fully.

The Committee began its report by observing that circumstances had changed radically since the period when the 1931 Committee made its report. Unemployment had dwindled, and both main political parties were 'publicly committed to a permanent policy of full employment'. Whereas in 1931 manufacturers were struggling with a deficiency of effective demand, in 1949 this was not the problem, but, instead, 'it must be a major objective of economic policy to secure the fullest use and best distribution of the men, materials and industrial capacity of the country'. The Committee had been specifically instructed 'to pay particular attention to present circumstances and to the need for efficiency and economy in production

[18] *The Distribution of Building Materials and Components: Report of the Committee of Enquiry appointed by the Minister of Works* (1948), para. 137.

[19] *Ibid.*, Recommendations, pp. 51–2.

and distribution'. A further change in circumstances was the 'recognition of the need to investigate monopolies and restrictive practices', marked by the passage in 1948 of the Monopolies Act.[20] Resale price maintenance, like other restrictive business arrangements, was now on the defensive; the accent was to be on efficiency in the use of resources, and restraints on competition were to be scrutinised with this end in view.

Save in one important respect – the case for preventing selective price-cutting of the loss-leader variety – the report is generally unfavourable to r.p.m. 'We are satisfied', the Committee concluded, 'that the elimination of price competition over the greater part of the distributive trades is not consistent with the need for the maximum efficiency and economy in production and distribution so necessary in the present economic circumstances.'[21] On distribution costs and margins, the report includes a forceful paragraph: 'In the first place, for many classes of branded product no "ordinary" or "average" distributor exists.[22] Secondly, there is nothing in the nature of the distributive trades which makes it likely that in conditions of free competition the cost of running a shop should always approximate to an average figure. Thirdly, so far as it is a fact that costs do not in practice vary between traders who conduct roughly similar types of business, this may be attributed to the fact that in the absence of price competition "excess" profits are consumed in competition on service. Fourthly, distributive margins on price maintained goods are principally determined not by reference to costs, but by a process of bargaining and by conformity to the demands of organised distributors'.[23] The Committee was particularly critical of r.p.m. where, as in many trades, it was administered and enforced by associations of manufacturers and distributors. The collective withholding of supplies and other aspects of collective enforcement involved 'the use of extra-legal sanctions which may deprive a trader of his livelihood', which in its view was not justified.[24] Collective administration led to an extension and intensification of

[20] *Report of the Committee on Resale Price Maintenance*, Cmd 7696 (1949), paras 8–13.

[21] *Ibid.*, para. 160. The reference to the 'greater part of the distributive trades' is a pardonable exaggeration.

[22] This was inserted presumably to counter the argument that manufacturers set the margins according to the costs of the 'average' trader.

[23] *Report* . . . , para. 69.

[24] *Ibid.*, para. 142.

r.p.m. Moreover, though the Committee noted that not all collective associations were equally inflexible in enforcement or complex and comprehensive in their control of price competition, it said that 'all . . . have a common purpose and an inquiry of this nature must to some extent consider them together, for it is in their combined effects that the most conspicuous dangers appear'.[25]

The Committee also considered the inter-relations between r.p.m. and arrangements restricting competition among manufacturers, though its terms of reference did not permit a full exploration. Without pronouncing on the merits of such restrictive arrangements, the Committee concluded: 'We wish . . . to record the fact that the evidence which we have heard shows that the agreements governing the maintenance of retail or wholesale prices are not infrequently accompanied by agreements to restrict competition among manufacturers . . . We have failed to trace any agreement to restrict competition in the manufacture of branded goods which was not accompanied by an agreement to maintain resale prices'.[26]

But whilst the Committee were severely critical of r.p.m. as a restrictive arrangement, it nevertheless saw some good in it. 'Past experience appears to have shown manufacturers that if a nationally advertised brand is sold at varying prices in neighbouring shops the demand for it – as reflected in the distributors' orders to the manufacturer – substantially decreases.'[27] 'Price reductions . . . may not reflect any actual or expected saving in operating expenses but may be used as an aggressive weapon of competition.'[28] 'The disruption of trade in popular lines which is brought about by these [loss-leader] activities appears to bear particularly heavily upon the retailer who, by carrying in addition a wide range of relatively slow selling lines and in some trades by offering skilled technical advice to his customers, provides a service whose value may not be recognised until it has disappeared.' Furthermore, the Committee accepted the argument 'advanced by some manufacturers that the uncertainty brought about by prolonged price-cutting may make it difficult and sometimes impossible for them to maintain the quality and continuity of production of their branded goods'.[29] In view of the

[25] *Ibid.*, para. 152.
[26] *Ibid.*, para. 158.
[27] *Ibid.*, para. 42.
[28] *Ibid.*, para. 81.
[29] *Ibid.*, para. 84.

importance attached by the Committee to these considerations, it is surprising that the report includes no specific examples of the harmful effects of selective retail price-cutting and presents no more detailed analysis of the purportedly relevant situations.[30] The absence of documentation is as notable in this report of 1949 as in its predecessor of 1931: in neither case, therefore, is it possible for the reader to assess the relevance of the evidence submitted to the committee, or the validity of the deductions drawn from it. The question of relevance is especially important since it is possible that both in 1931 and in 1949 manufacturers may have been recalling instances where their own r.p.m. arrangements had broken down temporarily while those of their competitors had not, or situations before they had introduced r.p.m. while some of their competitors had done so – types of situation which are not relevant for assessing the effects of conditions in which no one has any r.p.m. whatever.

The Committee's acceptance of the argument that selective price-cutting injures the reputation and sales of well-known brands placed it in a dilemma. On the one hand, r.p.m. as practised was found to have serious disadvantages from the point of view of both consumers and the national economy. On the other, however, retail price competition could be deleterious to manufacturers, distributors and 'to the wider interests of the public'.[31] Its recommendations were designed to reduce the disadvantages of r.p.m. without disposing of the safeguard against selective price-cutting. It recommended

[30] The Report referred to the chocolate trade as one where between 1927 and 1932 'the instability caused by cut-price traders was having an adverse effect on the demand for the better-known proprietary chocolates . . .' (*Ibid.*, para. 107). An examination of contemporary accounts of events and opinions raises doubts about this important finding. See B.S.Yamey, *The Economics of Resale Price Maintenance* (1954), pp. 67–72.

The earlier report, *Restraint of Trade . . .* (1931), also referred specifically to the confectionery trade. It noted (para. 30) that shops in the middle of big cities could distribute confectionery on a substantially lower margin than the $33\frac{1}{3}$ per cent. of the retail price which manufacturers customarily allowed. In consequence, the general observance of the prescribed prices had 'in some of these areas tended to break down. The leading chocolate manufacturers informed us that in London they now make no attempt to enforce the prices which they ask retailers to charge for their products'. In this report there is no linking-up of this account of contemporary retail price competition with the discussion of the general proposition that price-cutting has adverse effects on the sale of branded goods – a proposition which, as has been shown above, occupies a prominent place in the report.

[31] *Report . . . on Resale Price Maintenance*, para. 85.

that the most effective form of r.p.m., the collective enforcement of the practice, should be brought to an end. But 'no action should be taken which would deprive an individual producer of the power to prescribe and enforce resale prices for goods bearing his brand'. However, the Committee wanted the best of both worlds; it did not want to see these powers used in ways which would protect high-cost distributors and impede new developments in distribution. Individual r.p.m., it said, should not be used to 'deprive the public of the benefits of improvements in distribution'; public policy required that there be 'provision for such price reductions as are justified by low-cost distribution or by a regular policy of distributing surplus profit to the customer'. The Committee recommended that the appropriate government departments, in consultation with the main trade organisations, should consider the best way of implementing this policy.[32]

The compromise solution adopted by the Committee was accepted by one member, Mr Henry Smith, as 'a marked advance from the present position'; but he added a strong Note of criticism. He thought it unwise to leave it to the individual manufacturer to draw the line between 'ordinary' retail price competition and the use of loss leaders. He believed, moreover, that the disadvantages of r.p.m. outweighed the disadvantages of retail price competition: 'The influence of resale price maintenance is continuous and actual, while the disturbing effect of price competition upon the sale of branded goods may only operate occasionally'. He concluded that in his view 'even the power left to the individual manufacturer by these proposals may prove to be more harmful to the public interest than would be the complete restoration of free price competition in the distributive trades'.[33]

Following on the publication of the report discussions took place between the Board of Trade and the various price-maintenance and other trade associations on the voluntary implementation of the Committee's recommendation; but they came to naught. The 'trade organisations concerned . . . have not been able to suggest any means of carrying out' the second part of the recommendation concerning individual r.p.m., that is, 'that the practice should be operated with greater flexibility, so as to allow price reductions justified

[32] *Ibid.*, paras 159–67, for the recommendations.

[33] *Ibid.*, pp. 34–5, for Note by Henry Smith.

by low costs'. 'In the Government's view the economic objections to resale price maintenance are no less great when the practice is carried on by individuals . . . than when it is done collectively. For this reason the continuance of the practice would be acceptable only if the manufacturers concerned were able and willing to introduce the required degree of flexibility in its operation. The Government has decided, therefore, that the necessary modification must be achieved by statute.'[34]

The 'necessary modification' was to take the form of the prohibition of both the collective and the individual enforcement of r.p.m. Individual manufacturers would, however, be allowed to prescribe maximum resale prices, provided it were made clear that the resale prices were maximum prices. The Government undertook to make sure that traders would be able to exercise their freedom to make price reductions. The main qualification in these drastic proposals was the promise that in drafting the legislation the Government 'will take account of any cases where it may be established that exceptional conditions would render the operation of the proposed provisions unworkable or undesirable in the public interest'.[35] This cryptic expression of intent was never elucidated. The Government also undertook to take steps, where this would prove to be necessary, to deal with 'abuses' in retail price competition, though it was 'not disposed to accept the contentions – which are based on past history and not on up-to-date experience – that the absence of resale price maintenance would inevitably lead to excesses and abuses of competition and that the price reductions which resulted would disturb the production and distribution of branded goods'. In its view fears of the possible emergence of 'unfair or excessive methods of price competition' 'cannot constitute a valid reason for allowing harmful restrictive practices to continue'.[36]

[34] *A Statement on Resale Price Maintenance*, Cmd 8274 (1951), paras 38–9.

[35] *Ibid.*, para. 43.

[36] *Ibid.*, paras 28 and 44.

The White Paper contains, as well as the statement of government intentions, a useful short review of the arguments for and against r.p.m. This review is, however, marred by some careless comments. Thus (para. 18) the argument that people would suspect the quality of branded goods if they were subject to retail price-cutting is certainly very weak, but is not disposed of by saying that 'few people would expect two bicycles of the same make . . . to differ in quality merely because they were sold at different prices in different shops', and by claiming that consumers could in any event 'always pay the higher price'. This reasoning can counter only the crudest version of this particular argument. Again, the statement

The White Paper policy was not translated into legislation; before the end of the year the Government had been voted out of office. When legislation was introduced in 1956 by its successor, it took a different form, which reverted more closely to the programme advocated in the Lloyd Jacob Committee's report of 1949, without, however, incorporating its novel, but almost certainly impracticable, feature of allowing low-cost traders to cut the prices of price-maintained goods.

The Reports of the Monopolies Commission, 1948–57

While the Government was conducting its negotiations with trade organisations and working out its policy towards r.p.m., the Monopolies and Restrictive Practices Commission, set up in 1948, was busy on its examination of restrictive practices and monopolies in a number of industries referred to it for investigation by the Board of Trade. Resale price maintenance was found in several of these industries, and was the subject of comment and recommendation by the Commission.

The work of the Commission up to 1956 related to two types of situation: first, where two or more firms which together accounted for a third or more of the goods in question were engaged in restrictions on competition; second, where one firm alone accounted for a third or more of the goods (the single-firm monopoly). (After 1956, the scope of its operations was limited, broadly, to the second.) In fact, most of the inquiries instituted in the years up to 1956 related to the first kind of situation, and it was in these that r.p.m. was encountered. The reports of this group of inquiries are discussed together in this section. It will be seen that the Monopolies Commission was strongly opposed to a collective policy of r.p.m. as well as to its collective enforcement, but that it was, in general, tolerant of individually conducted r.p.m., except in one important case, that of the tyre industry. Its findings and recommendations thus gave a further push in the direction of splitting into two halves the problem of policy towards r.p.m., involving prohibition of the collective enforcement of r.p.m., and non-interference with the individual enforcement of r.p.m.

In its very first report, on dental goods, the Commission had to

(para. 26) that the practice of r.p.m. was built up in the years of deflation and unemployment (presumably the 1930s) is without foundation.

assess r.p.m. as part of a complex set of restrictive arrangements. Each manufacturer in the association had to fix the resale prices of all his dental goods, and each dealer had to maintain them. There were also provisions for exclusive dealing arrangements. Enforcement was collective. The Commission found that 'in this industry the system of collectively enforced resale price maintenance has had the effect of buttressing the general level of prices; manufacturers themselves claim that part of the value of resale price maintenance to them lies in the fact that, if dealers compete in price, the result very soon is a request for increased discounts (that is, for a reduction in the manufacturer's price)'. The Commission's criticisms of the entire system of trade control embraced the collective policy of implementing and enforcing r.p.m. But it did not 'on balance see any objection in this particular trade to the individual manufacturer maintaining the end prices of his goods when he so chooses'. Individual price maintenance was in order provided it was not obligatory under an agreement, and provided each manufacturer was free to decide his own level of discounts to hospitals and other large buyers such as dentists' co-operatives.[37]

The next report also involved r.p.m., and again the goods concerned were not goods bought by ordinary consumers and included non-branded lines. In the supply of cast iron rainwater goods (building components) the principal manufacturers had a set of agreements which involved the stipulation of fixed common delivered prices to be observed by both manufacturers and merchants. Both the manufacturers and the merchants claimed 'that price maintenance by foundries [that is, common pricing] is impracticable without resale price maintenance supported by carefully drawn provisions for enforcement'. The Commission criticised the network of restrictive arrangements in that it prejudiced the interests of non-member firms, retarded the introduction of low-cost methods of production, and discouraged more economical methods of distribution and procurement. It is not clear, however, how far the Commission approved or disapproved specifically the r.p.m. ingredient in the complex of restrictions; its main recommendation was that those concerned should change their arrangements so as to meet the Commission's objections.[38]

[37] Monopolies Commission, *Report on the Supply of Dental Goods* (1950), paras 229–30.

[38] Monopolies Commission, *Report on the Supply of Cast Iron Rainwater Goods* (1951), paras 171, 220–1.

The maintenance of uniform resale prices on a collective basis with enforcement 'by means of fines and a Stop List' was a prominent feature of the restrictive arrangements in the electric lamp industry. In this inquiry the Commission concluded that the common price agreement among the associated manufacturers was not against the public interest, though certain additional safeguards of the public interest were necessary. It considered, however, that collective enforcement of resale prices was against the public interest and should be brought to an end. It did not disapprove of individually enforced r.p.m., but expressed the view that the manufacturers' association should change its rules so that individual members could permit any retailer (and not only co-operative societies as was the practice) to give 'any general price reduction . . . by means of a dividend or other method which does not single out products of particular manufacturers'. It is not clear whether the Commission's approval of individual r.p.m. depended on its qualified approval of the manufacturers' own horizontal price agreement. The only clue given in the report is that the Commission thought that the recommended changes in the operation of r.p.m. would help to keep the manufacturers' agreed prices and distribution system 'reasonable'.[39]

In a later report, on metal windows, the Commission once more gave its approval to the common pricing agreement of the manufacturers. Here r.p.m. was included in the standard agreement between each manufacturer and his merchants, though there was no collective agreement. The Commission thought that without r.p.m. it would have been difficult or impossible to operate the manufacturers' price agreement, since a merchant selling one manufacturer's product might be competing directly with another manufacturer selling direct to the customer. 'Since there is no collective enforcement against the merchants . . . , we see no objection to this practice in present circumstances.'[40]

In three other inquiries, on the other hand, the Commission disapproved of the manufacturers' price agreements, and this disapproval carried over to the associated systems of r.p.m. (though not to individually conducted r.p.m.). In the case of certain semi-manufactures of copper, most of the associations stipulated, 'in contracts

[39] Monopolies Commission, *Report on the Supply of Electric Lamps* (1951), paras 263 and 294.

[40] Monopolies Commission, *Report on the Supply of Standard Metal Windows and Doors* (1956), para. 243.

with middlemen, that on re-sale the prices must not be less than those quoted by association members'. This stipulation was designed 'to re-inforce the associations' minimum price policy'. The Commission decided that the regulation of resale prices was no more than an incident of the common minimum price system, and hence was against the public interest in that context.[41] In two later reports the Commission went further. In its report on hard fibre cordage the Commission condemned the horizontal price agreement. A collective agreement to maintain resale prices (though without their collective enforcement) supported the common price system, and was, in that respect therefore, held to be against the public interest. The Commission went on to consider the r.p.m. arrangements 'in themselves', and concluded that they would be against the public interest 'even if there is no common price system'. 'The objection to collective agreement to maintain resale prices is the rigidity which it promotes in distribution'; and it rejected the argument that r.p.m. was necessary because manufacturers sold to users in competition with dealers.[42] In its report on electrical machinery and plant the Commission disapproved of the horizontal price agreements in the various parts of the industry. Collective arrangements to maintain resale prices, without collective enforcement, were of little significance, but served to support the common price arrangements, and were therefore against the public interest. Again, the Commission reported that by themselves the resale price arrangements, and some other practices, would 'create an undesirable degree of rigidity in the industry and might be expected to operate against the public interest'.[43]

[41] Monopolies Commission, *Report on the Supply and Export of certain Semi-Manufactures of Copper and Copper-Based Alloys* (1955), paras 129 and 311.

[42] Monopolies Commission, *Report on the Supply of Hard Fibre Cordage* (1956), paras 291 and 294.

[43] Monopolies Commission, *Report on the Supply and Exports of Electrical and Allied Machinery and Plant* (1957), paras 817 and 832.

One other report should be mentioned, although there was no specific recommendation concerning r.p.m. In its report on the supply of electric wires and cables, the Commission noted that one of the manufacturers' associations insisted that 'its [common] prices, terms and conditions are observed on resale by all customers'. The Commission recommended that the system of common prices should be terminated. There is no reference to r.p.m. in its recommendations; in the context, however, it seems that the Commission disapproved of the common policy as to resale prices. Monopolies Commission, *Report on the Supply of Insulated Electric Wires and Cables* (1952), paras 123 and 282.

In the group of reports discussed so far, the Commission in every case disapproved of collective measures requiring dealers to observe maintained resale prices, generally disapproved of collective undertakings by manufacturers to practise r.p.m., but did not disapprove of individually adopted and enforced r.p.m.

In a further three reports of the Commission the industries in question had neither a concerted policy about r.p.m. nor arrangements for collective enforcement. In the insulin manufacturing industry each manufacturer included r.p.m. in its trade terms, but none had taken enforcement action. Moreover, these terms did not apply to the great bulk of insulin sold by retailers under the National Health Service. The Commission decided that the arrangements did not operate against the public interest.[44] In the case of rubber footwear, the Commission ascertained that 'there is plenty of non-price-maintained rubber footwear on the market, there is no collective arrangement for maintaining resale prices and no collective enforcement. These facts all tend to ensure that there is a considerable measure of freedom for resellers'. The Commission accordingly considered that the practice of r.p.m. by some members of the manufacturers' association was not against the public interest.[45] The third report concerned the supply of tea. Here the Commission discovered that more than half the tea supplied in the United Kingdom was subject to individual r.p.m., and that the degree of enforcement varied. It concluded that there were 'no special circumstances or practices in the tea trade' which would warrant an adverse assessment of r.p.m. in that trade.[46]

The remaining report which included some discussion of r.p.m. was that on the supply of tyres. In this industry all the manufacturers practised r.p.m., and all resale prices in the retail market were identical, though there was no manufacturers' agreement to ensure this. There was machinery for the collective enforcement of these resale prices. 'The arrangements result in a completely rigid price system in which it is impossible for a customer in the replacement

[44] Monopolies Commission, *Report on the Supply of Insulin* (1952), paras 64 and 95.

[45] Monopolies Commission, *Report on the Supply of Certain Rubber Footwear* (1956), paras 293–5.

[46] Monopolies Commission, *Report on the Supply of Tea* (1956), paras 147–51 and 171.

[that is, retail] market to buy any make of new tyre except at the fixed price, unless at some point the system breaks down.'[47] The Commission showed that the abolition of collective enforcement alone would not achieve the desired object of stimulating price competition among traders because each of the major manufacturers was strong enough to secure compliance with its resale price stipulation; the abolition of collective enforcement would merely 'put the smaller tyre manufacturers at a disadvantage'. It therefore concluded that 'the only way to ensure a reasonable degree of price competition in sales to the public is to abolish the maintenance of retail prices, whether it be individual or collective'. This would have the added advantage that it might foster competition among the manufacturers in respect of their own selling prices to the trade, in spite of the oligopolistic structure of the industry.[48] 'In these conditions it will be easier for larger traders and users to bargain with manufacturers individually, and manufacturers themselves will have less incentive to make their own prices or their suggested resale prices identical if they have no assurance of what price the trader will ultimately charge.'[49] The theme of the working back of price competition from distribution to production was to recur in later reports of the Commission dealing with certain single-firm monopolies.

A minority of the Commission (four of the nine members who signed the report) were not prepared to endorse the drastic solution of total abolition. The minority thought that price competition at the manufacturing stage would be sufficiently stimulated if price

[47] Monopolies Commission, *Report on the Supply and Export of Pneumatic Tyres* (1955), para. 490.

The Report explains in some detail the arrangements in the industry for detecting price-cutting by traders and for applying collective sanctions. These methods had attracted adverse public attention. Though the investigating staff of the trade association were forbidden to act as *agents provacateurs*, the report notes that it is 'hardly surprising that they are sometimes accused of doing so', since some concealment was inevitably involved in making test purchases. 'Various methods of approach are used [by the test purchasers] and the roles assumed by the investigators are varied to suit the particular case and to conform with local colour. For example, on one occasion the investigator was "sooted up" to look like a coal man; in others they have appeared as farmers, commercial travellers and van drivers.' The trade association 'maintain a special van for this purpose so that the investigator may present himself at the trader's premises as if he were an ordinary would-be purchaser'. *Ibid.*, paras 493 and 238.

[48] On the significance of the structure, *ibid.*, para. 480.

[49] *Ibid.*, para. 497.

discussions among the manufacturers were abandoned (as recommended by the Commission) without the elimination of r.p.m. Moreover, since both the 1931 and 1949 committees which investigated r.p.m. had 'approved of the right of every manufacturer of branded goods to fix the price at which his goods are sold to the public' – a statement which ignores the qualification as to flexibility, regarded as important by the second committee – they were not prepared to make an exception of the tyre trade unless they were satisfied that in the particular case r.p.m. was detrimental to the public. They were not satisfied that this was so. Indeed, in their view abolition of r.p.m. would have adverse effects: distribution would be disorganised, and would be prejudiced especially in the smaller towns and villages; r.p.m. facilitated the provision of various services which contributed to road safety;[50] and the public would not be protected against over-charging if r.p.m. were to go.[51]

The Government was not called upon to adjudicate between the rival recommendations of the majority and minority of the Commission. New legislation affecting r.p.m., among other matters, was already on the way to the statute book. No action was taken specifically on the more recent reports of the Commission.

The Prohibition of Collective Enforcement, 1956

The monopolies legislation of 1948 entrusted the Monopolies Commission with the task of investigating monopoly conditions in the particular industries referred to it; several of these individual-industry reports have been considered in the preceding section. Additionally, the Board of Trade was empowered to direct the Commission to inquire into 'the general effect on the public interest of [restrictive or monopolistic] practices of a specified class', without, that is, confining the inquiry to any designated industry or industries. Late in 1952 such a general reference was made to the Commission, to cover an inquiry into collective arrangements which came to be called 'collective discrimination'. The Commission reported in 1955.

[50] The minority also approved, on grounds of its contribution to safety on the roads, the operation in the industry of a collective system of registered dealers. This particular restriction was later declared to be contrary to the public interest by the Restrictive Practices Court, which rejected the defence that it was reasonably necessary to protect the public from injury by road accidents resulting from tyre failures: *Re Tyre Trade Register Agreement* (1963), L.R. 3 R.P. 404.

[51] *Report . . . on Tyres*, paras 557–69.

Subject to a dissent by three of the ten members who took part in the inquiry, the Commission held that in general all these practices were against the public interest, that they should be prohibited by law, but that there should be provision for individual exemptions.[52] The dissenting minority rejected this root-and-branch approach, advocated the registration of collective agreements and their treatment on a case-by-case basis.[53]

Two of the six categories of collective discrimination related to r.p.m.: agreements among manufacturers to practise r.p.m. for (some or all of) their goods; and the collective enforcement of resale price stipulations.[54] The Commission, in this inquiry, was not concerned with r.p.m. as such: 'We express no views about the advantages or disadvantages of resale price maintenance itself'.[55] It was concerned with them only to the extent that they were 'relevant to the consideration of the collective obligations' undertaken by suppliers.[56]

As to concerted policies of maintaining resale prices, the Commission concluded that they extended the practice of r.p.m. The restrictive effects of r.p.m. 'are intensified by agreements between manufacturers which oblige the parties to them to fix the resale prices of their goods; and they will usually have the further restrictive effect of compelling manufacturers who might otherwise prefer not to sell their goods in this way to fall into line with the majority'.[57] Such agreements therefore had the effect of further limiting the consumer's freedom of choice; and they protected distributors in a way which in general did not promote economies in distribution and was not 'justified as a means of preserving standards of service'. These agreements therefore were against the public interest. This conclusion applied in general also to r.p.m. arrangements which formed part of horizontal price agreements. The Commission observed,

[52] Monopolies Commission, *Collective Discrimination: A Report on Exclusive Dealing, Collective Boycotts, Aggregated Rebates and Other Discriminatory Trade Practices*, Cmd 9504 (1955), ch. 9.

[53] *Ibid.*, paras 255–69.

[54] *Ibid.*, ch. 5. Besides analysis and assessment, this chapter contains a useful description of current practices. An Appendix (pp. 91–6) conveniently brings together the terms of reference, conclusions and recommendations of the committees on r.p.m. which reported in 1920, 1931 and 1949.

[55] *Ibid.*, para. 237.

[56] *Ibid.*, para. 135.

[57] This effect would come about because membership of the relevant trade association usually would have other advantages.

however, that common price agreements might exceptionally be found to operate in the public interest, and that their effective operation 'might depend upon the fixing of resale prices'.[58]

The Commission was very critical of the second type of collective discrimination, that is, collective arrangements for the collective enforcement of r.p.m. What was claimed by its supporters to be the main advantage of collective enforcement over other methods – its greater efficacy – was viewed by the Commission as a major disadvantage. It had adverse economic effects in that r.p.m. was more rigidly enforced and thus it prevented price competition more effectively than other methods of enforcement.[59] Moreover, the Commission had serious objections to collective action for enforcing contractual terms or trading stipulations. Associations had excessive and dangerous power over individual traders; and private collective enforcement proceedings could not be subject to the safeguards of court proceedings.

The minority disagreed. Because collective enforcement was the most efficient form, therefore it should not in general be regarded as contrary to the public interest. 'It seems to us illogical that, if it is lawful for individual manufacturers to prescribe the prices at which their goods must be resold (and for the purpose of the present reference [= inquiry] the desirability of this is not in issue) they should be debarred from enforcing the maintenance of the prescribed prices in the most effective manner consistent with the general law.' Whereas the majority of the Commission seem to have welcomed the possibility that, without collective enforcement, there might be more price competition because of more frequent deliberate or unintended failures to enforce, the minority did 'not feel that the retailer who sells below (or above) the prescribed resale price is deserving of any sympathy'. The minority also did not share the majority's uneasiness on the score of the 'private courts' used in collective enforcement. The minority therefore recommended that collective enforcement should not be prohibited, as the majority recommended, but should have the same treatment which they (the minority) thought

[58] *Ibid.*, paras 146 and 147.

In holding that the extension or intensification of r.p.m. was undesirable because of its effects on the use of resources and on the choices open to consumers, the Commission would seem to have been expressing disapproval of r.p.m. as such, notwithstanding its disclaimers.

[59] *Ibid.*, paras 169–72, especially para. 172.

appropriate for the other kinds of collective discrimination, namely, registration, and detailed examination of individual agreements to ascertain whether they were operating against the public interest.[60]

The Restrictive Trade Practices Act of 1956 was the expression of the Government's new policy towards monopolies and restrictive practices, influenced by the general report of the Monopolies Commission.

The most dramatic change referred to r.p.m. Collective enforcement of resale price stipulations was made unlawful. The most effective method of enforcement, introduced by William Glyn-Jones in 1896, was prohibited sixty years later. The major recommendation of the Lloyd Jacob Committee in 1949 was implemented, in this respect going beyond the recommendation of the majority of the Monopolies Commission in its general report of 1955[61] and against the recommendation of the minority. Public disquiet about the proceedings of collective enforcement agencies contributed to the enactment of the prohibition. But the outlawing of collective enforcement was not intended as a blow against r.p.m. as such. There was no new view as to the desirability of the economic effects of r.p.m. This is clear from the fact that the statute extended the powers of the individual manufacturer in the enforcement of his resale prices.

Until 1956 the individual manufacturer could enlist the help of the courts in implementing a policy of r.p.m. in that an action lay against price-cutting distributors with whom he was in direct contractual relations. This remedy was not, however, available (save in respect of patented articles) against price-cutting distributors with whom there was no contractual link. It was a remedy, therefore, which was of no avail against price-cutting retailers who had procured supplies from wholesalers or other retailers – that is, 'non-signer' distributors. The Act of 1956 gives the manufacturer the right to enforce his resale price condition against any distributor who 'acquires the goods with notice of the condition' as if he had been a party to a contract of sale with the manufacturer. This was designed to strengthen the hands of the manufacturer in his individual efforts at enforcement, since collective measures were no longer permitted.

[60] *Ibid.*, paras 262–9.

[61] The majority's recommendation was to the effect that prohibition should be made subject to the possibility of the exemption of particular exceptional cases.

The other and major innovations of the new legislation did not affect r.p.m. directly. Henceforth all restrictive agreements between two or more parties were to be registered publicly; and each agreement was in due course to be adjudicated by a new court, the Restrictive Practices Court, according to criteria laid down in the statute. Such agreements had previously been within the province of the Monopolies Commission. Its scope was now narrowed, and was to cover, broadly, 'single-firm monopolies', defined (as before) as situations in which one firm supplied (or bought) a third or more of the goods in question. The new position regarding inquiries into, and assessments of, r.p.m. was as follows: An agreement among a group of firms to practise individually enforced r.p.m. was an agreement to be registered under the Act and to be judged by the new court; the practice of r.p.m. in single-firm monopoly situations was to be examined by the Monopolies Commission in respect of industries referred to it by the Board of Trade.[62] The relevant decisions by the Court and reports of the Commission under the new statutory dispensation will be reviewed below. It is convenient to defer this review until after some discussion of the extent of r.p.m. in the late 1950s and early 1960s.

The Extent of Resale Price Maintenance

There are various difficulties of measuring the extent of r.p.m. Effectiveness of enforcement varies from trade to trade; and the degree of enforcement tends to fluctuate with economic conditions in the trade. Statistical assessments are therefore necessarily imprecise; but when carefully made, they can give a reasonable indication of the scope of the practice.

In 1960 the author estimated, roughly, that about one-quarter of

[62] Strictly, the Commission might also be required to examine r.p.m. in a situation in which there is no single-firm monopoly. This is so because monopoly conditions (within the meaning of the original act, as amended in 1956) include situations in which two or more firms, which together (but not separately) supply a third or more of the market, individually and without concerted action 'so conduct their respective affairs as in any way to prevent or restrict competition' between themselves, their suppliers or their customers. On this see B.S.Yamey, 'The Investigation of Resale Price Maintenance under the Monopolies Legislation', *Public Law* (1958), esp. pp. 370–2. The Commission has not, since 1956, been asked to investigate any monopoly situation in which there was no single-firm monopolist.

personal consumer expenditure on goods and services (or about 30 per cent. of expenditure on goods alone) was directed to price-maintained articles, about four-fifths of which were in commodity groups in which all or nearly all brands were price-maintained.[63] Another estimate, made independently, confirmed that the percentage was in the neighbourhood of 25 per cent.[64] Early in 1964 the President of the Board of Trade suggested that the r.p.m. affected 38 per cent. of consumer expenditure on goods,[65] which tallies broadly with another estimate published in the *Economist*.[66] If these figures are taken at their face value, they suggest that there had been a considerable increase in the scope of r.p.m. from 1960 to 1964 (before the Resale Prices Act was passed in the latter year). This is unlikely. It is safer to conclude no more than that all the estimates disclosed the same picture of the extensive sway of r.p.m.

In 1960 the consumer commodity groups most affected by r.p.m. were cigarettes and tobacco, chocolates and confectionery, motor cars and cycles, radio and television sets, electrical goods, gramophones and records, books, magazines and newspapers, chemists' goods, photographic equipment and supplies, sports equipment, watches and clocks, tyres and motor accessories, and beer, wines and spirits. In addition, many types of goods not bought by the public but by business firms or professional people were price-maintained. Some idea of the range of these goods is given by the following selection of classes of goods for which claims for exemption from the 1964 prohibition (discussed below) have been registered:[67] cement, carbon paper, filing cabinets and other office equipment, compressed air motors, typewriters, microphones and stands, dental goods, mercury, flocs, powders and papers for chromatography, industrial gloves, steel ventilators for strongrooms, permanent magnets, surveying, hydrographic and navigational instruments, and engineers' revolution counters.

It seems unlikely that the prohibition of collective enforcement in

[63] B.S.Yamey, *Resale Price Maintenance*, Hobart Paper No. 1, Institute of Economic Affairs (1960; 4th ed., 1964), pp. 7–9.

[64] P.W.S.Andrews and Frank A.Friday, *Fair Trade* (1960), p. 8.

[65] House of Commons Debates, 691, col. 258 (10 March 1964).

[66] *Economist*, 29 February 1964.

[67] The Registrar of Restrictive Trading Agreements has issued four lists of registered goods, from which the selection has been made. It does not follow that r.p.m. is comprehensively practised in respect of each of the listed goods.

1956 materially affected the extent of effective r.p.m.[68] Indeed, after 1956 r.p.m. became more important in certain trades, notably in footwear and hardware. Manufacturers individually were still able to cut off direct supplies of their goods to price-cutting retailers; and price-cutting of goods obtained indirectly could be stopped by means of court injunctions.[69] There was some weakening of r.p.m. in certain commodity groups such as toiletries, which were increasingly being handled by supermarkets and other stores primarily engaged in the grocery trade; and it also weakened in the tyre trade. The ending of collective enforcement may have contributed to these developments. The eventual ending of r.p.m. in the grocery trade may also have owed something to this prohibition, though the erosion of the post-war r.p.m. in this trade had begun before 1956 and represented little more than a reversion to the situation before 1939 when the practice also had been relatively unimportant. More generally, the prohibition of collective enforcement, by placing the burden of action against price-cutters on the shoulders of each manufacturer, gave rise to some measure of flexibility in enforcement; and the costs of legal action against price-cutters encouraged greater boldness on the part of some of them. At the same time, the

[68] '. . . Experience of the operation of the 1956 Act showed very soon that the move from collective to individual enforcement made comparatively little difference to the economic effects of the resale price maintenance system, and that those who said that by the removal of collective enforcement it would wither away were shown not to have been justified in their expectations.' President of the Board of Trade, House of Commons Debates, 691, col. 260 (10 March 1964).

[69] The extent to which manufacturers used their powers under the 1956 Act is discussed in J.F.Pickering, *The Restrictive Trade Practices Act (1956) and Resale Price Maintenance*, Ph.D. thesis, University of London, 1964, ch. v, on which I have drawn. According to this author's inquiries, in over 200 instances court injunctions against, or undertakings from, price-cutting distributors were obtained by manufacturers. The principal commodity groups involved were: chemists' goods 70; hardware 40; electrical appliances 30; motor vehicles and accessories 30; food 10; paint, etc. 8; tobacco products 5; confectionery 3; clothing and drapery 3; wines and spirits 1; other 10 (*ibid.*, p. 92). The author formed the view that for every one instance of recourse to the courts there were about nine instances where the manufacturers in question were able to stop price-cutting by obtaining informal undertakings.

For the judicial interpretation of the provisions relating to the enforcement of r.p.m. in the 1956 Act, see J.Lever, *The Law of Restrictive Practices and Resale Price Maintenance* (1964), pp. 76–9; also V.Korah, Note in *The Solicitor*, 1 (1962), pp. 191–3. It may be noted that the giving of gifts by the retailer, and the operation of general rebate schemes, entitle the manufacturer to take action.

right of action through the courts against 'non-signer' retailers strengthened the hands of manufacturers in trades in which there had not been machinery for collective enforcement.

The Reports of the Monopolies Commission, 1957–64

Since the division, in 1956, of the field of monopolies and restrictive agreements between the Restrictive Practices Court and the Monopolies Commission, the latter has issued three reports in which r.p.m. is discussed: these deal primarily with single-firm monopoly conditions in the supply of cigarettes, electrical equipment for motor cars, and wallpaper.

In its report on cigarettes the Commission discussed at some length the prevailing practice of r.p.m. The Commission concluded that 'so long as competition between manufacturers continues on the present scale', r.p.m. did not in its view operate against the public interest. This conclusion was criticised effectively in a trenchant note of dissent by one of its members, Professor G.C.Allen.[70] Resale price maintenance was practised both by the dominant firm (with about three-fifths of the trade in 1959) as well as by the next biggest firm (with just under one-third of the market) and the remaining firms.

The Commission's favourable view of r.p.m. was the more unexpected in view of two points made by the Commission itself. First, it said that it 'may be argued' that, through r.p.m., the largest firm could, 'in effect, determine the method of retail trading for the great bulk of the supply, and that it may be considered a disadvantage from the standpoint of the public interest that opportunities for doing business on terms other than those at present imposed should be so narrowly limited, since this produces uniformity and rigidity in trading methods to the detriment of experiment and innovation in distribution'.[71] Second, the Commission repeated a point made in its earlier report on motor tyres that the 'manufacturers [of cigarettes], who with few exceptions do not at present compete with one another in price for products of the same class, might be more willing to vary their own selling prices if there were no longer any standard

[70] Monopolies Commission, *Report on the Supply of Cigarettes and Tobacco and of Cigarette and Tobacco Machinery* (1961), paras 561–8; Professor Allen's Note of Dissent, paras 612–8.

[71] The dissenting member commented: 'I should have thought this [latter] proposition was self-evident'.

retail prices'. Professor Allen reinforced this observation as follows: 'It is possible, indeed probable, that retailers, if they themselves were subject to keen price competition,would bring pressure on the manufacturers to reduce prices to the trade. In other words, price competition among retailers might work back to the manufacturers. If, as is possible, the latter's marketing efforts were then to be diverted from the forms of competition that raise selling costs (for example, competitive advertising) to such forms as lead to lower prices, then the public interest would be promoted'.

The Commission concluded, however, that these disadvantages or conceivable disadvantages of r.p.m. were more than off-set by its advantages in the circumstances of the trade. Four main issues are referred to in the report. (1) In the Commission's view distributors' margins were in general not 'excessive', and any reductions in retail price by traders 'on an economic basis' 'could only be small'. The dissenting member pointed out, in rebuttal, that average margins were irrelevant. What he found to be significant was 'the divergence of costs among the various distributors in circumstances in which cost differences cannot be reflected in the retail prices charged'. He also referred to the likelihood that more economic methods of buying by consumers (for example, quantity purchases) would develop with suitable price incentives. (2) The Commission indicated that the benefits to some consumers of the small price reductions it foresaw would be counterbalanced by the inconvenience caused to others as a result of the reduction in the number of sources of retail supply. The dissenting member, however, could not see how any reduction in the number of supply points occurring in response to the preferences of consumers could be a disadvantage, particularly when contrasted with the alternative where, through r.p.m., the manufacturers prevented any exercise of consumer choice between convenience of shopping and price reductions. (3) The Commission predicted that cigarettes would lend themselves readily to loss-leader selling by retailers. Though the loss-leader selling was itself not improper, the Commission believed that it would be concentrated on the most popular brands, and that this would benefit their manufacturers, the dominant firm in the first place and the second-biggest firm secondarily, 'at the expense of other manufacturers'. (This, incidentally, is an interesting and realistic contradiction of the more common claim that loss-leader selling is prejudicial to the sales of the brands selected for this treatment.) While the Commission thought it would be undesirable to weaken competition on the manufacturing side for the sake of intensifying competition on the distributive side of the trade, the dissenting member, who was not convinced that the dominant firm would gain more than its main competitor, did not agree that restrictive practices should be kept in being in order to preserve a fringe of smaller manufacturing firms which, *ex hypothesi*, would not be able to supply the market as effectively as the two leading firms. (4) The Commission considered the claim that, without r.p.m., distribution of cigarettes would be more risky, bad debts would increase, manufacturers would be less willing to sell on credit, and distributors themselves would have to finance their stocks (of high value because of the high rate of excise duty) possibly on less favourable terms than those available to the manufacturers. It was doubtful whether the withdrawal of r.p.m. would be 'a determining factor' in the granting of credit to the trade; but in so far as this might be so, the effects of stopping r.p.m. 'might be disadvantageous'. The dissenting member pointed out that the credit standing of the successful retailers would be improved, and only that of the marginal firms would deteriorate. The dangers foreseen by the manufacturers 'would be confined to the period of transition to the new distributive system'.

The Commission's report on the supply of electrical equipment for motor vehicles (for example, batteries, headlamps and sparking plugs) deals with a number of separate firms, each the monopolist (within the meaning of the legislation) in one or more of the main categories of equipment. The major prevailing pricing practice was that of charging substantially lower prices on quantity sales of components as initial equipment to vehicle manufacturers than on sales to distributors for re-sale to motorists and fleet operators. In respect of the latter 'replacements' market, constituting in the aggregate over a third of manufacturers' sales receipts, r.p.m. was virtually complete, and it was accorded careful analysis by the Commission.[72] It decided that r.p.m. was against the public interest and recommended that it be terminated. The Commission did not 'entirely discount the various disadvantages which would attend the termination' of r.p.m. in the industry. But in its view they were outweighed by the advantages of such a measure.

It was urged on the Commission that standards of service by

[72] Monopolies Commission, *Report on the Supply of Electrical Equipment for Mechanically Propelled Land Vehicles* (1963), paras 1020–7.

distributors would suffer in the absence of a guaranteed and adequate margin. Since items of servicing (such as fitting) were separately charged for, the Commission gave its attention to the ordinary distributive services, namely the ability to identify the component required and the availability and accessibility of the necessary stocks. It saw no reason why these services should be adversely affected to the extent that they were required by the motoring public. It thought that there would be a danger of 'occasional exploitation by overcharging' when a motorist needed a component urgently and had to deal with an unfamiliar trader; but it pointed out that this could happen with r.p.m. also, since in such a situation the customer would almost certainly require the fitting or repair services of the trader, for which the charges were not controlled. The Commission also considered the danger that, with free retail pricing, pressure on prices would reach the manufacturer 'who may begin to produce an inferior article in order to save cost'. It rejected this possibility in respect of the major manufacturers whose products were also sold to the vehicle manufacturers who engaged in continuous testing and scrutiny. However, 'there is always the possibility that other manufacturers may try to exploit the replacement market with cheap and inferior products'; but to the Commission 'this risk appears . . . to be much greater when there is a maintained price level for the genuine products'.

Against these possible disadvantages of the abolition of r.p.m., the Commission set strong advantages. It thought that the distributors' margins were comparatively high, and was not satisfied that they were no higher than necessary. Without r.p.m., the prices charged by distributors would be tested by competition, which would press not only on their profits '– which may not be unreasonable at present in relation to existing costs – but on the costs themselves'. While it did not expect immediate reductions in retail prices generally, except for those paid by strong bargainers such as large fleet owners, in the longer term 'we would expect it to lead to more efficient and cheaper distribution with some variety in price, depending partly upon the kind of service required by the customer'. As a secondary effect, 'we think that distributors who could no longer expect to retain for themselves as of right a fixed percentage of a fixed retail price would exert greater pressure than they do at present upon the manufacturers to cut their own selling prices as a means of keeping the retail prices at a competitive level'. It attached some importance to this effect because, in so far as it operated, it would reduce the wide differences between the manufacturers' prices for initial-equipment sales and their prices for sales in the replacement market, which 'price differentiation' the Commission concluded was against the public interest 'in principle'.

The report on monopoly conditions in the supply of wallpaper is the most recent of the Commission's reports in which r.p.m. figures prominently. In this industry the dominant firm supplied about four-fifths of the market in recent years. Distribution of wallpaper took two different forms. A large part of the firm's output was handled by 'pattern book merchants' who re-sold wallpaper to decorators in room-lots to meet the ultimate customer's particular requirements. Selected patterns were made available for this trade. Every two years each merchant made up his own pattern book from these patterns, and stood ready to supply the needs of decorators. These pattern book papers were subject to r.p.m. This part of the trade was large but declining, and sales of pattern book papers were also made by ordinary retailers of wallpaper. The other method of distribution was through retailers. Wallpapers intended for this part of the trade (that is, not through pattern book merchants) were not price-maintained. Generally, they were cheaper and of lower quality than the other category, but there was a good deal of overlapping in price and quality.

The Commission concluded that the practice of r.p.m. by the dominant firm was against the public interest. Its judgment was influenced considerably by the special circumstances of the industry: r.p.m. was operated by the monopoly supplier and no other supplier; it applied to only one-half of that firm's products 'with a view to supporting a particular method of trading'; and it influenced the prices of non-maintained products.[73]

The practice of r.p.m. was defended by the dominant firm on the grounds that, without it, the pattern book method of distribution would decline substantially, because in the absence of guaranteed margins and prices, merchants would not be so ready to incur the heavy expenses of making up the pattern books, to accept the risk of tying themselves to the selected patterns for a period of two years, and to maintain the necessary stocks. The Commission was not

[73] Monopolies Commission, *Report on the Supply of Wallpaper* (1964), paras 159–61 and 176–81.

convinced that the high margins in the trade were necessary for these purposes. Those customers who found it convenient to buy wallpapers through decorators would continue to be able to do so. The Commission doubted whether the public interest was best served by a practice intended to support and preserve the particular method of distribution through pattern book merchants and decorators. Moreover, the Commission concluded that the practice of r.p.m. served to preserve the dominant firm's 'near monopoly in the trade through decorators', and that this was undesirable in the absence of any positive advantage to the public interest. The Commission explained the working of this monopoly effect. Pattern book merchants had a strong inducement to stock and sell the price-maintained lines, all of which came from the dominant firm. This firm was the only one with a scale of production large enough to set aside certain patterns for this branch of the trade; the other manufacturers were unable to do so. 'The small manufacturer who wishes to sell some of his patterns through decorators can hardly maintain his [resale] prices if, as is the case, he also wishes to sell the same patterns through retail shops in competition with [those of the dominant firm's patterns] which are not price-maintained.'[74]

The Commission could find no real disadvantage to the public interest in the abandonment of r.p.m. There might be some 'reorganisation of the distributive trade, but we see no reason why this should have an adverse effect on the public interest'. The pressure of competition should 'have a wholesome effect upon efficiency and costs in the distributive trade, and ultimately upon the retail prices not only of pattern book ways [that is, wallpapers] but of all wallpaper'. The dominant firm announced its abandonment of r.p.m. shortly after the report was published.

Decisions of the Restrictive Practices Court

Individually administered and enforced r.p.m. does not involve registrable restrictive agreements in terms of the Restrictive Trade

[74] About one-fifth of the sales of retail shops consisted of the pattern book wallpapers of the dominant firm. Thus r.p.m. did not price these wallpapers out of the retail-shop market. Presumably the Commission formed the view that the fact of their being price-maintained reduced the sales – without eliminating them – of price-maintained lines in that part of the market where there also were competing non-price-maintained lines.

Practices Act of 1956. The Restrictive Practices Court, created under this legislation, therefore has had to consider r.p.m. only in such cases where a group of manufacturers included in their registrable restrictive agreements an obligation on members of the group to prescribe and maintain resale prices; and the Court has had to judge whether the acceptance of such obligations was or was not contrary to the public interest in the particular circumstances.

In two cases, primarily concerning horizontal price agreements in the cement and metal windows industries respectively, the Court held that the common pricing arrangements were not against the public interest because in each case the public as users of the goods enjoyed specific and substantial benefits from them. The obligation to maintain resale prices was held to be a reasonably necessary adjunct to, or an essential part of, the horizontal price agreement, and hence also escaped judicial condemnation.[75] In another case, however, concerning a horizontal price agreement and collective control of channels of distribution in the carpets industry, the Court saw no virtue in the main restrictions, and the ancillary restrictions affecting resale prices (at the wholesale stage) went down with them.[76]

Resale price maintenance occupied a more central part of an agreement among motor manufacturers affecting the channels of distribution. The Court was 'satisfied that the true intention of the parties to the distribution scheme agreement . . . was, and continues to be, that each signatory shall in fact maintain the retail prices of his vehicles by the imposition of conditions of sale'. However, the adverse assessment of the Court is of little interest for present purposes: it followed automatically because the signatories of the agreement made no attempt to justify the undertaking to prescribe and maintain resale prices. Other parts of the agreement which did not involve r.p.m. were also declared contrary to the public interest.[77]

[75] *Re Cement Makers' Federation Agreement* (1961), L.R. 2 R.P. 241, at 291–2; *Re Standard Metal Window Group's Agreement* (1962), L.R. 3 R.P. 198, at 243. In the former decision, the Court also said: 'This condition is likely to have the effect of keeping down the price to the ultimate purchaser in what will probably continue to be a sellers' market . . .'

[76] *Re Federation of British Carpet Manufacturers' Agreements* (1959), L.R. 1 R.P. 472; see 486, 530–1.

[77] *Re Motor Vehicle Distribution Scheme* (1960), L.R. 2 R.P. 173, at 220–1. The Court declared, further, that an amended agreement, in which each manufacturer agreed to 'publish the retail prices of his products', was also contrary to the public interest. *Ibid.*, 228–9.

The judgment of the Court on the Net Book Agreement is by far the most important for present purposes, because it was primarily concerned with r.p.m. as such. This was so because it was agreed by both parties to the proceedings that, in the absence of the main agreement among publishers to prescribe and maintain resale (that is, 'net') prices, r.p.m. in books itself would come to an end. The Court therefore had to judge the effects of the Net Book Agreement in the light of its assessment of the effects of the *de facto* termination of r.p.m.

The Court concluded that r.p.m. was in the public interest because its abrogation would produce the following unfavourable results: 'The number of stockholding booksellers in the country would be reduced. The stocks held by the surviving stockholding booksellers would be less extensive and less varied than at present. Although in rare cases retail purchasers might be able to buy particular titles more cheaply . . . , the retail price of most books would be higher. Fewer titles would be published, and those which failed to find a publisher in consequence of the altered conditions . . . would include works of probable literary or scholastic value.'[78]

The analysis by which this conclusion was reached was built up of a number of steps. Stockholding booksellers stimulate sales of books by having stocks and wide selections available. Their numbers and the extent of their stockholding depend upon r.p.m. Without r.p.m. there would be fewer of them, and each would hold smaller stocks and narrower selections. In consequence, fewer books would be sold in total, and fewer copies of each title on the average. Publishers would therefore tend to publish fewer titles; and smaller editions of those published would have higher publication costs per copy. The process generating these adverse results would be initiated, therefore, by forces acting adversely on stockholding booksellers. The Court predicted that the termination of r.p.m. would injure those booksellers in two separate ways. First, there would be unstable, and largely occasional, retail price-cutting of a relatively small number of titles, which would increase the risks of stockholding, and hence discourage it. Stockholding booksellers would also require higher gross margins in these circumstances. Second, stockholding booksellers would lose to non-retailing firms part of their trade in supplying books to libraries; this reduction in their business would affect their stockholding for retail sale.

[78] *Re Net Book Agreement, 1957* (1962), L.R. 3 R.P. 246, at 322.

A detailed examination of the judgment would be out of place here, and has been published elsewhere.[79] Three points may be noted briefly. First, the Court appears to have been much influenced by events in the Canadian book trade since the abolition of r.p.m. in 1951; yet the judgment does not explain the relevance to the United Kingdom of the Canadian experience, which itself is discussed only briefly. Second, there is the paradox that although retail price competition was expected to be very limited, yet it was expected to have serious unfavourable implications. Third, the judgment includes no discussion of the possibility of differences in the costs of competing retailers, a matter which is generally regarded as central to the economics of r.p.m.

The favourable judgment of the Court was hailed as a signal victory for r.p.m. in books, though wider repercussions were limited by the Court's acceptance of the aphorism, 'Books are different'.[80] Its major repercussion outside the book trade itself is that it stands, together with the favourable judgments of r.p.m. in the earlier cases relating to cement and metal windows, as judicial authority for the view that r.p.m. in some trades and in some circumstances is in the public interest, and that the abrogation of r.p.m. in them would on balance have undesirable consequences.[81]

[79] R.B.Stevens and B.S.Yamey, *The Restrictive Practices Court: the Judicial Process and Economic Policy* (1965), pp. 94–5, 100–1, 102–4 and 224–35.

[80] See p. 251 of the law report, cited in footnote 78.

The dominant firm in the wallpaper industry claimed that it used similar arguments in support of r.p.m. to those accepted by the Court in the Net Book decision. The Monopolies Commission held that its case was not assisted by the comparison between the two trades: they 'differ widely in structure and in the latter [book trade] there is very fierce competition between a large number of suppliers none of whom predominates'. Monopolies Commission, *Report on the Supply of Wallpaper* (1964), paras 131 and 179.

It may be said, in passing, that a reading of the *Net Book* judgment does not support the view that 'many factors besides economic ones were considered by the tribunal when upholding the book trade arrangements' [G.Sawer, *Law in Society* (Oxford, 1965), pp. 141–2]. This is not a distinguishing feature of the particular judgment.

[81] It is interesting to note two reports of later criticisms of the Net Book system from the publisher's point of view.

'A more difficult bastion to be stormed, in the view of many progressive publishers, is the bookshop. Although publishers gave support to the chartered booksellers by siding with the principle of price maintenance a few years ago, the feeling is growing that bookshops, in their present form, are not an adequate means of getting books to buyers. In spite of all the traditional distaste for it,

The Prohibition of Resale Price Maintenance in 1964

When the new statutory provisions relating to r.p.m. were introduced in 1956, the Minister in charge of the legislation observed that they could not be regarded as a last step. Further legislation was in fact introduced in 1964. Public sentiment was moving progressively away from qualified or unqualified support of r.p.m., and there was a growing volume of criticism.[82] Experience of increasing retail price competition in the sale of groceries and some other goods showed not only that there was considerable scope for price reductions but also that apprehensions of disruption, instability and confusion were unfounded. Housewives and other shoppers discovered or re-discovered the benefits of price competition. At the same time there had not been any dramatic reduction in the number of small-scale shopkeepers in the affected trades; and there was evidence that many of them were sufficiently efficient, or could become so by means of co-operative activities with or without the assistance of wholesale dealers, to continue in business.

As early as 1958 there was authoritative questioning of the appropriateness of the policy solution which had been adopted in 1956. The government-appointed Council on Prices, Productivity and

the pressure to start mail-order selling by publishers is going to grow, and with it a new assault on the Net Book Agreement.' 'A Balanced Account', *Times Literary Supplement*, 27 May 1965.

'I reluctantly supported the Association's fight for the retention of the Net Book Agreement in the firm belief that if it is granted the trade will then take this opportunity to modernise itself and improve its services to booksellers and to the book-buying public. However, this has not happened. As a consequence, I am now reluctantly forced to oppose the retention of the Net Book Agreement. Let no one imagine that under the new legislation [of 1964] the Restrictive Practices Court will just approve the retention of the Net Book Agreement on the nod. I assure you this will not happen. In the opinion of many people, in the trade and outside, the retention of this agreement would not be in the interests of the trade or the nation as a whole.' Robert Maxwell, MP, a publisher, reported in *The Bookseller*, 12 June 1965.

Those trades in which r.p.m. has been approved in proceedings under the Act of 1956 are not exempted from proceedings under the Act of 1964 which is discussed below. However, in proceedings under the latter Act, 'the Court may treat as conclusive any finding of fact made in those proceedings [under the Act of 1956], and shall do so unless prima facie evidence is given of a material change in the relevant circumstances since those proceedings'.

[82] Successive editorials in *The Times* demonstrate the change in attitude towards r.p.m. of this influential newspaper.

Incomes (the 'Three Wise Men') in its first report suggested that this policy should be reconsidered: 'The great emphasis which has been placed recently by the Government on the need for price reductions – an emphasis with which . . . we largely agree – leads us to think that the matter ought to be carefully reconsidered'.[83] In its second report the Council reported that the Government had explained that it was too early to institute an inquiry into the consequences of the changes made in 1956; the Council suggested, in reply, that it was possible that the importance of r.p.m. (as well as other matters pertaining to competition) 'in the particular context of preventing general price inflation was not given much weight at the time the legislation was passed'.[84] In fact, during 1960 the Board of Trade did institute an extensive inquiry into the extent and operation of r.p.m. No report was published, but it is generally believed that its tenor was critical of the practice.

Further criticism of r.p.m. came from the Committee on Consumer Protection which inquired, *inter alia*, into measures 'desirable for the further protection of the consuming public'. The Committee was informed by the President of the Board of Trade in November 1959 that it was too early to 'warrant a judgment' on the working of the provisions relating to r.p.m. introduced in 1956 and that, if the need to review the provisions became evident, 'the problem could be referred to the Monopolies Commission'. (Instead, in the event the departmental inquiry, noted above, was initiated.) The Committee therefore regarded r.p.m. as being outside its terms of reference; nevertheless, it did not refrain from offering the view that the repeal of the provisions 'permitting enforcement of individual resale price maintenance might greatly benefit consumers'.[85] In December 1963 the Consumer Council, a body set up by the Government in implementation of a recommendation of the Committee on Consumer Protection, lent its weight to the mounting criticism. It expressed the opinion that 'in the interests of the consumer resale price maintenance should be made illegal in this country', though it added that certain safeguards were necessary.

The issue of r.p.m. finally sprang into the limelight early in 1964, and the subject was prominent in the press for the best part of the

[83] Council on Prices, Productivity and Incomes, *First Report* (1958), para. 155.

[84] *Ibid.*, *Second Report* (1958), para. 118.

[85] *Final Report of the Committee on Consumer Protection*, Cmd 1781 (1962), paras 7 and 902.

year. It began when a member of the Opposition in the House of Commons, Mr J.Stonehouse, introduced a private member's bill to abolish r.p.m. generally, the sole exceptions being those instances where the Restrictive Practices Court had found the practice not to be against the public interest. The bill did not survive its second reading. Its introduction may have helped to precipitate the (Conservative) Government's decision to legislate against r.p.m., as a first instalment of a programme of legislation designed to strengthen measures for the control of monopolies, restrictive business agreements and mergers, and to encourage competition in the economy.

The Resale Prices Bill was introduced on 10 March by Mr Edward Heath, the Secretary of State for Industry, Trade and Regional Development and President of the Board of Trade. After outlining the wider programme of legislation, Mr Heath turned to r.p.m., and he posed the major issue of policy in these terms: 'It is now apparent that there is no halfway house. The choice is as simple as this. We can permit resale price maintenance to go on in every case, with all that it entails in the way of higher costs, a less efficient distribution system and less opportunity for consumers' preferences to influence supply, or we can provide for price competition, and facilitate the introduction of new and improved methods of distribution by ending resale price maintenance, except when it can be shown that it helps the consumer and is not contrary to the public interest.'[86] It is interesting that in launching the bill, neither of the two Ministers speaking on its second reading attempted to justify the legislation as a measure against the rise of prices in an inflationary setting. Their emphasis was on its likely effect on efficiency, consumers' choice and the best use of resources.

It may be asked why another possibility might not have been considered: the complete prohibition of r.p.m. without any exceptions. Such an approach, however, was presumably ruled out for at least two reasons. First, it would have gone against the (by then) 'traditional' approach of having monopoly situations and restrictive arrangements judged on their individual merits in each particular case. Second, by 1964, r.p.m. itself had been found to be not against the public interest in respect of several classes of goods: books, cement and metal windows (by the Restrictive Practices Court), and tea, rubber footwear and tobacco products, *inter alia* (by the Monopolies Commission). Direct disregard of these assessments, and

[86] House of Commons Debates, 691, col. 260 (10 March 1964).

failure to provide at least in principle for these and other possible exceptional cases, was inconceivable.

The bill had a stormy passage through Parliament. 'Published in late January, the bill received a generally favourable public response, but thousands of small shopkeepers, egged on by the *Daily Express*, protested vehemently; and Mr Heath had to contend with a Tory back-bench rebellion which rumbled on from January through April. The rebellion reached its climax on 11 March 1964, when 21 Conservatives voted against the government and at least 17 others abstained; on a later division the government's majority fell to one.'[87] At one time it seemed as if the thrust of the bill might be blunted by compromise changes to placate the opposition within the Conservative ranks; but Mr Heath in fact managed skilfully to make some alterations in detail without having to deviate from the original design. Though the parliamentary troubles undoubtedly caused serious dissension within the party in office, Mr Heath emerged with an enhanced reputation as a skilled and determined politician and one who was willing and able to initiate and carry through reforms in the face of organised and vocal criticism inside and outside Parliament.

The Resale Prices Act, 1964, provides for the prohibition of individual r.p.m. save in respect of those goods which the Restrictive Practices Court has declared to be 'exempted goods' in terms of the statute. The Court may declare a class of goods to be 'exempted

[87] D.E.Butler and Anthony King, *The British General Election of 1964* (1965), p. 23.

See also A.Sampson, *Anatomy of Britain* (revised edition, 1965), pp. 46–7: 'A vivid example of lobbying in action was the campaign in defence of Resale Price Maintenance, after Edward Heath had announced his intention to abolish it early in 1963 [*sic*]. Here, all the interests that might be damaged by the new bill – the brewers, the chemists, the motor trade, and small shopkeepers of all kinds – tried to co-ordinate their protests in the "Resale Price Maintenance Coordinating Committee" in Wimpole Street. They supplied pamphlets and arguments, they lobbied M.P.s and they organised bombardments of letters from constituents. "The really disturbing part of the mail", wrote *The Times* political correspondent in February 1964, "comes handwritten or unevenly typed bearing his constituency postmark, . . . letters from newsagents, stationers, chemists, garage owners, tobacconists, wine and spirit merchants and all the rest of the small men in the constituencies can chill the backbenchers' blood . . ."'

It should be added that the government-appointed National Economic Development Council in March welcomed the bill on the ground that it 'should increase efficiency in distribution'. NEDC, *The Growth of the Economy* (1964), pp. 126–7.

goods' where it appears to the Court that without r.p.m. the consumers or users of those goods would suffer detriment greater than the detriment resulting from the maintenance of minimum resale prices. This approach is generally in accord with that adopted in 1956 in respect of restrictive agreements such as horizontal price agreements: the Court is required to assess the benefits and detriments flowing from the particular restriction, and to reach a decision. There are, however, two major differences. In the first place, whereas the Act of 1956 does not limit the relevant benefits and detriments to those affecting the consumers or users of the goods, but includes, for example, considerations relating to exports and unemployment, the later Act requires the Court to have regard exclusively to the interests of consumers and users of the goods in question. Mr Heath, who piloted the legislation on to the statute book, carefully resisted attempts to introduce additional grounds for exemption, such as the protection of the interests of retailers and their employees, the promotion of exports or the maintenance of employment. Second, whereas in the earlier Act the Court is required to take cognisance of any 'specific and substantial' benefits to consumers, users and purchasers flowing from the restriction, the Act of 1964 is more concrete in that it lists the particular kinds of benefit to consumers (and users) which alone are to be considered. There are five of these types of benefits: r.p.m. may be found meritorious where, in its absence, the quality of the goods or the varieties of the goods would be substantially reduced to the detriment of consumers; where the number of the outlets for the goods would be substantially reduced to the detriment of consumers; where the retail prices of the goods would in general and in the long run be higher to the detriment of consumers; where the goods would be sold under conditions endangering the health of consumers; or where necessary services provided with the sale of the goods would be substantially reduced to the detriment of consumers.

The Restrictive Practices Court has not yet made decisions under the new Act, and thus there is no authoritative interpretation of the criteria summarised in the preceding paragraph. It is the general view, however, that it will be difficult to secure exemption since the 'gateways' are narrow and likely to be so interpreted.

The Act includes provisions prohibiting the withholding of supplies from any dealer on the sole ground that that dealer has resold or is likely to resell such goods at prices lower than those recommended by the supplier. These provisions are widely drawn. There is a further provision to the effect that a supplier may nevertheless withhold supplies of goods from a dealer where he has reasonable cause to believe that within the previous twelve months the dealer (or any of his reseller customers) has been using as loss leader any goods of the same or a similar description. Loss leader is defined as referring to resales of goods 'not for the purpose of making a profit on the sale of those goods, but for the purpose of attracting to the establishment at which the goods are sold customers likely to purchase other goods or otherwise for the purpose of advertising the business of the dealer'. The influence of the Canadian precedent is apparent.[88]

Although the prescription and enforcement of minimum resale prices is prohibited except where exemption has been granted, a supplier may notify dealers or otherwise publish 'prices recommended as appropriate for the resale' of his goods. Such prices are in no way binding on resellers; and the supplier has no right of action against those who disregard them, either by selling above or below them.[89] The supplier's right to stipulate maximum resale prices also seems to be left unimpaired by the Act.

[88] See above, p. 39.

[89] The most recent report of the Monopolies Commission, on the supply of petrol to retailers, was published after the Resale Prices Act had reached the statute book. In this trade, r.p.m. had been practised by the main suppliers until 1962 or 1963, by which date all had given it up. Retail price competition had been initiated by retailers of lower-price petrol supplied by certain new companies which had begun operations in the UK market. (For an account of how a major supplier, Esso, had initiated r.p.m. following strong representations by organised retailers of petrol, and how it subsequently discontinued it, see report of *Esso Petroleum Co. Ltd v. Harper's Garage (Stourport) Ltd* in *The Times*, 16 June 1965.) The main companies then followed the practice of recommending resale prices in the various marketing zones. Although these recommendations did not create obligations, they were widely adopted, giving rise to a substantial uniformity of retail prices grade for grade and zone for zone. The Commission concluded that 'such a degree of uniformity . . . could not have prevailed without the recommendations'. The Commission was not required to make recommendations on this particular matter. One member of the Commission, Professor T.Barna, in a Note of Dissent, included among his recommendations: 'Suppliers should cease to fix, recommend or suggest retail prices'. Monopolies Commission, *Report on the Supply of Petrol to Retailers in the United Kingdom* (1965), paras 25, 67, 346–9 and Note of Dissent, para. 34.

It is by no means certain, however, that much additional price competition would have developed (or would develop) in the absence of resale price recom-

Suppliers of goods or trade associations of such suppliers are required under the Act to register goods in order to claim exemption from the prohibition. Until the Court has decided whether or not exemption should be granted, suppliers of the registered goods can continue to practise r.p.m. and enforce their rights against 'non-signer' resellers.[90] By the closing date for registration, the Registrar of Restrictive Trading Agreements had received some 700 applications from firms or associations, the goods being divided into about 500 classes. A supplier of a class of registered goods can continue r.p.m. even though he himself did not make an application: registration – and any eventual exemptions – relate to classes of goods, not to particular suppliers of the goods.

The widespread registration of applications for exemption disappointed those who expected the new Act to sweep the slate clean, with only a few cases to be left for adjudication. The Consumer Council issued a statement in which it deplored the fact that no less than 121 classes of goods were included in the first list of applications. (The three later lists are not so heavily weighted towards consumer goods as the first.) 'Such a massive attempt by British industry to avoid the abolition of resale price maintenance is unwelcome evidence of unwillingness to face up to the rigours of genuinely competitive trading.' It applauded the decision of a number of firms to 'allow their products to find their own price level'.[91]

Resale price maintenance has been abandoned by individual firms or by all firms in the manufacture of razor blades, furniture, certain items of glassware, tyres, certain rubber goods, domestic electrical appliances, power hand-tools, paint, spirits and wine, wallpaper, sports goods, motor accessories and motor cars. (This list cannot pretend to be complete.) Although it is far too soon to judge the full effects of these decisions to jettison r.p.m., sufficient time has elapsed to establish that appreciable numbers of retailers are able to make substantial and persisting price reductions on formerly price-

mendations, since competition in the retailing of petrol is seriously weakened by restrictions on the number of retailers resulting from planning controls on the establishment of new petrol-retailing sites. On this, see H.Townsend, 'Exclusive Dealing in Petrol: Some Comments', *Economica*, 32 (1965), pp. 410–23.

[90] See, for example, *E.M.I. Records Ltd v. Morris* (1965), L.R. 5 R.P. 254.

[91] Consumer Council, Statement issued 1 March 1965.

Similar sentiments have been expressed by spokesmen for the present (Labour) Government.

maintained articles. Price reductions of between 10 and 20 per cent. of the price-maintained lines have been common. Ample scope for price reductions and economies has been shown to be present. Even in trades in which there had been some *sub rosa* price-cutting before the abolition of r.p.m., the abandonment of price-fixing has led not only to open price reductions but also to bigger reductions by larger numbers of retailers. These price reductions have been particularly striking since they have been made at a time when retail prices generally have been moving upwards.[92] The evidence of these price reductions will probably make it more difficult for r.p.m. on other goods to be defended successfully in proceedings before the Court.

Two instances of abandonment call for more than passing reference. The first is the motor industry. In October 1964 the manufacturers decided not to seek exemption, and hence r.p.m. lapsed formally when the statutory prohibition came into effect in April 1965. The decision was reached after legal advice had been taken. The manufacturers undertook to maintain 'responsible marketing arrangements and the highest standards of service to consumers'. If experience were to show that consumers and users had suffered detriment because of abolition, the situation would be reconsidered (as is permitted under the Act). Price reductions by some traders of between £30 and £50 on the average family saloon car were expected.[93] It is difficult to assess how widespread and deep actual price-cutting has been. It has varied for different makes of car. A general impression is that many car buyers are shopping around more actively than before, and that price cuts in excess of £50 have not been uncommon except on makes which are in short supply. Price-cutting in tyres and accessories seems to have been more widespread than in cars.

The second instance is that of spirits. In February 1965 the

[92] This fact has been seized upon by the present (Conservative) Opposition. 'The only exceptions, broadly [to the widespread rise in prices], are the results of the courage of this side of the House in passing the Resale Prices Act last year, with no help from the Labour Party.' Sir K.Joseph, House of Commons Debates, 717, col. 490 (28 July 1965); also P.Goodhart, *ibid.*, col. 529.

The reference to the Labour Party harked back to that party's attitude towards the government party's difficulties over the Resale Prices Bill. 'The Labour Party, to its discredit, simply abstained and enjoyed the fun . . .' S.Brittan, *The Treasury Under the Tories 1951–64* (1964), p. 268.

[93] *The Times*, 16 October 1964.

Distillers Co. Ltd, which supplies over half of the home market for Scotch whisky, abandoned r.p.m. on its brands of whisky, gin and vodka. This decision was taken after legal advice had been sought. This was the signal for large price reductions, initiated in the first stages by supermarkets possessing the necessary licences for the sale of liquor. Price reductions spread, and were intensified by direct sales of case-lots to consumers by wholesalers. The profits of some companies with interests in the retailing of liquor were affected adversely. The impact of the price reductions would have been greater still had it not been for the fact that most supermarket establishments and other would-be price-cutters do not have the necessary licences. Nevertheless, the impact of Distillers' decision was great enough for r.p.m. in the sale of wines and spirits to dwindle into relative insignificance.

The political decision, taken in the Resale Prices Act of 1964, to leave it to a judicial body, the Restrictive Practices Court, to determine whether r.p.m. should or should not continue in particular trades, raises a number of important questions.[94] One of the most interesting questions concerns the kinds of evidence or information the Court may find acceptable and helpful in the course of its work.

In the trades in which r.p.m. is likely to be defended before the Court, it is likely that the practice has had a more-or-less uninterrupted reign for fifty years or more, so that there may be no one with direct personal experience of the particular trades in the United Kingdom before the advent of r.p.m.[95] In judgments given under the earlier Restrictive Trade Practices Act of 1956, the Court has sometimes taken cognisance of accounts of events and developments preceding the introduction of the particular restraint on competition before it for adjudication; and in other cases it has disregarded them as being irrelevant because of material changes in relevant circumstances.[96] In the r.p.m. cases under the Act of 1964, the most recent historical experience, relating as it would do to the late nineteenth

[94] The general question of the use of the judicial process in the making and implementation of economic policy is examined in detail, in relation to the work of the Restrictive Practices Court under the Act of 1956, in Stevens and Yamey, *op. cit.*, esp. chs 3, 4, 6 and 7.

[95] *Cf. Re Net Book Agreement, 1957* (1962), L.R. 3 R.P. 246, at 311 and 323.

[96] For a review of cases, see Stevens and Yamey, *op. cit.*, pp. 95–101.

or the early twentieth century, may well be regarded as having little or no value as an indication of what is likely to happen in the 1960s without r.p.m. (though any such disregard of past experience would seem to call for specification of the changes which have occurred and which are thought to rob the early experience of current interest). Moreover, there is the question of how 'evidence' relating to the early period could be introduced acceptably into the court proceedings.

Evidence of contemporary developments in foreign countries has generally had short shrift from the Court in proceedings under the Act of 1956.[97] The Court has stressed the difficulty of making valid inter-country comparisons, and of gaining a full appreciation of particular developments in a foreign country. The only important exception has been in the judgment on r.p.m. in books where, as has already been noted, Canadian experience was held to be of some relevance in indicating the likely effects of the abolition of r.p.m. in the United Kingdom.[98] It remains to be seen whether evidence of foreign experience will be more important in proceedings under the Act of 1964: the difficulty of introducing evidence in an acceptable form may be a serious obstacle.

Developments in other trades in the United Kingdom since the termination in them of r.p.m. provide another possible source of evidence. Evidence of this kind – events or developments in other industries not subject to the particular restrictions on competition under consideration – has been virtually of no account in cases under

[97] For a review of cases, see Stevens and Yamey, *op. cit.*, pp. 101–4. To the cases reviewed there in which the Court was not prepared to draw conclusions from evidence about foreign countries may now be added *Re British Heavy Steelmakers' Agreement* (1964), L.R. 5 R.P. 31, at 84: 'As regards the recent happenings in ECSC [European Coal and Steel Community], the differences are so many and so great . . . that no relevant inferences can be drawn from the volume of information – much of it can scarcely qualify to be called evidence – with which we were supplied'.

[98] See Stevens and Yamey, *op. cit.*, pp. 102–4. Experience in foreign countries has been held to be relevant in another case which is not considered in the cited book: *Re Glazed and Floor Tile Home Trade Association's Agreement* (1963), L.R. 4 R.P. 239, at 274–5. Experience in Italy and South Africa was held to be significant. Experience in Canada, on the other hand, was not: 'The Canadian market however is very small and it is difficult to draw any valid conclusions from its experience which would be appropriate to a large market'. It is interesting that the Court in the earlier *Net Books* case should have regarded experience in Canada to be of relevance for the United Kingdom.

the Act of 1956.[99] But whether or not specific evidence of this kind is to play a part, it may be recognised that proceedings under the Act of 1964 will be taking place after some of the effects of the termination of r.p.m. in various trades will be a matter of common knowledge.

It is widely thought that the implementation of the Resale Prices Act in due course will result in a substantial reduction in the extent of r.p.m. To date, under the earlier Restrictive Trade Practices Act of 1956, which applies (broadly) to all collective agreements and arrangements involving horizontal price-fixing, market-sharing or control of channels of distribution, no more than nine agreements have escaped the disapproval of the Restrictive Practices Court. The Resale Prices Act, which applies to r.p.m. alone, imposes more stringent criteria than the earlier statute; hence the view that the chances of the successful defence of r.p.m. arrangements are small.

When restrictive agreements subject to the statute of 1956 have been abandoned, either voluntarily or by order of the Court, it has generally been difficult to notice or ascertain the effects of the removal of the particular collective restraint on competition. This has been so partly because most of the agreements did not relate to consumer goods, so that the changes, if any, have not been readily visible to the outside observer. But in many cases it is likely that the effects of abandonment have been limited. The generally buoyant state of demand in the economy, the non-competitive structure of several branches of manufacturing industry, and recourse occasionally to forms of co-operation not subject to the provisions of the legislation, undoubtedly have served to neutralise or weaken the thrust of the legislation.

It may be predicted with some confidence that the progressive abandonment of r.p.m. will have more notable and noticeable effects. There can be little doubt that generally there is considerable scope for price competition in hitherto protected branches of the distributive trades, however modest the current average gross and net profit margins in them may appear to be. The restraining influences which have served to muffle or reduce the effects of the abandonment

[99] For examples of limited references to experience in other industries in the UK, see *Re Wholesale and Retail Bakers of Scotland Association's Agreement* (1959), L.R. 1 R.P. 347, at 384–5; and *Re Permanent Magnet Association's Agreement* (1961–2), L.R. 3 R.P. 119, at 161.

of restrictions under the Act of 1956 are likely to be absent or largely inoperative in respect of the abandonment of r.p.m. It is true that manufacturers are permitted under the Act of 1964 to have recourse to systems of distribution through distributor agencies, and that this can serve as a substitute for r.p.m.; but it is unlikely that this cumbersome and expensive method of distribution will be adopted for this purpose, save in exceptional circumstances.[100] Again, the legislation allows manufacturers to *recommend* resale prices, without being permitted to enforce them; but in the circumstances of the United Kingdom such a practice is more likely to have the effect of sharpening price competition than of moderating or curbing it. Only one general *caveat* should be entered: the implementation of central and local government controls over the establishment and the extension of shopping centres and sites may temper somewhat the intensity of price competition and the pace of structural change in some branches of distribution after the abandonment of r.p.m. Official controls over the expansion and adaptation of retailing facilities may well prove to be the most serious remaining constraint on competition and innovation in the distributive trades after the scope and extent of r.p.m. have been reduced.

[100] When formulating the details of the legislation, the Government deliberately refrained from inserting provisions to prevent the replacement of r.p.m. by agency arrangements between manufacturers and distributors. It was thought desirable not to do anything which might curtail the development of agency arrangements unrelated to the discontinuance of r.p.m. It was also thought that agency arrangements would not 'be used very much as an evasion. If it is, no doubt action can be considered later on'. E. Heath, House of Commons Debates, 695, cols. 311–2 (12 May 1964).

INDEX

For Product Safety Concerns and Information please contact our EU
representative GPSR@taylorandfrancis.com
Taylor & Francis Verlag GmbH, Kaufingerstraße 24, 80331 München, Germany

www.ingramcontent.com/pod-product-compliance
Ingram Content Group UK Ltd.
Pitfield, Milton Keynes, MK11 3LW, UK
UKHW040927180425
457613UK00010B/274

* 9 7 8 0 2 0 2 3 6 2 2 7 4 *